YES

Yoga *for* Emotional Support

*A Guided Journey
to Self-Love &
Emotional Harmony*

by Christine Shaw

ISBN: 979-8-35094-996-4 (print)

DEDICATION

This book is dedicated to all the remarkable individuals and challenging circumstances that have woven the tapestry of my life. To those whose presence brought forth the lessons of self-love and compassion, I extend my deepest appreciation.

To the countless souls who, like myself, have embarked on a journey of self-discovery and growth, seeking to better themselves by attending YES classes and workshops—I dedicate this work to you. Your commitment to learning and applying yoga techniques as a pathway to love yourself is an inspiration that transcends the pages of this book.

May these stories and teachings be a testament to the resilience of the human spirit and the transformative power of self-love. To everyone who has embraced the YES philosophy, may you continue to thrive in life and radiate the light of compassion and acceptance.

With gratitude and love,
Christine

PART I

INTRODUCTION

YES - Yoga for Emotional Support

Emotional support–it's something we all yearn for. Connection, compassion, abundance, and happiness are universal desires, yet the stresses of life often hinder us from fully embracing each moment. Introducing the Yoga for Emotional Support program, or YES, this book provides techniques for everyone to savor life's joys. Join me on this transformative journey as we explore the path to emotional well-being and the abundant life you deserve.

We all have experienced or are currently experiencing difficult and stressful life situations. These stresses can come from the loss of a loved one or a relationship, difficulty in the workplace, a mental or physical health diagnosis, trauma, worry about a child, spouse, friend, or yourself. They can lead to anxiety, grief, depression, anger, fear, worry, or other low vibrational states that keep us from enjoying this one precious life we have to live.

Emotions are energy in motion; the energy that propels us forward. When our vibrational energy is high, life brims with joy and enthusiasm. Discover your inner strength with YES–a guide designed to elevate your vibrational energy. Learn techniques not only to navigate challenging times but to infuse more peace, hope, and happiness into your life. YES empowers you to reduce stress, cultivate emotional balance, foster connections, embrace self-love, and blossom into the wonderful experience it is meant to be.

This book is designed to help you to recognize the beautiful person that you are by dedicating time daily to self-care. In sharing my story of resilience amidst life's challenges, you'll discover the genesis of YES–my journey of hope, courage, strength, and happiness. Drawing from researched techniques that transformed my life, you'll learn to prioritize your health and well-being, cleansing your mind and body from toxic thoughts and emotions. Through gentle yoga, mindful breathing, meditation, aromatherapy, sound therapy, affirmations, visualization, energy exercises, and more, you'll learn ways to de-stress from life's pressures. No prior yoga experience required.

When you see the word *Yoga* in *Yoga for Emotional Support*, chances are you might think about yoga as moving your body into pretzel-ey poses. Yoga postures are called asanas in Sanskrit (the language of yoga). Hatha Yoga refers to the physical practice of yoga utilizing asanas. There are many other types of yoga that are not centered around asanas. They are Jnana yoga (the practice of self-knowledge or self-realization), Mantra yoga (chanting), Kriya yoga (activity or movement of consciousness), Karma yoga (the path of action), Bhakti yoga (devotion to God or a supreme consciousness in any form), Raja Yoga (the practice of meditation, mental, and physical control), Kundalini yoga–a combination of bhakti, raja yoga, and shakti yoga (expression of power and energy), and Swara yoga (the nature of the breath and modes of breathing). YES practices learned here will focus on many of these forms of yoga to guide you to heal your heart and nurture your soul.

Yoga transcends mere physical movements. It's a practice that seeks to still the fluctuations of the mind, as expressed in Yoga Sutra 1.2: 'Yoga Chitta Vritti Nirodhah,' which translates to quieting or removing the mind's fluctuations. The Sanskrit components–chitta (mind-stuff), vritti (fluctuations), and nirodhah (suppression or restraint)–reveal the essence of this discipline. In the midst of our daily lives, our minds tend to wander, dwelling on past memories or fretting about an uncertain future, leading to stress and, ultimately, fear. Driven by both conscious and unconscious thoughts, our emotions become entwined with our thoughts. As Dr. Candace B. Pert notes in 'Molecules of Emotions,' 'Learning new positive thought patterns is facilitated so that we can permit conscious calm access to our 'bodyminds' below the neck. So often folks today are unnecessarily stressed out instead of blissed out, spending time and energy on subconsciously focusing on irrelevant frantic survival patterns which no longer serve us.'

Our emotions are carriers of energy, and within that energy, light emerges. Our thoughts, emotions, energy, and light can manifest as either positive, strong, and bright with high vibrations or negative, weak, and dim with low vibrations, or fall somewhere in-between. Experiencing positive emotions like peace, joy, contentment, and love generates vibrations of openness and self-acceptance. Conversely, uncomfortable emotions such as anger, jealousy, and fear create negative vibrations, fostering self-criticism and the painful belief of 'I'm not enough.' Recognizing this interplay allows us to navigate our emotions and energy, fostering a positive and vibrant inner landscape.

Engaging in yoga practices and meditation serves as a powerful tool to release low vibrational thoughts and emotions. Dr. Candace B. Pert emphasized the profound impact of emotions on the body, stating, 'Since emotions run every system in the body, don't underestimate their power to treat and heal.' Delving into our emotions and recognizing our capacity for healing is a transformative journey. By turning inward, examining the root causes of fears and stress, and altering our responses, one can cultivate peace and happiness. Restorative yoga, a practice that activates the parasympathetic nervous system, rest and digest, is instrumental in reducing low emotional states. Using props for support, like blankets and bolsters, it facilitates deep relaxation, fostering ease in body, mind, and spirit. Gentle flow vinyasa offers a slow-paced, breath-linked movement that promotes patience and kindness toward our bodies, emphasizing the importance of our moment-to-moment experience. Additionally, Yoga Nidra, known as yogic sleep, provides a unique state between waking and sleeping, encouraging conscious awareness of deep relaxation. In the YES program, you will explore and practice restorative yoga, gentle flow, and Yoga Nidra, which will assist in cultivating perseverance, strength, and resilience

Meditation, a practice spanning thousands of years, has empowered individuals to observe and calm the fluctuations of the mind. Scientific studies have validated its myriad benefits, including reducing anxiety and depression, countering addictive behaviors, enhancing memory, establishing new neural pathways, fortifying the immune system, promoting cardiovascular health, and boosting self-esteem. Dr. Shanida Nataraja's book, *The Blissful Brain: Neuroscience and Proof of the Power of Meditation*, serves as a testament to these benefits and the supporting research. Within the YES program, you'll explore the various meditation techniques crafted to aid in observing strong emotions as they arise. This heightened awareness fosters a response-driven approach, empowering you to navigate life's circumstances with resilience. Alongside asanas and meditation, this book introduces an array of tools and techniques, enhancing your journey towards emotional well-being. These include:

- **Mindful breathing:** Calms the body, mind and nervous system.

- **Aromatherapy:** Promotes relaxation, improves sleep, boosts the immune system, eases anxiety and depression, and enhances overall health.

- **Sound therapy:** Relieves pain and stress, balances the nervous system, and relaxes the body and mind by tapping into the vibrational frequencies of your body.

- **Creative visualization and positive affirmations:** Drawn from authors such as Louis Hay, Shakti Gwain, Esther Hicks, Joe Dispenza, and others help you to envision and create the present and future life you desire.

- **Energy exercises:** Based on Donna Eden's work, these exercises raise vibrations and invite in positive energy.

- **Chanting mantras:** Calms and soothes the mind and body, reduces stress and anxiety, balances the chakras, boosts the immune system, and opens us up to intuition.

- **Singing songs of inspiration:** Enhances self-expression and positivity as well as increases the 'feel good' hormones of dopamine and endorphins.

- **Acupressure:** Relieves physical and emotional pain.

- **MBSR (Mindfulness Based Stress Reduction) exercises:** Based on the work of John Kabat-Zin, improve emotional and social functioning.

- **EFT (Emotional Freedom Technique):** Reduces stress from trauma and promotes a deeper mind-body connection.

Discover these techniques and more within the pages of this book.

Emotional pain often finds its expression in physical discomfort, as unresolved past hurts become deeply stored within our cells. Left unaddressed, this pain can escalate, leading to various diseases such as heart and respiratory problems, high blood pressure, back pain, cysts, organ failure, and even cancer. The practices within the YES program are meticulously designed to guide you in understanding, feeling, and embracing your emotions, paving the way for a healthy life filled with peace, happiness, and self-love. YES is not only a means to alleviate physical ailments but also a unique program that combines proven practices aimed at relaxing both the body and mind. Crafted to facilitate a journey toward homeostasis, each themed session begins with letting go of what no longer serves us, progresses to the learning of techniques and yoga practices, and concludes with inviting in what nourishes us. Curated from esteemed sources like Esther Hicks, Byron Katie, Ticht Nacht Hahn, Louise Hay, Teal Swan, Donna Eden, and others, the YES program seamlessly integrates ancient wisdom from yoga and Ayurveda. This compilation creates a comprehensive 75–90-minute session, offering a seamless flow of self-care tools for your holistic well-being.

The Intention of *YES* is to provide you with:

1) **Tools for Self-Discovery:** Explore various yoga-based techniques that incorporate breathing with postures to enhance emotional balance as well as the variety of modalities listed previously.

2) **Community and Connection:** Experience a sense of belonging and support in an inclusive environment where rituals honor each individuals journey. In a group, everyone gathers together to release difficult emotions fostering a collective bond. Outside the group setting, this connection can be experienced through the YES community on social media or through virtual classes (see Y4ES. com)

3) **Empowerment and Confidence.** Cultivate strength, courage, hope, and faith through practices aimed at promoting self-love and unconditional acceptance. Yoga techniques guide you in focusing on your unique path, reminding you that you have control over your own behavior and responses. Embrace your journey with confidence, recognizing that you are love! Express it through your talents and personality in a way that resonates with your authentic self.

Note: This book is designed to empower you to follow the outlined techniques and choose themed classes based on your daily needs. Whether practicing alone, with a friend or small group, or following videos on www. Y4ES.com (which may differ from the book content), you have the flexibility to tailor your experience.

Another Note: Ayurveda, a Yogic practice derived from the Sanskrit words *ayus* meaning "life," and *veda* meaning "knowledge" or "science," offers ancient wisdom for healing the body and mind. While a few Ayurvedic principles are briefly mentioned in the book, they are not presented as techniques for emotional healing. I highly recommend exploring and incorporating Ayurvedic practices in your daily routines.

HOW TO USE THIS BOOK

The YES book is organized by five themed sessions - YES for Breathing, YES for Clarity, YES for Energy, YES for Heart Opening and YES for Relaxation - each offering three unique sessions, providing a total of 15 diverse practices. Within each themed chapter you will discover a wealth of yoga modalities, techniques, lessons, and readings all aimed at fostering self-connection. This book is your guide to discovering the right self-care methods for various situation or emotional state, complimented by illustrations depicting yoga postures for your reference.

You may skip around to find a themed class to practice that day, or you may refer to the charts listed after the Table of Contents that offer the practices you may need according to your emotional state or specific life circumstances that day.

You may wish to use the book as a part of your daily ritual, choosing which theme speaks to you that day and completing the entire 'class' or parts of it depending on the amount of time you have set aside. By making YES a part of your regular practice, you'll infuse self-love and positivity into the start or end of your day, enhancing your ability to navigate challenges.

How do I know? Because I have been through some very difficult life circumstances, as many have, and I emerged feeling self-empowered and confident. Continuously seeking ways to open my heart and nurture my soul, I've embraced self-acceptance as well as acceptance of others just as they are. It is a freeing and joyful journey. Thank you for choosing this book. Congratulations on taking this important step to managing your emotions and inviting more joy and serenity into your life!

YES - YOGA FOR EMOTIONAL SUPPORT
TABLE OF CONTENTS

1

Christine's Story:
From Adversity to Strength

Hi! My name is Christine Thea Shaw. Sure, that's my name, but who am I? I am a mom of two, a yoga teacher and yoga therapist, a singer and performer, a bicyclist, a spiritual leader, a certified elementary education teacher, a lover of nature, animals, and fitness, and a person who loves to inspire others to be healthy, happy, and strong. Those things are all true but is that who I really am deep inside? That's the question we all want to know. Who am I and what's my purpose? One of my favorite quotes by Wayne Dyer is "Don't die with your music still inside you. Listen to your intuitive inner voice and find what passion stirs your soul." We all have music inside of us, and I believe our passions and our life's purpose changes throughout our lives. As we live and experience life's challenges with all of its joys and sorrows, struggles and successes, we grow and discover unexpected, and sometimes unwanted, twists and turns. All of these lead us to know ourselves more and more. My journey has surely had some unexpected challenges that I never saw coming. I am actually grateful for them and all the new challenges that arise every day even though they were, and continue to be, painful. We all have our own challenges and struggles, and every one of us needs support from others and compassion from ourselves to get through the tough times and come out strong on the other side. My journey is about how I was faced with life challenges, sought support for my overwhelming emotions, and then created the

YES program to serve others in their search for emotional health and overall wellbeing.

I really struggled for weeks and months to write this next part about my story. I wondered if I should or even needed to tell all of the gruesome details or just stick to my feelings of fear, grief, and helplessness over things that were out of my control. I wondered if I should say that I know other people have experienced much worse things in life than I have, and what happened to me pales in comparison. One day after a meditation session, I pulled two angel cards from my deck. They gave me just the messages I needed. One was *vulnerability*. It read "Listen to your vulnerable feelings, as they contain wisdom and inspiration, and then pray for strength to focus on your priorities no matter what." The second card was *authenticity*. It read "Trust that your real self, whom God created divinely perfect, has the strength and knowledge needed for this situation." I interpreted these messages to mean that when I share my vulnerable feelings and am my authentic self, the story will flow. Telling my story is not what is most important. What came as a result of the events in my story is what really counts.

I always considered myself to be a happy person. I faced a few emotional upsets like losing friendships and boyfriends and not getting cast in shows, but it was when I faced some serious situations that literally brought me to my knees, that I understood what real emotional overload was. Whatever challenging life situations you may be going through, this book is a way to look inside and discover your true nature, heal from pain and troublesome emotions, find your inner strength and purpose, and live life to its fullest with the music inside of you playing for all to enjoy. Here is my story of adversity to strength.

When I was 49, my 13-year-old daughter's behavior had changed dramatically. I was frightened by the danger she was putting herself in with her use of alcohol and marijuana, which quickly progressed to other drugs. I experienced so many emotions over her transformation from an innocent child who was so talented, intelligent, and fun-loving, to an angry, scared, and troubled teenager. I was sad that this was happening to her and to our family. I was mad at the damn drugs and whoever sold them to her. I felt guilty for not being a better mom and for not keeping her safe. I felt scared that she would go to jail or die from an overdose. I felt shame for the stigma that goes along with drugs and addiction, and how people would view her and me. I worried about what led to her pain that caused her to numb out with drugs. I was confused about how this happened and worried about what I was going to do. The depth and variety of emotions I was feeling over what another person (my wonderful daughter) was doing began to bring up levels of stress and feelings of being totally overwhelmed that I truly had never experienced before in my life.

The emotional whammies really began with my marriage to my first husband. We were married for 14 years. As things began to fall apart, at around year seven, we tried marriage counselors, at-home programs, and separation for six months. We tried two more years together, but then our marriage ended in divorce. I remember experiencing mostly sadness over a broken marriage and deep concern about how the children would handle the split.

The second and most devastating emotional whammy for me was the discovery of my daughter's substance use disorder. I lived through nearly seven years of constant fear as a result of her actions. I tried to navigate ways to help her, wondering all the time if each new thing I tried was the "right" thing. I remember asking one of the leaders of a parent support group, "How do I know what the right thing is to help her?" And he said "You don't. There is no 'right' thing. We just do what we feel is best." So, I did what all of the people who "knew" what to do suggested. I sent her to numerous rehabs, found many counselors, said *yes* to psychiatrists prescribing drugs, sent her to a rehab high school, set rules and boundaries, told her I love her and support her but I don't support her using drugs, and on and on. All of these confusing choices and decisions set me on an emotional roller coaster of stress and worry. I began experiencing trauma from each new situation that came up. I wondered if the knock at the door was the police, if the phone ringing was a call from school asking me to come get my daughter, or if a car door slam and loud voices were drug dealers coming to the house. I remember crying hysterically on the bathroom floor thinking maybe I would try heroin to know what it's like. I felt anxious and on edge all of the time. I worried about what would happen next and wondered why I seemed to be the only one responsible for "fixing" this problem? I sought help for myself by attending all of the counseling sessions at each of her rehabs, as well as Al-Anon and Nar-Anon meetings. I even organized a parent support group with other parents. When I attended my first parent support group, it offered resources for the children. What I found was missing was emotional support for the parents. I needed something beyond what that group had to offer to help me for my anxiety and tension. I was looking for emotional support to find ways to calm myself and understand what I can do when other people are doing things that I have no control over. I read books about codependency and how parents of a teen with addiction can cope with their emotions and also help their child. When my daughter continued her drug use despite all the things I was putting time and energy into, I realized that it wasn't helping and it was even driving a wedge between us.

If all of this wasn't enough, the third emotional whammy was over the breakup of my second marriage. I met a wonderful man through Match.com, and we hit it off right away. He was handsome, fun, witty, and smart, and we had a lot in common. In addition to his positive attributes he was also struggling with the effects of childhood abuse. He lived with trauma every day. I knew about his trauma before we married, and thought that I would be able to help him to heal. I didn't know the depth of his pain and how deeply the love I had for him led to *my* pain when, after three years of marriage, he suddenly accepted a job in California. He packed up all of his things and moved to the

West Coast, saying that I could simply move out there and join him when I was able. I was pondering what all of these changes meant for me when two months later, he called to say he wanted a divorce. I was left to clean out our home, put it on the market to sell, find a new place to live, and figure out my finances. I was suddenly thrown back into being single again when I thought I would be married forever. A flood of emotions bombarded me after being blindsided by this dramatic life switch. I felt confused, rejected, angry, and sad. I was uncertain about what to do next. I did not want the things that were happening to be happening!

When we were first married, I didn't have training in how to support someone with trauma. I read books and did research online about childhood trauma to understand his responses and mine to the situations that arose surrounding communication, expectations, fear, blame, shame, and his feelings of not being good enough. We worked together to find therapists using traditional and non-traditional techniques including practicing yoga and meditation together. The happy person I always considered myself to be, enthusiastic for life and all it has to offer, was jeopardized by these life situations and my feelings that I was helpless to make changes. I didn't feel like my true self. I was worried all the time about things that I had no control over, like how other people were managing their lives. I struggled to control my anxiety and concerns about what my daughter was doing. I blamed myself and wondered what I could have done better in my relationship with my daughter and husband.

Right in the middle of my daughter's struggles and my husband wanting a divorce, my dad was dying of cancer. I visited him in the hospital and stayed by his bedside day and night. I got very little sleep and was exhausted and drained of all internal resources, and I didn't even care because at the time I believed that taking care of someone else was more important than taking care of me and my health and well-being. All of these people needed my love, care, and attention and

I didn't know how to take care of myself. I was being pulled by the gamut of emotions multiplied by the feeling that there was no time to process them or even bring up positive feelings of joy, peace, and calm within me. I felt totally out of control. I felt that no matter what I tried to do to help solve the situations in my life, nothing made a difference. My emotions had control over me. I felt desperate to have control over the things around me so that they would not be happening!

2

A Vision for Support: *YES* is created

My personal journey led me to seek support for my well-being. As a yoga instructor, I was aware of the profound impact that yoga has in alleviating stress and fostering mental and physical well-being. However, I yearned to research and explore additional techniques. I discovered a treasure trove of tools from some of my favorite teachers, including Donna Eden, Byron Katie, Esther Hicks, Teal Swan, Eckhart Tolls, Jon Kabat Zinn, and many others. Each of these teachers contributed unique perspectives and practices that enriched my understanding of holistic well-being. A pivotal influence in my journey was my revered guru, Swamini Shraddhananda Saraswati, from Kula Kamala Ashram in Pennsylvania. When deciding to offer support to others through the new program I was developing, I sought additional Yoga training. Under SwaminiJi's guidance I obtained certifications in Yoga Therapy and Spiritual Leadership, deepening my commitment to supporting others on their paths to wellness.

Through extensive research, dedicated study, and consistent practice, I came to a valuable realization: the techniques I had diligently learned became powerful tools during challenging moments. Confronted with adversity, I discovered the ability to not only acknowledge and understand my emotions but also to choose appropriate self-care methods. Instead of avoiding the emotions, I learned to navigate through them, emerging on the other side with a sense of calm, relaxation, happiness, and wholeness.

This journey also taught me a fundamental truth: I cannot change or fix others. When difficult situations arise, I need to start by asking "What do I need to do to take care of myself?" and then do it! By prioritizing self-care, I found the strength to support others through active listening and genuine love. Encouraging them to reflect on how they will address their own life challenges became a meaningful way to offer support. When asked for guidance, I can draw upon a wealth of proven techniques that have worked for me and countless others. Having incorporated these practices into my own life, I felt equipped to extend my support further by introducing individuals to the YES (Yoga for Emotional Support) classes.

I still experience difficult situations, thoughts, and emotions, but the difference is that now I know what to do when they arise. I am much better at observing them and not letting them control me or bring me down. I turn to the YES techniques that have helped me to not only manage difficulties, but come through them with grace, ease, and a new found love for myself and others. I can truly say that I've reclaimed my happiness! I feel like my true self again. This journey has inspired the creation of Yoga for Emotional Support, a platform designed to guide others in embracing self-love and nurturing their souls.

You are not alone. There's a path towards rediscovering your authentic joy and well-being. Yoga for Emotional Support is here to accompany you on your journey to self-love and emotional harmony!

3

YES - The Program: *Feeling for Healing*

The intention of *YES* is to offer you practices to heal your heart and nurture your soul. I call this emotional intelligence or emotional resilience. The Yoga sutras of Patanjali is a collection of 196 aphorisms (short sayings) outlining the eight limbs of yoga. Putting these into practice helps us to attain freedom or *moksha*. Knowing and practicing the eight limbs is a great start into the journey of self-love.

Self-care/Self-love = The practice of taking action to preserve or improve one's own health and well-being.

Maitri (Sanskrit) = Friendship with loving-kindness towards oneself

The Eight Limbs of Yoga:

1. Restraints - Yamas
    Non- Harming- Ahimsa
    Truthfulness- Satya
    Non- Stealing- Asteya
    Moderation- Brahmacharya
    Non- Attachment- Aparigraha

2. Observances - Niyamas
    Cleanliness- Saucha
    Contentment- Santosha
    Discipline- Tapas
    Self- Study- Svadhyaya
    Surrender to the Divine- Ishvara Pranidhana

3. Postures - Asana

4. Breath - Pranayama

5. Withdraw of the Senses - Pratyahara

6. Concentration - Dharana

7. Meditation - Dhyana

8. Liberation - Samadhi

When we move through the eight limbs, from the practice of ethical guidelines for our lives to the deeper inner sense of our true nature, we discover that place where our sense of self and self-love (*maitri*) lies. The intention of YES is to offer techniques to find a deep friendship with yourself, receive support through a community, and put into practice ways to thrive in life. The principles found in the Yoga Sutras, as well as other modalities and spiritual teachings, can help us to find healing. Feeling for healing means that instead of avoiding feelings that arise from our conditioned mind, thought patterns, and beliefs, we feel them. We become still and observe what is happening as the emotions arise, and then use the lessons to connect to our true nature, which is love. With regular practice, YES will help you to discover your true and loving self and improve all relationships, especially the one with yourself.

Now begins the instruction on the practice of yoga (*Atha yoganusasanam*). This is the translation of the first of 196 Yoga Sutra in The Yoga Sutras of Patanjali. Sutra means rule or aphorism. The second sutra, as stated earlier, translates as quieting or removing the fluctuations of the mind. The word Yoga literally translates as "to yolk or join." When we practice yoga, we are yoking or joining together the individual spirit with the universal spirit. Yoga is about quieting the mind and drawing within to discover your true nature through self-study (*svadhyaya*). Yoga helps us to find balance and ease in the mind, body, spirit, and emotions. Yoga postures (*asanas*) help us to move our physical bodies that house our non-physical selves (consciousness). When exploring Yoga for Emotional Support, following a format makes learning and practicing the variety of yoga techniques simple and easy. The goal is to experience total body wellness or homeostasis. The following is the format of each session followed by a detailed description.

4

YES Session Outline

I created each *YES* session with a theme and nine sections. The first section is the opening where you can ask yourself what you wish to let go of and then affirm what you wish to invite in. The next seven sections include 3 restorative yoga postures, 3 techniques or lessons and 1 gentle yoga postures sequence. The final section is the closing which allows you to burn or dissolve away what does not serve you and invite in positive energy and focus with some quotes of inspiration.

1. Opening
   Theme for the sessions:
   Breathing, Clarity, Energy, Heart Opening, Relaxation,
   Letting Go Question. What can you let go of today?
   Affirmations, gratitude, and energy you wish to invite in.

2. Restorative Yoga Asana (posture) #1 & Breath Assessment

3. Technique, Lesson or Reading #1

4. Yoga Asana (postures)

5. Technique, Lesson or Reading #2

6. Restorative Yoga Asana #2; aromatherapy and sound, or music

7. Technique, Lesson or Reading #3

8. Restorative Yoga Asana #3 Lounge Chair Savasana;
   aromatherapy, a reading, yoga nidra and/
   or music or other techniques

9. Closing. Burning or Dissolving Ritual to Let Go of what's not serving us and Inviting-In Ritual to invite in positivity
    What will you invite into your life today?
    (something based on the theme)
    A statement to the universe about what you wish for today
    Two quotes of inspiration (based on the theme)

1. Opening. Theme for the Session.

There are five themed sessions: Breathing, Clarity, Energy, Heart Opening, and Relaxation. Follow the outline for each session to learn a variety of techniques and yoga postures for befriending yourself. Choose the session or techniques that speak to you on any given day for a specific situation or emotion.

◊ **Letting-Go Question**

A *YES* session begins by letting go. There are always things we can let go of that currently stand in the way of being our best self. What are the limiting beliefs, worries, doubts, and negative self-talk that keep you stuck in the same old mindset and thoughts that don't serve your best life? For each session there are three questions to ponder about what you wish to let go. My suggestion is to choose one question that speaks to you. Write your answer on a small piece of paper, explore the feelings around it and why it's important to let it go. At the end of the session, you can perform the fire ritual or dissolving paper ritual to release what you wrote down that no longer serves you and then invite in what will serve you. When we let go we open up space to invite in what we need.

◊ **Affirmation/Mantra, Gratitude, and Energy**

What is an affirmation? It is anything we continually say or think. If we think "I'm not important" enough times, we will begin to believe it. Likewise, when we think and say kind things to ourselves like "I am deserving of love", we will believe that too! Here, the affirmation is a declaration repeated for emotional support or encouragement. A mantra (Sanskrit for "mind tool") is a word or phrase that you repeat to invite the energy of that phrase. It can be chanted 108 times (or less) followed by quiet reflection or meditation.

After writing down what you wish to let go of, create a deep connection with yourself by placing your hands over your heart. Say your affirmations/ mantras for the day. State them in the present moment to invite in the positive seeds of what you wish to create in your life. For example: "I feel the positive possibilities all around me," "I am discovering my true and loving nature every day." Sample affirmations are offered for you to use in each *YES* session.

Next, think or say out loud what you are grateful for and also what positive energy you wish to invite into your life today that will boost your mood and help to guide your day in the direction you desire. Choose words like ease, clarity, joy, patience, wonder, delight, inspiration, fortitude, strength, forgiveness, faith, passion, etc. (You can purchase angel cards with positive energy words to offer you guidance. https://www.amazon.com/Original-Angel-Cards-Inspirational-Meditations/dp/0934245517)

2. Restorative Yoga Asana #1 & Breath Assessment

After the beginning rituals, the best way to settle the body and mind is to tune into your breath in a relaxing and restorative posture. You will learn a variety of restorative postures to help you relax. Illustrations throughout the book will show you how to set up and get into the postures. You may choose the suggested ones or one of your choice for total support and relaxation. When you come into the posture, begin to release any past or future thoughts. Breath assessment is designed to help you to notice what your natural breathing pattern is like in the moment without trying to change anything. Notice the rise and fall of the belly and chest. Notice the length of the breath and how smooth or rough it is. Is it flowing naturally, helping you to become calmer, or does noticing it give you a tense feeling? Just observe. Next, count your inhales and exhales, working towards a longer exhale. When you lengthen the exhale, a signal is sent to the brain to activate the parasympathetic nervous system (the rest and digest or relaxation response) and turn down the sympathetic nervous system (the fight or flight response). Beginning each practice with this awareness of the breath will prepare your mind and body to receive the techniques that follow.

3, 5, and 7. Technique, Lesson, or Reading

In each session, learn a technique, lesson, or reading to assist in finding harmony and peace in your life. They will help you to improve the way you feel and offer you confidence to control your responses to your inner and outer world so you can thrive in life! There are a variety of ways to calm and heal the body and mind, observe and quiet the ego and monkey mind, reframe past traumas, reduce anxiety, and manage grief and other stressors. As you try these practices, see which ones you enjoy and practice them regularly as mental, physical, and emotional situations arise.

4. Yoga Asana

Gentle and flowing postures that link breath with movement can help bring ease and flexibility to the body. Held postures assist with focus, breath, mindfulness, stillness, clarity, and calm.

6 and 8. Restorative Yoga Asana #2 & #3

The yoga postures (asanas) that are best for relaxing the body and mind are restorative ones. Restorative yoga uses props like bolsters, blankets, blocks, straps, and eye pillows. In restorative postures, your body is fully supported to assist in total relaxation. It is important to come into this relaxation state while still conscious, so you are aware of what deep relaxation feels like. These postures activate the para-sympathetic nervous system or rest and digest response. We are all so busy in our lives that we may be unfamiliar with the effects of lying down just to rest. Learning and practicing restorative postures helps our body to enjoy stillness and a deep sense of presence, noticing the subtle energies of the body when in a relaxed state.

◇ **Aromatherapy, Sound Therapy, Music, or Chanting**

Throughout a session essential oils (aromatherapy) are sug-gested to help open blocked or stuck areas in the body and mind. There are two main categories of essential oils (relaxing and uplift-ing) to assist in emotional support. The end of the book highlights many essential oils and their benefits.

Sound therapy is beneficial in calming the body and mind and tapping into vibrational brain waves. The five types of brain waves are:

- gamma - learning and processing information (frequency of 400-100hz)
- beta - conscious thought and logical thinking (frequency of 12-40hz)
- alpha - place between conscious thinking and the subconscious mind (frequency of8-12hz)
- theta - involved in daydreaming and sleep (frequency of 4-8hz)
- delta - associated with deep sleep (frequency of 0-4hz).

Nature sounds, ocean sounds, Tibetan singing bowls, gongs, native American flutes, shruti box, harmonium, chimes, drumming, binaural beats (which means having or related to two ears) are all used for deep relaxation.

Music in the form of singing or recorded music is very healing. Creating your own songs is a powerful way to remember affirmations and to sing when you are feeling in low vibrational states. The sound and vibrations from chanting mantras induce the relaxation response, lowers blood pressure and heart rate, and calms brainwave activity.

To add music to your experience, go to www.y4es.com

9. Closing. Burning or Dissolving Ritual for Letting-Go and Inviting-In

At the end of your session, perform the "Letting-Go" ritual. Take the paper that you wrote on in the beginning and follow the ritual below to let go of what is not serving you, followed by the "Inviting-In" ritual to invite inspiration into your life from a quote or reading from a book of your choice.

Letting-Go Ritual:

After you write the answer on a piece of paper (regular paper for fire ritual and dissolving paper for the water ritual), perform the fire or dissolving paper ritual:

1. Place the paper in the bowl

2. Read the words about letting go

3. Burn or dissolve the paper and resolve to learn the lessons in a different way that will help you to feel better and open your heart

Letting-Go Burning or Dissolving Ritual Supplies:

1. "Letting-Go" words: *"I no longer need these thoughts, feelings, or circumstances that do not serve my highest and best good. I vow to be open to the lessons present to me in order to create positive habits and improve my outlook on life."*

2. A small heat resistant bowl or a small
bowl filled with warm water

3. A long handled lighter or dissolving paper (purchase
online) with what you wish to let go of written on it.

Inviting-In Ritual:

When the Letting-Go Ritual is complete read the sample quotes of inspiration or choose your favorite quote. Find some online or from your favorite book.

Performing the Inviting-In Ritual:

1. Read the Inviting-In words: *"Dear Universe–I invite this message of inspiration into my life at this time to serve my highest and best good. I promise to be kind to myself and more present every day."*

2. Read the quote/inspiration of the day

YES Techniques, Lessons, Readings

This table shows the practices in each session –
techniques, restorative, and yoga postures

Themed Class	Practice	Practice	Practice
Breathing #1 **Technique**	T#1: 8 Breaths to Joy	T #2: Emotional Guidance Scale	T#3: Kapalbhati and Sitali Breathing
Breathing #1 **Restorative**	Basic Relaxation Pose	Incline legs with Strap and Body Scan EO: Peppermint	Lounge Chair. Yoga Nidra EO: Lavender
Breathing #1 **Yoga**	Focus on the Breath		
Story #1	Carrying the Poop		
Breathing #2 **Technique**	T#1: Alt. Nostril	T#2: Grounding taps	T#3: R.A.I.N.
Breathing #2 **Restorative**	Gentle heart opener w/Blanket brush and Bolster	Seated Forward Fold EO: Eucalyptus	Lounge Chair EO: Cardamom
Breathing #2 **Yoga**	Breath of Joy		
Story #2	Losing the Keys		
Breathing #3 **Technique**	T#1: Crocodile	L#2: 12 Pathways	T#3: 4-7-8 Breath
Breathing #3 **Restorative**	5 Blanket Relaxation Pose	Side Twist w/ Bolster EO: Cedarwood	Lounge Chair Sandbag EO: Clary Sage
Breathing #3 **Yoga**	Hara Breathing with Tai Chi		
Story #3	The Angry Driver		
Clarity #1 **Technique**	T#1: Progressive Muscle Relaxation	T#2: Mantra and Mudra, Chanting Sat Nam	R#3: Detachment

Clarity #1 **Restorative**	Basic Relaxation Pose	Bolster Line up & Vagus Nerve Activation EO: Patchouli	Lounge Chair Guided Nature Visualization EO: Coriander
Clarity #1 **Yoga**	Small movement Series		
Story #4	Drop the Story and End the Worry		
Clarity #2 **Technique**	T#1: EFT	T#2: The 4 Agreements & 5 Sights/5 Sounds	T#3: Body Sensation Visualization
Clarity #2 **Restorative**	Triple Towers or Legs on a Chair	Side Lying EO: Sandalwood	Lounge Chair. Yoga Nidra EO: Grapefruit
Clarity #2 **Yoga**	Focus		
Story #5	The Ego is Loud! Pay Attention!		
Clarity #3 **Technique**	T#1: Pratyahara	T#2: The Hook up and Heaven & Earth	T#3: Happiness Bubble
Clarity #3 **Restorative**	Forward Fold w/ Bolster or Chair	Leaning Tower/ Incline legs with Strap EO: Tea Tree	Bound Angle EO: Jasmine
Clarity #3 **Yoga**	Drishti		
Story #6	I'm on the Edge of my Emotions		
Energy #1 **Technique**	L#1: Prana, Chakra, Vayus, Nadis	T#2: Eden Energy; Daily Routine	L#3: Raise your Frequency Lessons from Teal Swan
Energy #1 **Restorative**	Basic Relaxation Pose	Deer Pose w/Chest on a Low Bolster EO: Lemon	Lounge Chair. Chakra Meditation EO: Juniper Berry
Energy #1 **Yoga**	Chakras, Vayus, Nadis		

Story #7	Release the Pain with a Crack!		
Energy #2 **Technique**	T#1: Qi Gong: 5 Animal Frolics	L#2: Cure for Fear by Albert Brooks	T#3: Mantra Parusha
Energy #2 **Restorative**	Legs up the Wall	End to End Bolsters with Guided Nature Visualization EO: Rosemary	Lounge Chair. Mantra Parusha EO: Lime
Energy #2 **Yoga**	Mountain Viz. and Energy Rich Asanas. Sun/Moon		
Story #8	Don't Let the Rats Ruin your Life		
Energy #3 **Technique**	T#1: Acupressure	L#2: Chanting Mantras	L#3: Create your Reality
Energy #3 **Restorative**	Supported Torso	Side Lying w/ Bolster at the Back EO: Lemongrass	Lounge Chair w/ Visualization EO: Melissa
Energy #3 **Yoga**	Yoga Asanas and Emotions		
Story #9	The Yo-yo Day. It's All OK		
Heart Open #1 **Technique**	T#1: Positive Affirmations and Song of Affirmation	T#2: Octopus Technique	T#3: The Five Kleshas
Heart Open #1 **Restorative**	Basic Relaxation Pose	Mountain Stream EO: Rose	Lounge Chair EO: Orange
Heart Open #1 **Yoga**	Heart Opening Flow		
Story #10	What Someone Else is Doing is Affecting Me		
Heart Open #2 **Technique**	L#1: Tendency to Judge	T#2: Byron: The Work	T#3: Heart Coherence Meditation
Heart Open #2 **Restorative**	Basic Heart Opener	Pillow Fest or Bridge with Block EO: Bergamot	Lounge Chair w/ Snake Blanket and Bound Angle EO: Sage

Heart Open #2 **Yoga**	Heart Openers and Counter Poses		
Story #11	Be Proud of Yourself		
Heart Open #3 **Technique**	T#1: 8 Limbs of Yoga	L#2: The 5 Invitations (Discernment)	L#3: Metta Meditation
Heart Open #3 **Restorative**	Flying Flapping Fish	Twist with Chest on Bolster EO: Sweet Orange	Lounge Chair w/Metta Meditation EO: Sweet Marjoram
Heart Open #3 **Yoga**	Heart Focus		
Story #12	Sit with It		
Relaxation #1 **Technique**	T#1: Singing "I Have Arrived" song and others	L#2: 3 Granthis: Untie the Knots	R#3: Buzzing Bee Breath
Relaxation #1 **Restorative**	Basic Relaxation Pose	Forward Fold with a Bolster EO: Frankincense	Lounge Chair and A Visualization Treat for your Cells EO: Spearmint
Relaxation #1 **Yoga**	Granthis		
Story #13	The Female Brain		
Relaxation #2 **Technique**	T#1: The Joy of Letting Go	T#2: Guided Nature Visualization	T#3: Brainwave Frequencies and Binaural Beats
Relaxation #2 **Restorative**	Incline Legs	Side Lying w/Bolster EO: Lavender	Lounge Chair with Binaural Beats or Relaxing Music EO: Tangerine
Relaxation #2 **Yoga**	Yin Yoga		

Story #14	Be Nice. Think Twice.		
Relaxation #3 **Technique**	T#1: Samskaras and The Untethered soul	T#2: Walking Meditation	T#3: Point-to-Point Breathing for Relaxation
Relaxation #3 **Restorative**	Child's Pose	Twist with Chest on Bolster EO: Ylang Ylang	Lounge Chair with Point-to-Point Breathing EO: Pine/Thyme
Relaxation #3 **Yoga**	Relaxation Flow		
Story #15	I Could Easily Freak Out Right Now...But I Won't.		
Story #16	1 or 1,000 Breaths		
Story #17	Poop on the Path		

PART II

5

Themed Classes & Stories

Breathing

Yay for breathing! As long as I can remember I have loved to sing. I would sit for hours listening to albums like The Carpenters and the Broadway recording of Cinderella. I sang in talent shows, concerts and musicals all throughout school and my whole life. I sang on cruise ships, in theme parks and with Opera Delaware for 20+ years. To sing effectively and efficiently, a profound awareness and control of breath are essential. Fortunately, diaphragmatic breathing, or deep belly breathing, came naturally to me through my journey in singing. When I embarked on teaching yoga, I already understood the transformative power of breath. I was surprised to discover that many individuals unknowingly engage in reverse or chest breathing, a shallow breathing pattern that induces a stress state in the body. Diaphragmatic breathing not only relaxes the body but also lowers blood pressure and releases stress.

My gratitude for singing extends beyond the joy of music; it has imparted invaluable knowledge and the countless benefits of deep breaths. Personally, diaphragmatic breathing has been a powerful tool for calming myself in moments of feeling out of control or helpless. I've learned to pause first and utilize the most potent resource available to me in those moments – my breath!

One of the most powerful resources for cultivating presence and calming the entire being is the simple act of focusing on the breath.

Pranayama, derived from the Sanskrit word for breathing, translates as breath control. During some of life's most challenging moments, taking a moment to pause, turn inward, and just breathe can serve as a powerful antidote to worry and anxiety.

I vividly recall waking up in the middle of the night, gripped by concern for my daughter's safety. In those anxious moments, I found solace by directing all my attention to my breath – a practice that allowed me to let go of tension and embrace relaxation.

To enhance my breath-focused moments, I enjoy the app called Insight Timer, which offers a treasure trove of guided breathing and calming sessions. It has become a valuable companion on my journey to tranquility.

May we all find moments to center ourselves through the gift of conscious breathing.

Let's practice:

Sit tall and take a long, deep, focused breath in and a long, full breath out. Observe where the breath began. Did the abdomen move out on the inhale and in on the exhale? This is diaphragmatic breathing and is essential in yoga and in receiving the most benefits from your breaths. With just that one slow deep breath, did you feel a bit calmer and more present? If so, wonderful! That is the magic of breath. If not, learning and practicing different types of breathing exercises can help you to move towards a state of calm in a variety of life situations.

In this section you will learn many voluntary breathing techniques and yoga postures to reduce stress and calm your emotions. You will learn diaphragm breathing the three-part breath, alternate nostril breathing, ocean breath, cooling breath, bee breath, breath of fire, and fierce lion breath . A focus on the breath encourages everyday emotional management. It is the primary way to be present and heal.

YES for Breathing #1

1. Opening

◇ Letting Go

Questions of the day. On a piece of paper, that you will burn or dissolve at the end, write your answer to the question(s) below about what you wish to let go:

- *What stands in the way of being my best self?*
- *What do I find myself complaining about that I can release a grip on?*

◇ Hand on Heart Affirmations

"Breathing helps me to feel positively energized."

"Deep breathing gives me a peaceful feeling."

"I am mindful of my breathing in each moment."

◇ Personal Mantra

Choose a mantra of your own that speaks to you today. Begin with "I am," and say it in the present moment as if it already exists! Your personal mantra should be something you truly believe. Say it out loud with energy, emotion, vigor, enthusiasm, and intention to grow these positive seeds within you!

Example Mantra: *"I am filled with great power, focus, and energy and anything is possible when I am in a high vibration and happy state!"*

◇ **Gratitude and Energy**

Say to yourself or out-loud what you are grateful for and what positive energy you wish to invite into your life today. You may also choose an angel card with a word or message of inspiration for the day.

2. Restorative Yoga Asana #1 and Breath Assessment

Basic Relaxation Pose

Set-up: Lie down on the floor or on a yoga mat with a blanket or pillow under your head. Place a rolled-up blanket or bolster under your knees. You may also place blankets under your arms. You may place an eye pillow over your eyes. Make sure you feel fully supported and relaxed.

◇ **Breath Assessment:**

Come into the posture and begin to release any past or future thoughts. Relax and surrender more and more with every breath. Notice your breathing pattern without trying to change anything. Notice the rise and fall of the belly and chest. Observe the length of the breath. Is it flowing naturally and helping you to become calmer? Or does your breath feel rapid or shallow, creating tension? Just observe for 3-5 minutes. Now, count your inhales and exhales. Extend the exhales to assist your body in coming to a deeper state of relaxation, activating the parasympathetic nervous system (rest and digest). Allow your body and mind to surrender to the present moment and just be.

3. Technique #1: 8 Breaths to Joy [1]

I love to use this simple breath technique to focus on inviting in joy. One breath, one word. In 8 breaths and 8 words I can feel much more ease and calm. Remain in the restorative posture for 8 Breaths to Joy. Cultivation of joy is a vital part of mindfulness practice. Joy helps us to be more fully present in life, and gives us the motivation we need to embrace and transform our suffering. Use this practice for cultivating joy anytime and anywhere. You may wish to record your voice saying the following and then listen while you relax or go to www.y4es.

Let's practice:

1. **With the first breath**, bring your awareness to the sensation of your breathing. Pay close attention to the physical sensation of your breath as it moves in and out. Say to yourself *breath*.

2. **With the second breath**, bring your attention to all of the sensations in your body. Allow your awareness to completely fill your body, and notice what you find. Some sensations will be pleasant, some unpleasant, and some neutral. *Feel* these sensations without trying to change them at all. Say to yourself *body*.

3. **With the third breath**, actively release all of the tension, or agitation in your body. Imagine tension is being washed out of you with the exhale breath. Say to yourself *release*.

4. **With the fourth breath**, fill your heart with love and generosity toward yourself. Bring forth the feeling of kindness and compassion to your body and mind. Say to yourself *love*.

5. **With the fifth breath,** notice if there are any attachments or aversions present in you. Is there any part of you that wants reality to be different than it is right now? Are you not accepting things-as-they-are or fighting against them? Just notice and let yourself feel them without trying to make them go away. They are not your

1 https://www.mindful.org/8-breaths-to-joy-a-guided-practice/

enemy. They are a part of you that needs love and caring. Say to yourself **attachments**.

6. **With the sixth breath,** become aware that everything you need to be happy is already present in this moment. All of the conditions that are needed for peace, joy, and freedom are already here. In every moment of life, there are infinite reasons to suffer, and infinite reasons to be happy. Where are you putting your attention? Focus on the positive conditions that are available in this moment. Let go of any suffering or low vibrational energy. Say to yourself **let go**.

7. **With the seventh breath,** become aware that you are alive. As you breathe, feel the energy of life moving through you. With this breath, we recognize the miracle of being alive. Say to yourself **alive**.

8. **With the eighth breath**, become aware of all of the beauty within and around you. As soon as we let go of our desires and bring awareness to the present moment, we see that reality is beautiful. All of our senses–our sight, sound, smell, taste, touch, and mental perception–deliver this beauty to us like a precious gift. All we have to do is enjoy. Say to yourself **beauty**.

Practice the eight breaths to joy by saying one word for each in and out breath like this:

1. Breath (In/Out)
2. Body (In/Out)
3. Release (In/Out)
4. Love (In/Out)
5. Craving (In/Out)
6. Letting Go (In/Out)
7. Alive (In/Out)
8. Beauty (In/Out)

4. Yoga Asanas: Focus on the Breath

Let's practice:

Come to all 4's: Cow/Cat pose. Inhale and arch the back into cow pose, open the heart, and look up. Exhale and round the back into cat pose, look down. Move through cow and cat pose 4-6 times to feel the movement with the breath to wake up the spine. Notice how the inhale and arching of the back in cow pose opens the whole front body and heart. It extends or expands the spine. Notice how the exhale and rounding of the back in cat pose opens the back body. It contracts the spine. All breathing is a flow of expansion and contraction. Tuck your toes under and straighten the legs to **Downward Facing Dog.** Take five long, slow, deep breaths here as you focus on the expansion and contraction of the breath. Walk the feet towards the hands into a forward fold. Take five more deep breaths and then roll up to standing.

Stand into Mountain Pose. Wake up the spine by moving it in all five directions.

Spinal Extension: Inhale and reach the arms up.

Side Stretch: Exhale and stretch to the right side. Inhale to the center. Exhale and stretch to the left side. Inhale to the center. Exhale interlace the hands behind the head.

Upper Back Bend: Rest the head back in your hands. Hold this position as you inhale and lift the heart and gaze up for an upper back bend and then exhale and bring your head back to center.

Forward Fold: Exhale and fold forward. Release the hands to the earth and allow the head to relax. Inhale to stand.

Twist: Exhale and twist to the right with prayer hands or extending the arms out. Inhale to the center. Exhale and twist to the left with prayer hands or extending the arms out. Inhale back to center and stand in mountain pose. Feel the energy and the awakened spine. Take six deep breaths for one minute.

Fierce lion[2] Breath with High Lunge: This Breathing technique helps to relieve tension and stress and to let go of what is not serving you in your life like worry, anxiety or emotional pain. Stand in High Lunge pose. Reach your arms straight up and then throw your arms back as you stick your tongue out and release the air out in a forceful breath out or with a growl like a lion! Do this 4-6 times until you feel a great sense of release within.

Secondary Fierce Lion Breath posture:

Stand in Goddess Pose and reach arms straight up and then throw your arms through the legs as you fold forward and stick your tongue out to release the air and the accompanying tension with a "Ha!" or a growl like a lion.

2 Name and action from Sadie Nardini, founder of Core Strength Vinyasa. www.Sadienardini.com

5. Technique #2: Emotional Guidance Scale[3]

Emotions are important and necessary. All emotions are to be felt and expressed in healthy, non-harmful ways. High vibrational feelings of love and joy feel good. When we are in this state, we feel open and alive and free to express ourselves. We feel happy and compassionate. Low vibrational feelings of fear, anger, and depression don't feel good. We feel closed off and sluggish. Our body responds with tightness or pain. We all find ourselves in varying emotional states all through our lives. Staying stuck in any one, especially the low vibration ones, for too long is not healthy. The Emotional Guidance Scale created by Abraham Hicks can help.

At the top of the scale is love and at the bottom is fear. Whenever we respond to the situations in our lives, we are either responding from a place of love or fear. Love encompasses the "good feeling" emotions listed from 1 to 7 and fear covers the "not- so- good-feeling" emotions listed from 8 to 22.

Let's Practice:

Here is how to use the Emotional Guidance Scale. Picture a current or recent situation where feelings of anger, fear, blame, insecurity, jealousy, or any low vibration emotion came up. Find this emotion on the scale. Really feel this emotion fully and completely. Say out loud or think about why you feel/felt it and where in your body you feel/felt it. Next, choose the next emotion up the scale and sit with that emotion. Your goal is to move from feeling bad to feeling better, one emotion at a time. Speak and think yourself up on the scale.

---

3 Abraham Hicks - Emotional Guidance Scale. www.abraham-hicks.com

EMOTIONAL GUIDANCE SCALE:

1. Love/Joy/Freedom

2. Passion

3. Enthusiasm/Eagerness/Happiness

4. Positive Expectations/Belief

5. Optimism/Trust

6. Hopefulness

7. Contentment

8. Boredom

9. Pessimism

10. Frustration/Irritation/Impatience

11. Overwhelmingness

12. Disappointment

13. Doubt

14. Worry

15. Blame

16. Discouragement

17. Anger

18. Revenge

19. Hatred/Rage

20. Jealousy

21. Insecurity/Guilt/Unworthiness

22. Fear/Grief/Depression/Despair/Powerlessness

6. Restorative Yoga Asana #2: Incline legs with Strap and Body Scan

Essential Oil Suggestion: Peppermint

Set-up: Use two blocks. Place one on the highest level and the other on the medium level in front of it. Lean a bolster or a tightly rolled blanket against it. Lie down on the floor with your legs up on the bolster. Take a yoga strap or belt, wrap it around your legs and secure your legs to the bolster for support. Lie back with a pillow or blanket for your head.

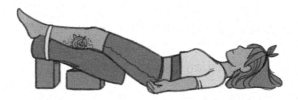

EO: You may place peppermint essential oil on your wrists or diffuse it in the air. Breathe in the essential oils to open up the passageways in the nostrils and the whole body. Take long, deep relaxing breaths. Play relaxing spa music, theta music, Tibetan singing bowl sounds or nature sounds. Rest and Relax.

Let's Practice:

Body Scan. Visualize a nice warm light moving down your body from the crown of your head to your feet. As you picture each body part, imagine all tension releasing.

There is no need to narrate. Just *feel,* as the warm, healing light calms and relaxes the whole head. Visualize the light moving down to the forehead at the third eye center, easing and releasing all tension or lines there. It moves down to the eye sockets bathing them in warmth and comfort. Feel as the light moves down to the cheeks and nose, ears, and jaw letting all tension go. Feel as the light moves to the neck and chest and shoulders bringing a feeling of ease and surrender.

The warm, bright light moves down the torso, healing and nourishing all of the internal organs. A sense of peace washes over the whole upper body. Picture the light moving down the hips helping them to settle and sink deeper into a restful state. The warm light moves down the legs, thighs, and calves, and all the way to the feet and toes. Now the light washes over the whole body, creating a sense of deep peace, relaxation, and equanimity. Remain here in this relaxed state for as long as you like.

7. Technique #2: Skull Shining (Kapalbhati Breath) and Cooling Breath (Sitali)

Skull Shining breath is a forceful exhale of air with passive inhales.

It improves circulation, sharpens memory, lowers blood pressure, helps reduce acid reflux, tones digestion, supports the immune system, energizes the body and brain, and balances and strengthens the nervous system.

Note: There are many contraindications (conditions that make something inadvisable) for Skull Shining breathing including but not limited to: pregnancy, high or low blood pressure, hernia, epilepsy, vertigo, and more. Do not practice this if you are experiencing any of these. Skull Shining breathing should be practiced on an empty stomach.

Let's practice:

To begin, sit crossed legged on a cushion on the floor if possible or in a chair. Throughout this practice, breath through the nose. Close your eyes and take a few relaxing breaths.

Exhale the air forcefully through your nose (without strain) while simultaneously pulling the navel towards the spine, contracting the abdominal muscles

- Release the abdomen and let the inhale happen naturally

- Continue this at a medium rate (not too quick or too slow) that feels natural and energizing. Repeat approximately 20 times.

You may begin with a slower rate of 1 exhale breath every 2 or 3 seconds. With practice, future sessions may be faster with 1 breath per second and up to 40 or more repetitions.

- When finished, pause and take note of how you are feeling. Notice sensations in your body and how you feel mentally and physically.

Cooling breath is a breath technique to relax and cool the mind and body. It expels toxins and cleanses and moistens the system. It involves breathing in through a curled tongue to instantly cool the mouth on the inhale. This is a nice practice to do when you are feeling angry or physically hot.

Let's Practice:

- Begin by sitting in a relaxed upright posture. Curl the tongue or, if unable to, make an "O" shape with your lips like sipping through a straw
- Inhale through your tube-shaped tongue or "O" shape for 6 counts
- Lower your chin to your chest, close your mouth and exhale through your nose. Repeat these steps 3 to 8 times
- When finished, pause and take note of how you are feeling. Notice sensations in your body and how you feel mentally and physically

8. Restorative Yoga Asana #3: Lounge Chair Savasana with Yoga Nidra

Essential Oil Suggestion: Lavender

Set-up: Place two blocks next to each other—one on the highest level and the other on the medium level, or one on the medium level and one on the lowest level. Lean a bolster or a tightly rolled blanket against it. Lie down with your bottom close to the bottom edge of the bolster and recline back. Use rolled blankets or pillows under your arms for arm rest support. Place a rolled blanket or bolster under your knees if you wish. Place an eye pillow on your eyes.

EO: You may place *Lavender* essential oil on your wrists or diffuse it in the air. Breathe in the essential oils to open up the passageways in the nostrils and the whole body. Take long, deep, calming breaths. Play relaxing spa music, theta music, Tibetan singing bowl sounds or nature sounds. Rest and relax.

Yoga Nidra. Now begin the practice of Yoga Nidra. Yoga Nidra is translated as "yogic sleep." It is a relaxing hypnagogic state between wake and sleep to assist your body in relaxing and turning the awareness inward by listening to spoken instructions. During the practice of Yoga Nidra, you will be asked to move your awareness to various body parts, sensations, emotions, and images. Try not to concentrate too intensely, as this may prevent you from relaxing. If the mind becomes overactive with thoughts and worries, just come back to the guiding sound of the voice.

You may find many guided Yoga Nidra practices on YouTube or on the Insight Timer App. You may record yourself reading a Yoga Nidra script from a Yoga Nidra Book [4] (See Footnote for recommended book). You may also listen to a recorded Yoga Nidra session by Christine Shaw on www/y4es.com/practices.

---

4 Yoga Nidra by Swami Satyananda Saraswati. Yoga Publications Trust, 2001

9. Closing. Burning or Dissolving Ritual

◇ **Letting Go.**

Get a lighter and a heat resistant bowl (for the burning ritual) or a bowl filled with room temperature or warm water (for the dissolving ritual). Take the paper with the answer to the letting go question and say the following out loud:

> *"Dear Universe–I no longer need these thoughts, feelings, or circumstances that do not serve my highest and best good. I vow to be open to the lessons presented to me in order to create positive habits and improve my outlook on life."*

Now place the paper in the bowl, light it on fire and watch it burn or take special dissolving paper and place it in the water and watch it dissolve. Let it go.

◇ **Inviting- In.**

Read one of the following quotes of inspiration below or choose your own. You may choose to print it on a paper or sticky note to post where you will see it. Say the following out loud:

> *"Dear Universe–I invite this message of inspiration into my life at this time to serve my highest and best good. I promise to be more present and kinder to myself every day."*

What will you invite into your life today?

1. Statement of gratitude to the Universe:

> *"Thank you, universe for allowing me to attract love and understanding into my life today with every breath."*

2. Quotes of inspiration:

    "Breathe. Let go. And remind yourself that this very moment is the only one you know you have for sure." ~ *Oprah Winfrey*

    "Breathe in deeply to bring your mind home to your body." ~ *Thich Nhat Hanh*

Story #1. Carrying the Poop
(Release past and future thoughts)

One bright sunny summer day I went out for a morning walk with my dog, Sosa. We walked along together enjoying the beautiful sky, puffy clouds, and gentle breeze. The sun was shining and I was just enjoying the present moment with nothing to do but take a nice walk. Then Sosa paused, sniffed, turned in a few circles and pooped. As usual I got out my poop bag and scooped up his business, tied a knot in the bag and we continued on our way. On this day in particular though I became really aware of the fact that I was holding a bag of poop. It was a little heavy (a bigger dump than usual) and I could smell the not-so-lovely odor coming from inside.

I started to feel like I just wanted to get rid of it as fast as I could. I began to notice all of the turmoil running through my head about carrying this bag of poop. I had forgotten about the lovely day that I was, not two minutes ago, really enjoying. Then suddenly an "ah-ha" moment arose and I began thinking of this as a great life analogy. "Here I am carrying this poop. Yes. The bag of poop is in my hand and I don't really like carrying it, but can I go ahead and carry it and still enjoy this nice walk with my wonderful dog and the beautiful day? Can I have crap that I am carrying around and still be content?"

We all carry crap around in our minds. You know, the things in life that we don't really like or enjoy, or may even hate and want to get rid of. We can choose to focus on and be distracted by the poop and miss out on the present moment, or just know that it is there and enjoy the present despite the tough stuff. I continued to think about this analogy and how I wished to get rid of the poop. I began to look for a trash can to put it in, but there wasn't one around. I thought, "What if I put it in someone's yard and just walked away?" Then I would be making my poop someone else's problem to handle. Sometimes we do that when blaming someone else for our problems or the emotions that arise in us. Then I thought, "It could be worse. I could have forgotten to bring a bag and I could be holding the poop directly in my hand right now! Fortunately, I can hold it neatly over here in this bag that is not a part of me but something separate, and do something about it later." In life we may have a problem we need to solve but we don't have to carry it with us all the time and ruin the moment we are in.

With all of these realizations, I began to enjoy the walk even more, looking around with Sosa when he paused to rest under a tree, talking to the mailman, noticing the shapes in the clouds, and taking deep breaths of contentment in the present. I enjoyed the rest of the walk, forgetting completely (almost) about the bag of poop. When I got home I threw it in the trash with a sigh. "That was easy," I thought and continued on with my day.

YES for Breathing #2

1. Opening

◇ **Letting Go**

Questions of the day. On a piece of paper, that you will burn or dissolve at the end, write your answer to the question(s) below about what you wish to let go:

1. *What interactions or situations do I worry about from the past or future that cause me stress?*

2. *Finish this sentence: "There is nothing so bad that (a negative thought or reaction) won't make it even worse."*

◇ **Hand on Heart Affirmations**

"I bring awareness to my breath to reduce stress of any kind. "

"I am comforted by my breathing."

"I can relax my body and mind through deep breathing."

◇ **Personal Mantras**

Choose a mantra of your own that speaks to you today. Begin with "I am,"

and say it in the present moment as if it already exists! Your personal mantra should be something you truly believe. Say it out loud with energy, emotion, vigor, enthusiasm, and intention to grow these positive seeds within you!

Example Mantra: *"I am the creator of my life! I love learning and growing and serving every day! I choose and surround myself with positive thoughts and feelings!"*

◇ **Gratitude and Energy**

Say to yourself or out loud what you are grateful for and what positive energy you wish to invite into your life today! You may also choose an angel card with a word or a message of inspiration for the day.

2. Restorative Yoga Asana #1 and Breath Assessment: Gentle Heart Opener with Blanket Brush and Bolster

Set-up: Take a Blanket Brush (a yoga blanket folded in half twice and rolled up so the fringe is on the end) and place it along the length of your yoga mat. Sit on the end of the blanket and lie back resting your spine along the length of the blanket. Reach under the blanket part that is under your neck and make a little blip (a fold in the blanket) to support the curve of your neck. Place a rolled blanket or bolster under your knees if you wish. Place an eye pillow on your eyes. Another option for a heart opening pose is a rolled blanket across the upper back and a rolled blanket or bolster under your knees if you wish. Make sure you feel fully supported and relaxed.

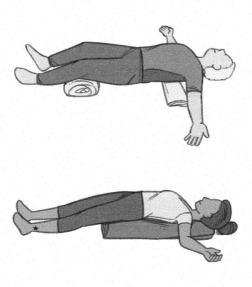

◇ **Breath Assessment:**

Come into the posture and begin to release any past or future thoughts. Relax and surrender more and more with every breath. Notice your breathing pattern without trying to change anything. Notice the rise and fall of the belly and chest. Observe the length of the breath. Is it flowing naturally, helping you to become calmer, or does your breath feel rapid or shallow, creating tension? Just observe for 3-5 minutes. Now count your inhales and exhales. Extend the exhales to assist your body in coming to a deeper state of relaxation, activating the parasympathetic nervous system (rest and digest). Allow your body and mind to surrender to the present moment and just be.

Technique #1:
Alternate nostril breathing (Nadi Shodhana)

Alternate nostril breathing, or Nadi Shodhana, is a subtle energy clearing, breathing technique that settles the mind, body, and emotions. It also reduces stress, balances the right and left brain, improves focus, supports lung function, and removes toxins. Streams of energy radiate through us in what is called the nadis. The nadi ending in the right nostril is called pingala. The nadi ending in the left nostril is called ida. The central nadi, sushumna, ends at the point between the nostrils where the nasal septum joins the upper lip. The activity of these nadis is reflected in the flow of breath within the nostrils. When pingala is active, the breath flows more prominently through the right nostril. Right nostril activity represents the masculine energy, more activity and internal heat. When ida is active, the breath flows more freely through the left nostril. Left nostril activity represents the feminine energy, and a calm mind and body, rest, and internal coolness.

When the central nadi (sushumna) is awakened, the two nostrils flow equally.[5]

When you are feeling overwhelmed or anxious, try this yoga breathing technique to find balance in the body, rejuvenate the nervous system, and calm the emotions.

Let's Practice:

- Sit up comfortably with a tall spine.
- Take your right hand and cross it over towards your left nostril.
- Rest your middle finger and index finger on the forehead between the eyebrows.
- Take a long deep breath in through both nostrils and exhale out.
- Place the thumb of your right hand onto the right nostril.
- Close your eyes and take a long deep inhale breath in through the left nostril.
- Close the left nostril with your ring finger, and retain the breath for a pause.
- Release the thumb from the right nostril and exhale out; pause at the end of the exhale.

---

5 Content from https://yogainternational.com/article/view/self-study-nostril-dominance

- Inhale through the right nostril.
- Close the right nostril with the thumb, and retain the breath for a pause.
- Release the ring finger from the left nostril and exhale out; pause at the end of the exhale.
- Repeat for 5-10 cycles.

When you complete the cycles, release the hand and take long, slow, deep breaths in and out through both nostrils. Notice any changes in your mental state, body and emotions.

4. Yoga Asana: Breath of Joy

This breath energizes the body, gives you a pick-me-up, and lifts your mood.

Let's Practice:

Stand in Mountain Pose. Take three short inhale breaths through the nose, filling up the belly, middle of the body, and the chest, respectively. Exhale everything out through your mouth. So–breathe in, in, in, out. The following arm movements go along with these breaths.

Inhale Breath #1 - Reach the arms forward and across the chest.

Inhale Breath #2 - Reach the arms out to the side of the body.

Inhale Breath #3 - Reach the arms all the way up overhead.

Exhale Breath #4 - Throw the arms beside the body as you fold forward.

Repeat 5 to 8 times. When finished, pause to feel the energy flowing in the body.

Do you feel more energy? More focus? More joy? You can use this technique whenever you need a little pick-me-up of energy, focus, and joy! (You may feel a bit dizzy. If so, you can fold only part way forward when expelling the air.)

5. Technique #2: Grounding taps[6]

This technique from Donna Eden and Eden Energy Medicine is designed to help you feel grounded in your body. Have you ever felt so unsure, overwhelmed, or just out of sorts that you felt like you were floating and not in a good way? A feeling of instability can lead to stress and tension. Grounding oneself spiritually, mentally, and physically helps us to feel stable and able to handle whatever comes our way.

Let's Practice:

Stand firmly in Mountain Pose. Tap, thump, or rub the following four areas of the body as you take three deep breaths with each one.

1. Cheekbones - Associated with the stomach. Helps with digestion.

2. Under the Collarbone - Associated with the kidneys. Helps to reduce toxins.

3. Center of the chest - Associated with the thymus. Helps boost the immune system.

4. Sides of the body by the rib cage - Associated with the Spleen. Helps improve metabolism.

---

6 Donna Eden Energy Medicine Technique

Stand still and notice if you feel more centered and grounded.

Another great and fun way to feel grounded is to go outside in your bare feet and walk in the wet grass!

6. Restorative Yoga Asana #2: Seated Forward Fold

Essential Oil Suggestion: Eucalyptus

Set-up: In a seated position with wide legs extended or in a wide knee child's pose, place a bolster propped up by blocks, blankets, or pillows, on the floor in front of you. You may place multiple blankets on top of the bolster to raise it up so your chest can lie comfortably on top. Rest your chest on the bolster and use another blanket or pillow for your head. Your arms may be propped with blocks or blankets at your sides. Another option is to place a blanket on the seat of a folding chair and rest your arms and head on the chair.

EO: Place eucalyptus essential oil on your wrists or diffuse it in the air. Breathe in the essential oils to open up the passageways in the nostrils and the whole body. Take long, deep, relaxing breaths. Play relaxing spa music, theta music, Tibetan singing bowl sounds or nature sounds. Rest and relax.

7. Technique #3: R.A.I.N. by Tara Brach[7]

The acronym R.A.I.N. is a four-step process to use when feeling overwhelmed, insecure, or unworthy. Practicing R.A.I.N. will help us to cultivate self-compassion.

You can take your time and explore R.A.I.N. as a stand-alone meditation or move through the steps whenever challenging feelings arise.

Let's Practice:
R.A.I.N.
Recognize what is happening (roots of understanding)
Allow life to be just as it is (grounds of love)
Investigate with gentle attention (deepens understanding)
Nurture (awakens love)

R–Recognize What's Going On
Recognizing means consciously acknowledging, in any given moment, the thoughts, feelings, and behaviors that are affecting you.
A–Allow the Experience to be There Just as It Is
Allowing means letting the thoughts, emotions, feelings, or sensations you have recognized to simply be there, without trying to fix or avoid anything.
You might recognize fear, and allow by mentally whispering "it's ok" or "this belongs."
I–Investigate with Interest and Care
To investigate, call on your natural curiosity and direct a more focused attention to your present experience. You might ask yourself:

7 tarabrach.com/rain

What most wants attention? How am I experiencing this in my body? What am I believing? What does this vulnerable place want from me? What does it most need? Whatever the inquiry, your investigation will be most transformational if you step away from conceptualizing and bring your primary attention to the felt-sense in the body.

N–Nurture with Self-Compassion

Self-compassion begins to naturally arise in the moments that you recognize you are suffering. It comes into fullness as you intentionally nurture your inner life with self-care. To do this, try to sense what the wounded, frightened, or hurting place inside you most needs, and then offer some gesture of active care that might address this need. Does it need a message of reassurance? Of forgiveness? Of companionship? Of love? It might be the mental whisper: *I'm here with you. I'm sorry, and I love you. I love you, and I'm listening. It's not your fault. Trust in your goodness.*

8. Restorative Yoga Asana #3: Lounge Chair Savasana

Essential Oil Suggestion: Cardamom

Set-up: Place two blocks next to each other–one on the highest level and the other on the medium level, or one on the medium level and one on the lowest level. Lean a bolster or a tightly rolled blanket against it. Lie down with your bottom close to the bottom edge of the bolster and recline back. Use rolled blankets or pillows under your arms for arm rest support. Place a rolled blanket or bolster under your knees if you wish. Place an eye pillow on your eyes.

EO: You may place *Cardamom* essential oil on your wrists or diffuse it in the air. Breathe in the essential oils to open up the passageways in the nostrils and the whole body. Take long, deep, calming breaths. Play relaxing spa music, theta music, Tibetan singing bowl sounds or nature sounds. Rest and relax.

9. Closing. Burning or Dissolving Ritual

◇ **Letting Go.**

Get a lighter and a heat resistant bowl (for the burning ritual) or a bowl filled with room temperature or warm water (for the dissolving ritual). Take the paper with the answer to the letting go question and say the following out loud:

> *"Dear Universe–I no longer need these thoughts, feelings, or circumstances that do not serve my highest and best good. I vow to be open to the lessons presented to me in order to create positive habits and improve my outlook on life."*

Now place the paper in the bowl, light it on fire and watch it burn or take special dissolving paper and place it in the water and watch it dissolve. Let it go.

◇ **Inviting In.**

Read one of the following quotes of inspiration below or choose your own. You may choose to print it on a paper or sticky note to post where you will see it. Say the following out loud:

> *"Dear Universe–I invite this message of inspiration into my life at this time to serve my highest and best good. I promise to be kind to myself and more present every day."*

What will you invite into your life today?

Statement of gratitude to the universe:

> *"Thank you, Universe, for every breath I take. With each breath, I remain present to 'what is' so I may enjoy each person, conversation, activity, and opportunity."*

Quotes of inspiration:

> *"When you inhale, you are taking the strength from God. When you exhale, it represents the service you are giving to the world." ~ BKS Iyengar*

> *"Who will tell whether one happy moment of love or the joy of breathing or walking on a bright morning and smelling the fresh air, is not worth all the suffering and effort which life implies." ~ Erich Fromm*

Story #2. Losing the Key
(Expectations)

I had a long to-do list and about an hour before I needed to move on to the next thing, teaching a yoga class. I took one look at Sosa who had been inside all day and looked bored. I thought I had just enough time to go to the dog park for a quick walk. We got in the car and zipped over to the dog park, eight minutes away. We jumped out of the car and I grabbed the necessities, gloves (it was cold), cell phone (to know the time), my single car key, the leash, and poop bags, and we were off. As we walked towards the park, essentially a giant field near a big pond, I realized I had no pockets in my coat or yoga pants, so I carried all my stuff in my hands. There were lots of people there and their dogs were running around sniffing, barking, chasing balls and frisbees, playing, and having fun! I let Sosa off of the leash and he enthusiastically ran to sniff and play with the dogs in the field.

I go to the dog park a lot where most folks stand around talking, drinking coffee, or texting on their phones. On this day, one person was sitting on a little stool that he brought and others were standing around talking as their dogs exercised like crazy! I made some small talk and kept an eye out for Sosa. When he gets tired after running around, he usually heads for the pond to get a drink. Today was no different. I headed down to the water after him. I threw a stick and played for a while and then we made our way back up the hill where the rest of the people and dogs were. I checked the time and realized I had just enough time to head home, drop off Sosa, and get to the studio to teach.

I clipped Sosa's leash on and began to leave, saying goodbye to everyone. I reached in my pocket for my key and ... no pocket. No key! Ahhhhhh! I realized that I must have dropped it somewhere in this huge field. I began looking all around in a small panic, knowing I really had no time to spare. There were lots of people around and so I called out to everyone: "I just lost my key! Can you help me find it?" Someone said, "Where did you lose it?" With a sweeping motion of my arm in a full circle across my body from left to right, I said, "Somewhere in this entire area!"

Nobody moved an inch. One person said, "I guess you will have to sleep in your car." Another person said, "You should hide a key under your car." I said that I did have one hidden but it only unlocks the car. It won't start the car. After a few more of those comments and watching nobody moving from their positions, I thought to myself: *What?? Nobody is going to help me?! I can't believe it! Stupid, uncaring people. Geez! Now I am not going to make it to the studio.*

Then I immediately had another thought: *It's not their responsibility to help me. I was the one who lost my key. I have an expectation they will help, but why am I getting mad that they aren't?* I kept looking as I pondered what I should do about getting to the studio to teach if I didn't find my key soon. I made my way down to look near the water on the other side of the hill where I had been playing with Sosa. No key.

I started to walk back to the field, and when I came up over the hill, I saw a lovely sight! *Every* person, including the guy who had been sitting on the stool and suggesting I sleep in my car, was looking for my key! They all had their heads down and were wandering in the fields, searching. I was so happy! I immediately thought about how just a few minutes ago I was calling them names and judging them for not helping me.

In just a few seconds a woman calmly looked at me with her hand up holding a single key and said, "Is this it?" I said, "Yes!!" and gave her, a stranger, a big hug and thanked her! I hurried to the car, dropped the dog off, and got to the studio on time! Of course, my class message and theme that night was all about the lost key and how we can have expectations of people or things. We never know how things will turn out. I believe that my immediate change of thought from *stupid uncaring people* to *why am I having these expectations of others? I'm going to let that go*, helped me to send out good vibes that rippled through the dog park and to the person who found my key. Thank you for your random act of kindness, people of the dog park.

YES for Breathing #3

1. Opening

◇ **Letting Go**

Questions of the day. On a piece of paper, that you will burn or dissolve at the end, write your answer to the question(s) below about what you wish to let go:

1. *What judgements do I hold about myself or others that keep me from experiencing peace and joy?*

2. *What negative mantra or affirmation do I say to myself that does not serve my best good? "I am... (insert negative thoughts)."*

◇ **Hand on Heart Affirmations**

"Deep relaxed breathing gives me strength and courage."
"I am more focused because of my breathing."
"I am more in touch with my body when I take long, slow breaths."

◇ **Personal Mantra**

Choose a mantra of your own that speaks to you today. Begin with "I am," and say it in the present moment as if it already exists! Your personal mantra should be something you truly believe. Say it out loud with energy, emotion, vigor, enthusiasm, and intention to grow these positive seeds within you!

Example Mantra: *"Lord, I am an instrument of your peace. I spread light and love wherever I go and turn doubt into faith. I am giving and loving."*

Prayer of Saint Francis
Lord, make me an instrument of your peace:
where there is hatred, let me sow love;

where there is injury, pardon;
where there is doubt, faith;
where there is despair, hope;
where there is darkness, light;
where there is sadness, joy.

O divine Master, grant that I may not so much seek
to be consoled as to console,
to be understood as to understand,
to be loved as to love.
For it is in giving that we receive,
it is in pardoning that we are pardoned,
and it is in dying that we are born to eternal life.
Amen.

◇ **Gratitude and Energy**

Say to yourself or out loud what you are grateful for and what positive energy you wish to invite into your life today! You may also choose an angel card with a word or a message of inspiration for the day.

2. Restorative Yoga Asana #1 and Breath Assessment: Five Blanket Relaxation Pose

Set-up: Place two folded blankets on top of each other and place this at the top of your yoga mat or on the floor. Make a Captain's Cap[8] pillow for your head. Fold blankets into thin armrests for each arm. Lie down on the floor or mat and rest your back on the blankets, your head on the pillow, and your arms on the arm rests. You may also choose to place a rolled-up blanket or bolster under your knees. Enjoy this restful, supportive position.

---

8 Term from Judy Curiel, Restorative Yoga Teacher. Take a folded blanket and fold two corners in towards the middle making a point. Fold this part over the blanket and then flip the whole thing over to make a "nest" for your head.

◇ **Breath Assessment:**

Come into the posture and begin to release any past or future thoughts. Relax and surrender more and more with every breath. Notice your breathing pattern without trying to change anything. Notice the rise and fall of the belly and chest. Observe the length of the breath. Is it flowing naturally helping you to become calmer, or does it feel rapid or shallow creating tension. Just observe for 3-5 minutes. Now count your inhales and exhales. Extend the exhales to assist your body in coming to a deeper state of relaxation, activating the parasympathetic nervous system (rest and digest). Allow your body and mind to surrender to the present moment and just be.

3. Technique #1: Crocodile Breath

This breathing technique is designed to strengthen the diaphragm muscles and helps you to breathe more effectively and deeply. Breathing deeply and fully is a key to optimal health.

Let's Practice:

Lie prone (on the belly) with your hands stacked and the forehead resting on the back of the hand to help the head and neck remain in a neutral position. Begin to inhale for 5-6 counts, pause for 2-4 counts, and exhale for 7-8 counts. On the inhale, feel the belly move towards the floor and the lower back and sides expand. Repeat this cycle 6-30 times or for 1-5 minutes.

4. Yoga Asana: Hara Breathing with Tai Chi

Hara (Japanese) or Dantian (Chinese) or Chi simply means breath or the energy in the center of the body below the navel in the lower abdomen. Oxygen moving around the body increases concentration, enhances the immune system, calms the body, emotions and mind, and helps to reduce stress. Noticing the breath in this area helps you to feel more grounded, rooted, and centered.

The basic breathing principles in Tai Chi are storing and delivering energy. Tai Chi movements alternate between gathering, storing, and delivering energy. When you inhale, taking in life-giving oxygen into the body, you are gathering and storing energy. When you exhale, you are delivering energy or force.

Let's Practice:

Begin by placing the hands on the lower abdomen with fingers touching in the center. As you breathe in, the fingers come apart and expand. Notice where the breath is moving in your body. Where do you notice it expanding? Exhale and notice the breath leave the body as you contract. Notice how this feels. Continue breathing this way, filling up the lower abdomen with energy and releasing it for another few minutes. Now, follow these steps to add movement with the breath:

- Move your hands up to the center of your chest and hold them apart from each other, palms facing, as if you are holding an invisible ball of energy.

- With your knees slightly bent, pick up your right foot and place it two feet in front of the left.

- Lean forward and place weight on that foot as you move your hands down and away from your body on the exhale and then back up and towards your chest on the inhale, drawing a circle in the air in front of your body. Repeat this 6-12 times on one side, and then switch so the left leg is forward.

5. Technique #2:
The 12 Pathways to Higher Consciousness[9]

In Ken Keyes' book, *The Handbook to Higher Consciousness*, he lays out the afflictions we have that block us from achieving our highest good. They come in the form of seven centers of consciousness: the security center, the sensations center, the power center, the love center, the cornucopia center, the conscious awareness center and the cosmic consciousness center. Our consciousness can be dominated by our past programming that makes us either attach to things or have an aversion to things in our lives. At any given time in our days, we are operating from one of these centers. We can use each of the 12 Pathways to Higher Consciousness as affirmations to help us to be more present.

My sister told me about this book in the early 90's. I loved the idea of being in a higher state of consciousness and I tried to memorize all

---

9 From the book *The Handbook to Higher Consciousness* by Ken Keyes Handbook to higher consciousness. Eden Grove Editions, Publication Year 1997

of the pathways, but settled on remembering the four categories: Freeing Myself, Being Here Now, Interacting with Others, and Discovering my Conscious Awareness. I try to remember which one I am operating from as I move through life.

The 12 Pathways to Higher Consciousness:

FREEING MYSELF

1. I am freeing myself from security, sensation, and power addictions that make me try to forcefully control situations in my life, and thus destroy my serenity and keep me from loving myself and others.

2. I am discovering how my consciousness-dominating addictions create my illusory version of the changing world of people and situations around me.

3. I welcome the opportunity (even if painful) that my minute-to-minute experience offers me to become aware of the addictions I must reprogram to be liberated from my robot-like emotional patterns.

BEING HERE NOW

4. I always remember that I have everything I need to enjoy my here and now—unless I am letting my consciousness be dominated by demands and expectations based on the dead past or the imagined future.

5. I take full responsibility here and now for everything I experience, for it is my own programming that creates my actions and also influences the reactions of people around me.

6. I accept myself completely here and now and consciously experience everything I feel, think, say, and do (including my emotion-backed addictions) as a necessary part of my growth into higher consciousness.

INTERACTING WITH OTHERS

7. I open myself genuinely to all people by being willing to fully communicate my deepest feelings, since hiding in any degree keeps me stuck in my illusion of separateness from other people.

8. I feel with loving compassion the problems of others without getting caught up emotionally in their predicaments that are offering them messages they need for their growth.

9. I act freely when I am tuned in, centered, and loving, but if possible, I avoid acting when I am emotionally upset and depriving myself of the wisdom that flows from love and expanded consciousness.

DISCOVERING MY CONSCIOUS-AWARENESS

10. I am continually calming the restless scanning of my rational mind in order to perceive the finer energies that enable me to intuitively merge with everything around me.

11. I am constantly aware of which of the Seven Centers of Consciousness I am using, and I feel my energy, perceptiveness, love, and inner peace growing as I open all of the Centers of Consciousness.

12. I am perceiving everyone, including myself, as an awakening being who is here to claim his or her birthright to the higher consciousness planes of unconditional love and oneness.

How to Use these 12 Pathways:

You may wish to take time to memorize all of these to discover where your thoughts and emotions are at any given time. The idea that we are freeing, discovering, welcoming, and reminding ourselves about our past programming continually throughout our days helps us to set an intention to create new ways of showing up in the world and moving to a higher state of conscious awareness.

Let's Practice:

Which of the twelve pathways resonate with you the most? I like #4 under the category of Being Here Now. To me, this is a powerful one and acts as a great affirmation. "I always remember that I have everything I need to enjoy my here and now unless I am letting my consciousness be dominated by demands and expectations based on the dead past or the imagined future." Choose your favorite one that speaks the most to you. Relax the mind and body and come to understand this powerful affirmation. Say the pathway that you chose to yourself throughout your day or anytime you notice the message from that pathway. Observe, reflect, and create new ways of experiencing life, expanding your awareness and living in a higher plane of consciousness.

6. Restorative Yoga Asana #2: Side Twist with Bolster and Blankets

Essential Oil Suggestion: Cedarwood

Set-up: Place a blanket on the floor or mat and another one for the head. Lie on your right side with a bolster in front of your body from the hips down. Keep the right leg straight and place your left leg on the bolster. You may also sandwich a bolster or rolled blanket between both legs. Rest your head on the blanket or on your arm for support. You may stay in this position for 5-10 minutes and then roll to the other side if you wish.

EO: You may place cedar wood essential oil on your wrists or diffuse it in the air. Breathe in the essential oils to open up the passageways in the nostrils and the whole body. Take long, deep, calming breaths. Play relaxing spa music, theta music, Tibetan singing bowl sounds or nature sounds. Rest and relax.

7. Technique #3: 4-7-8 Breath[10]

This breathing technique, developed by Andrew Weil, helps to bring the body into a state of deep relaxation. It helps to reduce the fight or flight response when in a state of stress and can help ease anxiety from a state of worry. If you are in a difficult situation, use this technique before responding. It can also assist in falling asleep.

Let's Practice:
Begin the technique by exhaling all the air out. Place the tongue just behind the upper teeth.

- Inhale through the nose for a count of 4
- Retain (hold) the breath for a count of 7
- Exhale the air out through the mouth w/a 'woosh' sound for a count of 8
- Repeat the cycle 4-8 times (8 is the maximum number of times)

---

10 Technique developed by Andrew Weil, MD https://www.drweil.com/videos-features/videos/breathing-exercises-4-7-8-breath.

8. Restorative Yoga Asana #3: Lounge Chair Savasana with Sandbag

Essential Oil Suggestion: Clary Sage

Set-up: Place two blocks next to each other; one on the highest level and the other on the medium level, or one on the medium level and one on the lowest level. Lean a bolster or a tightly rolled blanket against it. Lie down with your bottom close to the bottom edge of the bolster and recline back. Use rolled blankets or pillows under your arms for arm rest support. Place a rolled blanket or bolster under your knees if you wish. Place an eye pillow on your eyes.

Place a sandbag or a heavy folded blanket across the belly. This extra weight will offer you a sense of grounding, stability, and comfort. It will also help to strengthen the diaphragm. If the sensation is unpleasant, then you do not have to use it.

EO: You may place *Clary Sage* essential oil on your wrist or diffuse it in the air. Breathe in the essential oils to open up the passageways in the nostrils and the whole body. Take long, deep, calming breaths. Play relaxing spa music, theta music, Tibetan singing bowl sounds or nature sounds. Rest and relax.

9. Closing. Burning or Dissolving Ritual

◇ **Letting Go.**

Get a lighter and a heat resistant bowl (for the burning ritual) or a bowl filled with room temperature or warm water (for the dissolving ritual). Take the paper with the answer to the letting go question and say the following out loud:

"Dear Universe–I no longer need these thoughts, feelings, or circumstances that do not serve my highest and best good. I vow to be open to the lessons presented to me in order to create positive habits and improve my outlook on life."

Now place the paper in the bowl, light it on fire and watch it burn or take special dissolving paper and place it in the water and watch it dissolve. Let it go.

◇ **Inviting in.**

Read one of the following quotes of inspiration below or choose your own. You may choose to print it on a paper or sticky note to post where you will see it. Say the following out loud:

"Dear Universe–I invite this message of inspiration into my life at this time to serve my highest and best good. I promise to be more present and kinder to myself every day."

What will you invite into your life today?

Statement of gratitude to the Universe:
"Thank you for helping me to feel centered and calm with every breath."

Quotes of inspiration:

"Feelings come and go like clouds in a windy sky. Conscious breathing is my anchor." ~ Thich Nhat Hanh

"There is one way of breathing that is shameful and constricted. Then there's another way; a breath of love that takes you all the way to infinity." ~ Rumi

Story #3. The Angry Driver
(I, too, am like that)

I used to live in a neighborhood that was near a busy road. The speed limit on the main road was 50 mph. I remember that waiting to leave the neighborhood to ascend on this main road always made me a bit nervous. There was lots of traffic going pretty fast so I had to wait a long time until it was clear to move out into the stream. There was also a blind hill leading up to the neighborhood entrance which added an additional challenge to exiting. Most of the time I would estimate the speed and the distance between cars pretty accurately. On this one particular day though, I did not.

I was patiently waiting and looking both ways and saw my opportunity, or so I thought. I exited out into the stream of traffic and right away realized that my timing was off. The car behind me was approaching fast! I pressed my foot on the gas so I could get up to the 50 mph as quickly as possible. As I did so I looked into my rear-view mirror and was surprised to see the look on the face of the driver in the fast-approaching car. Boy, was she mad! I think I saw steam coming out of her ears and there was a big scowl on her face. I felt so bad I had cut her off. I waved an apology. She still seemed so angry. I was proud of the next thought that occurred to me. Instead of thinking, *'Geez, calm down'*, or *'Why are you so uptight?'*, or some sort of expletive, I thought, *'You know, I too can be like that. I too have felt annoyed and frustrated by someone else's actions. I have gotten mad when someone cut me off or was going too slow. I get it.'* Then I got up to speed and continued down the road. I didn't wait for her to pass to send her a scowl back, or a specific finger gesture, or lay on the horn, or complain about it in my head which would have made my day worse. I just continued on with my day and a bonus: A good lesson learned.

Clarity

I tend to be a very busy person always looking for the next thing that interests me. At my 15 year high school reunion when they handed out superlative awards, I won for person with the most jobs since graduation. I was proud of that fact! I have been a camp counselor, group exercise instructor, a singer at theme parks, on cruise ships, and in the opera, a librarian and classroom teacher, a waitress at pizza joints, fancy restaurants, and even a roller skating waitress at the Dolphin hotel in Disney World. I am an entrepreneur, business owner, yoga instructor and most importantly a mom. I choose not to limit myself in what I wish to invite into my life. When I work on the computer I can have 18 tabs open all at once and I don't want to close any of them because I know I'm going to get to it soon. This quality of mine is uplifting and it can also lead me to become distracted and lose focus on what is most important to me on any given day. My sister recommended a book to me called "Refuse to Choose". It's all about people like me who love to be involved in tons of things and refuse to pick one. The author, Barbara Shur, calls these people scanners. We are always looking for the next cool, exciting or interesting thing to do. The good news for me is that I settled in on three main areas that I continue to focus on. The top one is YES. Every day I put effort towards spreading the word and serving others to heal and be happy. The second focus is singing. I love to use my voice to bring happiness to others. Music is a huge part of my life and a universal way to connect. The third important area of focus for me is teaching. I enjoy working with children. They are pure joy! They are vibrant and eager to explore, learn and have fun. I learn as much or more from them than they learn from me. I enjoy tutoring and substitute teaching because I love helping children especially those who struggle and may fall through the cracks in school. I love teaching fitness and yoga classes as well as sharing my knowledge through private sessions with fun and humor. Through clarity and focus I am able to create and see the results of my efforts come to fruition.

What does clarity mean to you? The dictionary definition is "The quality of being coherent and the quality of transparency or purity." I like these, especially the idea of being transparent. Transparency means vulnerability and staying true to yourself. When we are open we see things clearly as they are in the present moment. Jon Kabat-Zin, who teaches meditation and mindfulness says "mindfulness is the awareness that arises through paying attention, on purpose, in the present moment, and non-judgmentally." Clarity allows us to be with and accept the 'what is' of the moment. In this state we can come to our true nature and show up as our authentic self. In this section you will cultivate clarity with focused practices like PMR; Progressive Muscle Relaxation, a joint freeing series, as well as tapping, chanting, and Yoga Nidra, a body scan visualization. Enjoy the benefits of finding clarity that can lead to peace and ease.

Let's Practice:

Sit up tall on a chair, on the floor or on a meditation cushion and just be still and quiet. That's it. No movement. No thinking. No doing or thinking about doing. Can you just sit there? Be still. Focus. Breathe. Sit for at least one minute and up to as many minutes as you like. You may think this is meditation. It is. Did you feel increased clarity in the stillness? Take this relaxed state of mind and body into the next sections' practices and allow clarity in.

YES for Clarity #1

1. Opening

◇ Letting Go

Questions of the day. On a piece of paper, that you will burn or dissolve at the end, write your answer to the question(s) below about what you wish to let go:

1. *What can I let go of that will bring more clarity and calmness into my life?*

2. *What is the usual topic of my negative self-talk?*

◇ Hand on Heart Affirmations

"I am worthy of good things. It is ok to want the best for myself and to pursue the things that bring me joy and happiness."

"I choose positive thoughts. I understand that I create my own reality and I choose thoughts that are uplifting and positive."
"I live in a sea of acceptance and gratitude."

◇ Personal Mantra

Choose a mantra of your own that speaks to you today. Begin with "I am," and say it in the present moment as if it already exists! Your personal mantra should be something you truly believe. Say it out loud with energy, emotion, vigor, enthusiasm, and intention to grow these positive seeds within you!
Example Mantra: *"I am enjoying accessing my personal power without having to compromise for anyone!"*

◊ **Gratitude and Energy**

Say to yourself or out loud what you are grateful for and what positive energy you wish to invite into your life today! You may also choose an angel card with a word or a message of inspiration for the day.

2. Restorative Yoga Asana #1 and Breath Assessment: Basic Relaxation Pose

Set-up: Lie down on the floor or on a yoga mat with a blanket or pillow under your head. Place a rolled-up blanket or bolster under your knees. You may also place blankets under your back. You may place an eye pillow over your eyes. Make sure you feel fully supported and relaxed.

◊ **Breath Assessment:**

Come into the posture and begin to release any past or future thoughts. Relax and surrender more and more with every breath. Notice your breathing pattern without trying to change anything. Notice the rise and fall of the belly and chest. Observe the length of the breath. Is it flowing naturally helping you to become calmer or does it feel rapid or shallow creating tension? Just observe for 3-5 minutes. Now count your inhales and exhales. Extend the exhales to assist your body in coming to a deeper state of relaxation, activating the parasympathetic nervous system (rest and digest). Allow your body and mind to surrender to the present moment and just be.

Stay here and move to technique #1 PRM - Progressive Muscle Relaxation.

3. Technique #1: PMR - Progressive Muscle Relaxation[11]

PMR is used for stress relief. It consists of tensing and then relaxing a muscle group. This process is repeated throughout the entire body. Inhale when you tense the muscles and exhale when you release the muscles. There are many benefits of progressive muscle relaxation. It releases tension, lowers blood pressure, reduces fatigue and anxiety, and calms the body and mind. When your body is physically relaxed you cannot feel anxious. Following this script to guide you through the process:

Let's Practice:

- Find a quiet place to relax, either lying down or sitting in a comfortable chair

- Begin with a long inhale breath and tense the muscles of your right hand and forearm. Hold for 5 seconds and release with an exhale and a sigh.

- Tense your right upper arm and shoulder blade. Hold for 5 seconds and release with an exhale. Relax your upper arm and shoulder blade.

- Tense your left hand and forearm. Hold for 5 seconds and release with an exhale.

- Tense your left upper arm and shoulder blade. Hold for 5 seconds and release. Relax your upper arm and shoulder blade.

- Tense your forehead. Hold for 5 seconds and relax your forehead.

- Tense your eyes and cheeks. Hold for 5 seconds and relax your eyes and cheeks.

- Tense your mouth and jaw. Hold for 5 seconds and relax your mouth and jaw.

11 Script for PMR can be found here: : https://positivepsychology.com/progressive-muscle-relaxation-pmr/

- Tense your neck. Hold 5 seconds. Relax your neck.

- Tense your shoulders. Hold 5 seconds. Relax your shoulders.

- Tense your shoulder blades and back. Hold 5 seconds. Relax your shoulder blades and back.

- Tense your chest and stomach. Hold. Relax your chest and stomach.

- Tense your hips and buttocks. Hold. Relax your hips and buttocks.

- Tense your whole right leg. Hold. Relax your right leg.

- Tense your right foot. Hold. Relax your right foot.

- Tense your whole left leg. Hold. Relax your left leg.

- Tense your left foot. Hold. Relax your left foot.

- Stay relaxed for a while. Notice how your body feels.

4. Yoga Asanas: Joint Freeing Series

These movements are based on the Pawanmuktasana sequence. A series of postures from the Satyananda tradition. It helps relax the body and mind and stimulates the natural healing processes. This series is more a mental practice than a physical one. It is great for beginners because it's easy to learn. This practice helps with concentration, clarity and patience. It moves all of the joints of the body to help with mobility and to assist in sitting in meditation. Follow the postures below for this nurturing and relaxing series.

Let's Practice:
Sit on the floor with legs straight out. Repeat each movement 4 to 6 times.

Inhale, point toes.

Exhale, flex toes.

Inhale,
soles face in

Exhale
soles face out.

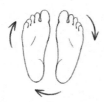

Inhale, circle
ankles out. Exhale,
circle ankles in.

Inhale,
extend the leg out.

Exhale,
draw the heel in.

Inhale, rotate
legs out. Exhale,
rotate legs in.

Inhale,
arch the back.

Exhale,
round the back.

Inhale,
extend the leg.

Exhale, draw the
knee to chest.

Inhale, all 4's.

Exhale,
shift hips right.

Inhale, all 4's.

Exhale,
shift hips left.

| Sit on heels. | Inhale, | Exhale, |
| Reach arms out. | point fingers up. | point fingers down. |

Inhale fingertips   Exhale, fingertips
point out.   point in.

Circle wrists right and left

Inhale, arms out,   Exhale,
palms up.   touch knuckles
                        to shoulders.

Inhale, elbows wide.

Exhale, elbows together.

Inhale, bend elbows, palms forward.

Exhale, bend elbows, palms face back.

Inhale, arms reach up.

Exhale, arms reach back.

Inhale, arch the back.

Exhale, round the back.

Inhale, sit tall. Exhale, stretch right.

Inhale, sit tall. Exhale, stretch left.

Inhale, sit tall. Exhale, twist right.

Inhale, sit tall. Exhale, twist left.

Inhale, head up.

Exhale, head down.

Inhale, head center. Exhale, head right.

Inhale, head center. Exhale, head left.

5. Technique #2: Mantra and Mudra. Chanting Sat Nam

The word mantra means a "tool for the mind". The following practice is called Kirtan Kriya used in kundalini yoga. It is intended to bring mental balance. It clears the subconscious mind of traumas and negative emotions. It improves concentration and brain function, increases intuitive abilities and brings peace and understanding to the practitioner. It awakens divine love and light.

In this practice you will chant Sat Nam with mudras (hand gestures). The meaning of Sat Nam is "true essence or name."

The word is split into its parts Sa -Ta - Na - Ma. Press each finger to the thumb as you say each word out loud. Each finger represents an element:

	Thumb represents fire
"Sa" represents birth	Index finger represents air
"Ta" represents life	Middle finger represents space
"Na" represents death	Ring finger represents earth
"Ma" represents rebirth	Pinky finger represents water

When chanting mantras, you may chant out loud, whisper or say them silently to yourself. Begin by sitting up tall on the floor or in a chair. Breathe deeply in through the nose and out through the nose. Place the back of your hands on the knees with your palms up. Say each word as you touch your thumb to each finger.

Let's Practice:

- *Touch thumb to index finger and say "Sa."* This increases the air element within the body. It has a positive effect on the emotions and the endocrine system
- *Touch thumb to middle finger and say "Ta."* This increases the space element within the body. It has a positive effect on thoughts and intuition
- *Touch thumb to ring finger and say "Na."* This increases the earth element and decreases the fire element within the body. It has a positive effect on the tissues, muscles and bones.
- *Touch thumb to pinky finger and say "Ma."* This reduces the water element within the body. It helps with clear communication.

Repeat slowly or quickly or somewhere in between 10 times or more until you feel a sense of relaxation within. When you finish the mantra pause and meditate for 5 to 10 minutes feeling the effects of the mantra.

6. Restorative Yoga Asana #2: Bolster Line up & Vagus Nerve Activation

Essential Oil Suggestion: Patchouli

Set-up: Place two bolsters end to end. Place one blanket down the length of both bolsters for comfort. Fold or roll two blankets for arm rests. Place these on either side of the bolsters. Sit on the end of the bolster and lie back. Rest your arms on the blankets to feel fully supported. Use an eye pillow to help stimulate the Vagus nerve. Tune into sensations in your body. Relax a little bit more with each exhale.

What is The Vagus Nerve?

The vagus nerve is so named because it "wanders" like a vagabond, sending out sensory fibers from your brainstem to your internal organs. The vagus nerve, the longest of the cranial nerves, controls your inner nerve center and contains parasympathetic nerve fibers. It runs through the brain, face, thorax and abdomen and it oversees a vast range of crucial functions, communicating motor and sensory impulses to every organ in your body. When one increases their vagal "tone" it means that the body can relax faster after experiencing stress. There are many ways to stimulate the vagus nerve. Here are a few:

- Exposure to cold. Take cold showers or go out in the cold with minimal clothing. Dunk your face in ice water.
- Take long slow deep breaths. Most of the time we take 20 breaths per minute. Slow down to 6 yoga breaths per minute.
- Sing, hum, chant, and gargle to activate the nerve.
- Meditate to relax the mind
- Exercise
- Laugh

Another way to activate the nerve is by resting in a restorative posture and placing an eye pillow on the eyes. This places a bit of pressure there and shuts out the light to assist the body in relaxing.

EO: You may place *patchouli* essential oil on your wrists or diffuse it in the air. Breathe in the essential oils to open up the passageways in the nostrils and the whole body. Take long, deep, calming breaths. Play relaxing spa music, theta music, Tibetian singing bowl sounds or nature sounds. Rest and relax.

7. Reading #3:
Light on Yoga Sutras by B.K.S. Iyengar[12] Detachment

The Yoga Sutras of Patanjali are 196 aphorisms (short sayings) in 4 chapters that outline the purpose and practice of yoga. The sutras follow the eight-limb path of yoga, guiding us to go within. The eight-limb path is a roadmap to our own self-discovery and love. Stress can be an obstacle to our spiritual progress. One of my favorite teachings from the sutras is non-attachment or detachment. Detachment is one wonderful way to reduce stress.

The first reading is page 17 from *Light on the Yoga Sutras* by B.K.S Iyengar: *"Non-attachment is the deliberate process of drawing away from attachment and personal affliction, in which, neither binding oneself to duty nor cutting oneself off from it, one gladly helps all, near or far, friend or foe. Non-attachment does not mean drawing inwards and shutting oneself off, but involves carrying out one's responsibilities without incurring obligation or inviting expectation." "Detachment brings discernment: seeing each and every thing or being as it is in its purity without bias or self-interest."*

The second reading is from page 61: Yoga Sutra 1.12 "abhyasa vairagyabhyam tannirodhah." Translation: Practice and detachment are the means to still the movements of consciousness.

> repeated practice - abhyasa
> freedom from desires, detachment,
> renunciation - vairagyabhyam
> their restraint- tannirodhah

This passage is from page 62: *"Practice is the path of evolution; detachment and renunciation, the path of involution. Practice is involved in all the eight limbs of yoga. Evolutionary practice is the onward march towards discovery of the self, involving yama, niyama, asana and pra-*

---

12 *Light on the Yoga Sūtras of Patañjali* - B.K.S. Iyengar – Patanjali - Harpercollins-2005

85

nayama. The involutionary path of renunciation involves pratyahara, dharana, dhyana, and samadhi. This inward journey detaches the consciousness from external objects."

The message in Sutra 1.12 is important to our emotional healing because it reminds us that our healing and self-discovery are an inside job. When we practice detaching from external objects like what other people do or say or what situations we find ourselves in then we are able to observe our responses. We can look inward to a still, calm place where no drama or reaction occurs. This is a lifelong practice; not letting outside circumstances disturb our inner environment. This is detachment.

Let's Practice:

Meditation. Meditation is the first step to practicing detachment. Sit quietly in a room with very little distractions. Quiet the mind and still the body. Breath and relax. Stay in this meditation for five minutes or more. Maybe add a mantra that you will stay open and detached from wishing for things to be one way or another.

Interactions. Now go about your day interacting with the world and people and see what you tend to be attached to. Are you attached to material things, expecting people to be or act a certain way? Usually, we are attached to things being different than they are. Use the practice of meditation to stay present in the here and now and experience everything as it is.

8. Restorative Yoga Asana #3: Lounge Chair Savasana with Guided Nature Visualization

Essential Oil Suggestion: Coriander

Set-up: Place two blocks next to each other; one on the highest level and the other on the medium level or one on the medium level and one on the lowest level. Lean a bolster or a tightly rolled blanket against it. Lie down with your bottom close to the bottom edge of the bolster and recline back. Use rolled blankets or pillows under your arms for arm rest support. Place a rolled blanket or bolster under your knees if you wish. Place an eye pillow on your eyes.

EO: You may place *Coriander* essential oil on your wrist or diffuse it in the air. Breathe in the essential oils to open up the passageways in the nostrils and the whole body. Take long, deep, calming breaths. Play relaxing spa music, theta music, Tibetan singing bowl sounds or nature sounds. Rest and relax.

Go to www.Y4ES.com. You may also use the app, Insight Timer or go to YouTube to find your favorite guided nature visualization.

9. Closing. Burning or Dissolving Ritual

◇ **Letting Go.**

Get a lighter and a heat resistant bowl (for the burning ritual) or a bowl filled with room temperature or warm water (for the dissolving ritual). Take the paper with the answer to the letting go question and say the following out loud:

> *"Dear Universe–I no longer need these thoughts, feelings, or circumstances that do not serve my highest and best good. I vow to be open to the lessons presented to me in order to create positive habits and improve my outlook on life."*

Now place the paper in the bowl, light it on fire and watch it burn or take special dissolving paper and place it in the water and watch it dissolve. Let it go.

◊ **Inviting in.**

Read one of the following quotes of inspiration below or choose your own. You may choose to print it on a paper or sticky note to post where you will see it. Say the following out loud:

"Dear Universe–I invite this message of inspiration into my life at this time to serve my highest and best good. I promise to be more present and kinder to myself every day."

What will you invite into your life today?

Statement of gratitude to the Universe:

"Thank you, universe for helping me to see things clearly as they are and to appreciate each present moment."

Quotes of inspiration:

"Gratitude unlocks the fullness of life. It turns what we have into enough, and more. It turns denial into acceptance, chaos to order, confusion to clarity. Gratitude makes sense of our past, brings Peace for today and creates a vision for tomorrow." ~ Melody Beattie

"The soul always knows what to do to heal itself. The challenge is to silence the mind" ~ Caroline Myss

Story #4. Drop the Story and End the Worry
(The stories we tell)

Did you ever have something terrible happen? Something that really brings up strong emotions? I mean something small and wee or something that's really huge? Of course, you have. We all have. A small thing might be that your neighbor's dog barks a lot and it drives you crazy or someone just gave you a mean look or your friend won't talk to you over something that happened a long time ago. A big thing might be that your long-time partner left you and you struggle getting over the heartache or you were just diagnosed with a critical infection or disease or you just got laid off and have no job prospects. These are all difficult and challenging life situations that can cause us suffering. What makes the suffering worse? Telling everyone your woes or as I say "telling your terrible story." These are the stories that are always present on your mind. They are about the terrible thing that is happening now or happened in the past or that might happen soon. These stories only bring us more worry, stress and dis - ease!

"But wait," you might say, "I *need* to share my story with people. It gives me comfort to be able to tell others. I need to vent and I need some confirmation that I am right or justified. I want to receive sympathy from others and that tells me that they care about me when they can confirm that I am right! Letting it out, complaining, worrying and stressing over these terrible situations helps me." But does it really? How does it make you feel emotionally and physically every time you "tell your story" to someone? It may seem to make you feel better temporarily to receive that confirmation or sympathy but in the long run it only creates more suffering for you and for others. Sharing our heartache or difficult situations and receiving support from a trusted and close friend or family member is good and necessary sometimes for our healing. But I am speaking of the endless "storytelling" of who or what happened to you that you repeat over and over until it manifests as physical illnesses that may start as something small and grow and grow as the negative talk continues. The body holds all of this emotional pain or as a popular book by Bessel Van der Kolk, MD., says "The Body Keeps the Score."

I read somewhere once that you get to tell your story three times and after that you must drop it! If you can tell it just once then that's even better. So, what can you do once you drop the story? You can begin to focus on your new "story." The new story will be all about the solution instead of the problem. What does focusing on the solution look like? It's voicing what you wish for and intend to happen. It's using affirmations and gratitude to think and speak about what you intend. For example, whenever I speak about my eye surgery from a retinal detachment, first I remember to say "I experienced a retinal detachment" instead of "I had a retinal detachment." I don't own the story. I don't complain about the difficulties of experiencing compromised sight or the long process of healing as the bubble they placed in there was doing its job, instead I say, "My eye is healing every day and my vision is even better than before." Now I have just put the energy out into the world of positive results and what I desire to happen. Another thing we can pay attention to is the lessons that are being offered to us through life's difficulties. Find the lesson in everything that happens to you especially the challenging and upsetting things. Only through those situations will the doorway to change open up the most.

So, the next time you hear yourself beginning to tell your story remember that no problems were ever solved by complaining. Pause and ask yourself, *"Will complaining solve the problem or bring me more peace and happiness?"* and when the answer is "No!" begin to set your thoughts on what will! Set all of your thoughts, attention, emotions, and energy on the solution. As you practice this–catching yourself telling the story and then finding solutions through positive affirmations and intentions on what you desire–all conflict and worry will begin to cease and your body, mind, spirit, and emotions will be more at ease. You will move through each present moment with lightness and more conscious awareness. The energy you create and then send out through your thoughts, words and actions will help the happiness to rise within you.

I work on this every day. I have caught myself getting ready to meet with a friend and thinking *what juicy gossip can I share?* Then I think again. I end up sharing stories of insight I had or a book I read or I ask them some deep questions about life or about their favorite vacation or memory. The visit ends up bringing us closer and I leave feeling joyful and more connected. This simple practice of not repeating a story of woe, can solve many of life's problems. We may become aware of how many stories or scenarios we create in our mind throughout the day aren't even happening and may never happen. Stay present. Find the gratitude in every moment and drop the story to end the worry!

The "woe is me" story. Sometimes we find ourselves in trouble and wish for help but will only accept specific help. If it's not the kind we were imagining then we don't want any help at all.

YES for Clarity #2

1. Opening

◇ **Letting Go**

Questions of the day. On a piece of paper, that you will burn or dissolve at the end, write your answer to the question(s) below about what you wish to let go:

1. *What conditions do I place on my peace of mind? "I can only be happy when..."*

2. *What mindless activities do I engage in that take me away from being fully present?*

◇ **Hand on Heart Affirmation**

"I can see things clearly when I remain open to new experiences."

"My purpose is clear and my path is opening before me."

"I appreciate the abundance in my life and I allow myself to expand in gratitude, success and joy every day."

◇ **Personal Mantra**

Choose a mantra of your own that speaks to you today. Begin with "I am," and say it in the present moment as if it already exists! Your personal mantra should be something you truly believe. Say it out loud with energy, emotion, vigor, enthusiasm, and intention to grow these positive seeds within you!

Example Mantra: *"I am a badass and I kick butt in life every day!"*

◊ **Gratitude and Energy**

Say to yourself or out loud what you are grateful for and what positive energy you wish to invite into your life today! You may also choose an angel card with a word or a message of inspiration for the day.

2. Restorative Yoga Asana #1 and Breath Assessment: Triple Towers OR Legs on a chair

Set-up: Create a tower with 3 yoga blocks lined up next to each other on the highest level. Place a bolster, pillow or rolled blanket on top of them. Another option is to set yourself up near a chair. Lie down on the floor or mat with a blanket under your back for comfort and a blanket or pillow under your head. Scootch (it's a word) your bottom close to the tower or chair and rest your calves or legs up on it. Relax in this restful, supportive position.

◊ **Breath Assessment:**

Come into the posture and begin to release any past or future thoughts. Relax and surrender more and more with every breath. Notice your breathing pattern without trying to change anything. Notice the rise and fall of the belly and chest. Observe the length of the breath. Is it flowing naturally helping you to become calmer or does it feel rapid or shallow creating tension? Just observe for 3-5 minutes. Now count your inhales and exhales. Extend the exhales to assist your body in coming to a deeper state of relaxation, activating the parasympathetic nervous system (rest and digest). Allow your body and mind to surrender to the present moment and just be.

3. Technique #1: EFT: Emotional Freedom Technique

This technique is based on ancient Chinese medicine and practices that use acupressure and energy meridians to heal the physical body. Doctor Roger Callahan and later, Dr. Gary Craig developed TFT (Thought Field Therapy) and EFT (Emotional Freedom Technique) to help a person overcome the effects of negative emotions, fears and thought patterns. EFT helps to create balance in your body and energy systems when faced with a difficult problem and accompanying emotions.

EFT is one of my favorite practices. It is easy to learn and do. I use it when I am in the midst of a difficult emotion that begins to arise in me. I just pause and tap. I say positive words to myself to help calm my body and mind, release tension and overwhelm and assist me in moving forward in my day without letting the fearful emotion snowball out of control. It really does help me to bring my body and mind back into a state of calm and to release the intense feelings I may be experiencing.

Let's Practice:
Begin by locating the places on your body to tap. Read each spot listed and tap with your fingertips on each one. The tapping meridians are: The edge of the pinky fingers (tap with your fingers or tap both edges of the pinky fingers together), the top of the head, eyebrows, side of the eyes, cheekbones, upper lip, chin, collarbone, center of the chest, and ribs under the armpits.

The Five EFT steps are:

1. *Focus on the problem.* Focus your attention on one area or problem you are experiencing.

2. *Test the level of discomfort, fear or anxiety.* On a scale from 1-10, with 10 begin the most difficult or uncomfortable, choose where you are in that moment.

3. *Choose a phrase.* The phrase will begin with "Even though I am feeling (insert problem and associated emotion), I love and accept myself where I am."

4. *Begin the tapping sequence and dialogue.* Tap each location one at a time and say the following (examples): "Even though I feel overwhelmed and stressed, I love and accept myself where I am." "Even though it is difficult to accept myself, I am open to feeling calm and relaxed." "I am feeling ... (anxiety, fear, anger, regret, stress, jealousy)" "I am open to feeling and releasing these emotions. I forgive myself for..." "I know what it feels like to feel calm. I am allowing my body to feel calm. This is only temporary."

5. *Test the final level of discomfort, fear or anxiety.* After tapping and saying your affirmations check to see what your number is. The number should be lower. Repeat the process until you get to a zero.

4. Yoga Asana: Focus

Dharana, the sixth limb of Patanjali's eight limbs of yoga, translates as concentration. In this yoga sequence find clarity by choosing one object to concentrate on during each posture. Choose to focus on your breath, your drishti (gaze), your core muscles, your shoulders, your right big toe, or anything. Choose one thing to softly concentrate on. Notice when your mind begins to wander and bring your attention back to that particular focus. In this practice there is a suggested point of focus for each pose. You may choose any focus.

Let's Practice:

Yoga Asana (Posture)	Suggested Focus
Begin in **Table Top or All 4's**	On the mat between your hands
Cow and Cat pose. Arch and round the back	The breath. (Inhale to arch/ exhale to round)
Send your hips back to your heels for **Child's Pose** (Balasana)	The tip of your nose
Straighten your legs and lift your hips into **Downward Facing Dog** (Adho Mukha Svanasana)	The thigh muscles engaging
Walk your feet to your hands and hang in a **Forward Fold** (Uttanasana). Release any tension	The space between your big toes
Roll up to standing in **Mountain Pose** (Tadasana)	Imagine roots moving into the earth from your legs and feet to support you
Rise up to the balls of your feet to lift the heels and lower down. Repeat 4-6 times. Hold.	The calf muscles or arches of the feet
Lower the heels and move into **Tree Pose** (Vrkasana) balance with one foot off the floor, resting on the lower leg	A spot directly in front of you to hold a soft gaze
Transition to a seated crossed legged position in **Easy Seat** (Sukhasana)	The third eye between the eyebrows
Twist (Ardha Matsyendrasana) to the right with the left hand on your right thigh and the right hand behind your back. Repeat to the left	The muscles of the upper back stretching
Transition center and extend the legs straight out in **Staff Pose** (Dandasana)	Straight ahead
Move into a **Forward Fold** (Paschimottanasana)	The shins
Sit tall and roll slowly down to your back in **Corpse Pose** (Savasana)	With eyes closed focus on your inner environment of energy, breath, a quiet mind and a still body

5. Lesson and Technique #2:
The Four Agreements by Don Miguel Ruiz[13]
– A Guide Map to Living a Positive Life
Bonus Technique: 5 Sights and 5 Sounds

The Four Agreements:

I love this book and these four simple reminders. I refer to them often especially when processing my emotions. I look inward to see how I was responding to a situation or person. I analyze to see if I was being impeccable and kind with my words or if I was blaming someone for purposely trying to hurt me. I notice if I was making something all about me or making assumptions about the meaning of someone's words. I like the 'always do your best' agreement because it reminds me of the first lessons we learn in kindergarten. We are all always just doing our best to be kind and happy in the world and we can definitely mess up and that's ok. Here are the Four Agreements. The author added a Fifth Agreement about listening which is an important and necessary skill to guide us to our inner intuition and discernment.

1) Be Impeccable with your Words

The word "impeccable" comes from the Latin word peccatus meaning "sin." The "im" in the beginning of impeccable is the Latin prefix that means "without." Impeccable means "without sin." Ruiz says that sin is anything that goes against oneself and taking responsibility for one's actions. He says that the first agreement is the most important one and the most difficult one to honor. Through your words you express your creative power. What you say will manifest. Words can either make or break your life. *Never* use negative words against yourself or others. Never gossip about others. In essence, this agreement focuses on the significance of speaking with integrity and carefully choosing words before saying them aloud. ***Use your words to express empathy, love, care and respect.***

---

13 https://www.miguelruiz.com/

2) Don't Take Anything Personally

The second agreement is a way to deal with hurtful treatment from others that you may experience in life. It advocates the importance of having a strong sense of self and not needing to rely on the opinions of others in order to be content and satisfied with your self-image. Each individual has a unique worldview that alters their own perceptions. The actions and beliefs of a person is a projection of their own personal reality. ***Anger, jealousy, envy, and even sadness can lessen or dissipate once an individual stops taking things personally.***

3) Don't Make Assumptions

Assumptions can lead to suffering. When one assumes what others are thinking, it can create stress and interpersonal conflict because the person believes their assumption is a representation of the truth. Ruiz believes that a solution to overcoming the act of making an assumption is to ask questions and ensure that the communication is clear between the persons involved. ***Individuals can avoid misunderstandings, sadness, and drama by not making assumptions.***

4) Always Do Your Best

The fourth agreement helps in achieving progress towards your life goals. This agreement entails integrating the first three agreements into daily life and also living to one's full potential. Ruiz says to avoid self judgement and regret and understand that your best will change moment to moment. ***Do your best without striving to be perfect.***

Ruiz states in his book "You don't need to judge yourself, feel guilty, or punish yourself if you cannot keep these agreements. If you're doing your best, you will feel good about yourself even if you still make assumptions, still take things personally, and still are not impeccable with your word. If you always do your best, over and over again, you will become a master of transformation."

Don Miguel Ruiz wrote another book called *The Fifth Agreement*. Here it is.

The Fifth Agreement:
5) Be Skeptical but Learn to Listen

Be skeptical because most of what you hear isn't true. When you learn to listen, you understand a person's story, and the communication improves a lot. Being skeptical uses the power of doubt to discern the truth. Whenever you hear a message from yourself, or from another simply ask: Is it truth, or is it not truth? Is it reality or is it a virtual reality? By being skeptical, you don't believe every message; your faith is in yourself.

What will you not believe? You will not believe all the stories that we create with our knowledge. You know that most of our knowledge isn't true so don't believe me, don't believe yourself, and don't believe anybody else. The truth doesn't need you to believe it; the truth simply is, and it survives whether you believe it or not. Lies need you to believe them. If you don't believe lies, they don't survive your skepticism, and they simply disappear.

Every person distorts the truth, but you don't need to judge what somebody says, or call that person a liar. All of us tell lies in one way or another, and it's not because we want to lie. It's because of what we believe, Once you are aware of this, the fifth agreement makes a lot of sense, and it can make a very big difference in your life.

Let's Practice:

My suggestion is to write these agreements down or simply remember them and use them as a guide for your daily interactions with yourself and others. Ask yourself if you are practicing these in all situations. When you falter, simply love yourself through the process of learning and growing every day.

Bonus Technique: 5 Sights and 5 Sounds

When feeling anxious or overwhelmed or beginning to experience a panic attack, pause and place all of your attention on the sights and sounds in your environment. This will help you to release the worry or panic thoughts that your mind can create and bring your full attention on to one simple thing at a time.

I remember my daughter learning and teaching this to me. It helped her to calm down in the face of fear, anxiety or panic. I have used it many times to quiet my racing mind and return to the present moment.

Let's Practice:

Begin by sitting up tall and find something in your environment to settle your gaze upon. Look at all of the details of that object without any commentary and without becoming distracted by anything else. Hold your attention on it for 30 seconds to one minute. Now shift your attention to a second object. It can be a leaf on a tree, a picture on the wall, a small object you are holding in your hand or even the lines on your hand. Hold your attention there. Now shift your awareness to a third object and repeat the same focused attention. Repeat with a fourth and a fifth object. Notice how this exercise kept you in the present moment where all is well.

Next, stay seated or lie down. Close your eyes and begin to listen to the sounds in your environment. Choose one sound like a bird call or a car driving by and bring your full awareness to that one sound. Listen for 30 seconds to one minute and then shift your awareness to a second sound, holding your full attention on that sound. Choose three more sounds to focus on. Remember to use this simple practice whenever you need to release a grip on anxious feelings that arise.

6. Restorative Yoga Asana #2: Side Lying

Essential Oil Suggestion: Sandalwood

Set-up: Prepare a blanket or pillow to place under your head and under your shoulder. Place a bolster or blanket between the thighs or just rest the top leg over the bolster or blanket with the bottom leg straight, and roll to your side. You may also choose to hug a bolster or pillow. Rest your head down and make sure your shoulder and head feel comfortable and fully supported. Relax and release any tension. Focus on the breath, silence, and stillness. After 5 minutes or so you may roll to the other side and relax there for 5 minutes or more.

EO: You may place *Sandalwood* essential oil on your wrists or diffuse it in the air. Breathe in the essential oils to open up the passageways in the nostrils and the whole body. Take long, deep, calming breaths. Play relaxing spa music, theta music, Tibetan singing bowl sounds or nature sounds. Rest and relax.

7. Technique #3: Body Sensations Visualization

This body sensation meditation is a way to be present with our physical form. Our body is our home. It's where we live. It's our temple. Our top priority is taking care of our physical body. It houses our consciousness, our soul. Without it we would not be able to express ourselves or communicate or give. Take good care of your body with aerobic exercise, yoga, eating healthy foods and drinking plenty of water. Also understanding that whatever we hold onto emotionally will manifest as dis-ease in the physical body. The first step to optimal health is to be aware, moment to moment of the body. This meditation will help you to tune into sensations and the five senses to assist you in noticing when body disturbances arise throughout your day and then how to take care of it before it develops into chronic pain or disease. If you make it a habit of scanning your body throughout the day for sensations and accompanying thoughts and emotions you will be aware of your emotions all the time.

Let's Practice:

1st - Begin by sitting tall in a comfortable position. Use your imagination to envision a relaxing and peaceful place, preferably in nature. Picture all of the details and how you feel when you picture being here. This is a place you can always go to when you are feeling out of balance or anxious.

2nd - Now begin to notice sensations in the physical body.

3rd - Bring your awareness to the breath and the accompanying body sensations. Breath in through the nose and out through the nose. Say to yourself "Breathing in I'm aware I'm breathing in, breathing out I'm aware I'm breathing out." Whatever the breath feels like is fine. No judgements.

4th - Notice your five senses.

Sight. Open your eyes and take a look around in your environment. Just observe what you see without inner dialogue arising. You may close your eyes and notice what shapes or colors arise.

Sound. Pause and listen carefully to the sounds in your environment or even to your own breath and heartbeat.

Touch. Feel your bottom resting on the cushion, your hands resting on your legs and other touch sensations.

Taste. What taste sensations do you notice in your mouth?

Smell. Breath in and notice what aromas are in the air.

5th - Notice other sensations: tingling, itchiness, tightness, pressure, ease. You may also tune into your 6th sense which is your intuition. Trust in this subtle or sometimes no-so-subtle 'voice' in your body. Your intuition mostly comes in the form of sensation in your stomach (your 'gut instinct') or your heart.

If you're struggling, it means something is going on that you're not accepting. The struggle is the feedback. Instead of pushing through, ask yourself "What am I not open to?" Often you'll see that the struggle dissipates right there. Notice where you feel it in the body. Where is the wave of tension in the body? Where do you notice softening? If it is too uncomfortable then return to that relaxing and peaceful place you imagined in the beginning. Stay here observing sensations as long as you wish.

6th - Begin to ease your way out of this body sensation visualization by returning your awareness to your breath and the space in the room and when you are ready gently open your eyes and bring your awareness back into the room.

8. Restorative Yoga Asana #3: Lounge Chair Savasana with Yoga Nidra

Essential Oil Suggestion: Grapefruit

Set-up: Place two blocks next to each other; one on the highest level and the other on the medium level or one on the medium level and one on the lowest level. Lean a bolster or a tightly rolled blanket against it. Lie down with your bottom close to the bottom edge of the bolster and recline back. Use rolled blankets or pillows under your arms for arm rest support. Place a rolled blanket or bolster under your knees if you wish. Place an eye pillow on your eyes.

Yoga Nidra. Now begin the practice of Yoga Nidra. Yoga Nidra is translated as "yogic sleep." It is a relaxing hypnagogic state between wake and sleep to assist your body in relaxing and turning the awareness inward by listening to spoken instructions. During the practice of yoga nidra you will be asked to move your awareness to various body parts, sensations, emotions and images. Try not to concentrate too intensely as this may prevent you from relaxing. If the mind becomes overactive with thoughts and worries, just come back to the guiding sound of the voice.

You may find many guided yoga nidra practices on YouTube or on the Insight Timer App. You may record yourself reading a yoga nidra script from a Yoga Nidra Book [14] (See Footnote for recommended book). You may also listen to a recorded Yoga Nidra session by Christine Shaw on www/y4es.com

EO: You may place *Grapefruit* essential oil on your wrists or diffuse it in the air. Breathe in the essential oils to open up the passageways in the nostrils and the whole body. Take long, deep, calming breaths. Play relaxing spa music, theta music, Tibetan singing bowl sounds or nature sounds. Rest and relax.

9. Closing. Burning or Dissolving Ritual

◊ **Letting Go.**

Get a lighter and a heat resistant bowl (for the burning ritual) or a bowl filled with room temperature or warm water (for the dissolving ritual). Take the paper with the answer to the letting go question and say the following out loud:

"Dear Universe–I no longer need these thoughts, feelings, or circumstances that do not serve my highest and best good. I vow to be open to the lessons presented to me in order to create positive habits and improve my outlook on life."

---

14 Yoga Nidra by Swami Satyananda Saraswati. Yoga Publications Trust, 2001

Now light the paper on fire and place it in the bowl and watch it burn or take the special dissolving paper and place it in the water and watch it dissolve. Let it go.

◇ **Inviting in.**

Read one of the following quotes of inspiration below or choose your own. You may choose to print it on a paper or sticky note to post where you will see it. Say the following out loud: *"Dear Universe–I invite this message of inspiration into my life at this time to serve my highest and best good. I promise to be more present and kinder to myself every day."*
What will you invite into your life today?

Statement of gratitude to the Universe:

> *"Thank you universe/God for granting me the serenity to accept the things I cannot change, the courage to change the things I can and the wisdom to know the difference."* ~Reinhold Niebuhr (The Serenity Prayer)

Quotes of inspiration:

> *"I am not the richest, smartest, or most talented person in the world, but I succeed because I keep going and going and going"* ~ Sylvester Stallone

> *"Happiness is when what you think, what you say, and what you do are in harmony."* ~Mahatma Gandhi

Story #5. The Ego is LOUD! Pay Attention!

(Observe your inner voice)

The other day I was just taking a stroll with the dog when my thoughts started taking over. I caught myself complaining, doubting, worrying, nit picking about this and that. And it was all going on in my head while I was simply walking along. Then I said out loud "My Ego is loud!"

I used to think the ego was just that selfish part of me that told me I was right and good and better than others, like the time I took a yoga class from another teacher and I began to judge her and think about how I could cue people into the poses better. The more I delve deep into this idea of universal energy and how thoughts create our reality the more I really pay attention to the thoughts...all of them. *That's* the Ego...All of our thoughts! Good. Bad. Right. Wrong. Judging. Controlling. Pondering. Hoping. Grasping. Cheering. Wishing. Poking. Prodding. Celebrating. Wondering, and on and on.

I figure since there is all of this ego thinking going on all the time and I wish to be happy and free of the endless cycle of negative thoughts that I can and will decide to choose what those thoughts are going to be!! Duh! To take it a step further, if I know that thoughts are energy and that energy expands to the universe and that the universe answers whatever we are thinking then holy crap! I better get my thoughts in check!

So, a moment after I said, "Wow! my ego is loud!" I chose new thoughts. I chose ones that helped me to feel positively charged and pleasant in that moment and therefore, in my future. I chose to focus on what I wish for and not on what I don't wish for. I now do my best, when the negative or worry or complaining thoughts creep in, to re-frame my thoughts from "why is this happening to me?" to "I am moving forward in a great direction." I change "I am disorganized and always mess things up" to "I am becoming more organized every day and am able to meet tasks with focus and attention." This reframing of thoughts, also called positive affirmations, takes consistent effort and mindful awareness and the results are outstanding!! They show up all the time in what I call "The Universe Every Day." I notice the energy of my thoughts manifest in many ways every day. I am given the name of a person and it turns into an excellent connection. I hesitate going into a store just long enough so that I bump into someone I haven't seen in years and we are able to help each other in a special way. I teach a yoga class and feel drawn to talk to someone afterwards who becomes a great friend and support. So, how can you quiet the ego and manifest what you wish for? Trust. Trust in the process. Trust in the universe. Trust in yourself! Soon you'll be saying, "The ego is just the right volume." It is filled with all the thoughts that create the life I desire!

The Ego is that annoying inner roommate that can be hard to ignore

YES for Clarity #3

1. Opening

◇ **Letting Go**

Questions of the day. On a piece of paper, that you will burn or dissolve at the end, write your answer to the question(s) below about what you wish to let go:

- *What limiting belief or thought keeps me from manifesting whatever I wish for in life?*
- *What opportunities have I passed up because of fear?*

◇ **Hand on Heart Affirmations**

> *"I see all there is to be grateful for in life. I acknowledge the blessings I have received in my life with gratitude."*

> *"I am focused and have clarity and energy in all I do."*

> *"I follow my own true purpose with clarity of mind."*

◇ **Personal Mantra**

Choose a mantra of your own that speaks to you today. Begin with "I am," and say it in the present moment as if it already exists! Your personal mantra should be something you truly believe. Say it out loud with energy, emotion, vigor, enthusiasm, and intention to grow these positive seeds within you!

Example Mantra: *"Nothing can hold me back from experiencing all the love, joy, creativity, and abundance in my life today and every day!"*

◇ **Gratitude and Energy**

Say to yourself or out loud what you are grateful for and what positive energy you wish to invite into your life today! You may also choose an angel card with a word or a message of inspiration for the day.

2. Restorative Yoga Asana #1 and Breath Assessment: Forward Fold with Bolsters or a Chair with Pratyahara (Technique #1)

Set-up: Sit tall with legs extended wide and place two yoga blocks on the floor in between the legs; one on the high level and one on the medium level. Stack two bolsters, or one bolster and many blankets or pillows across the blocks. Rest your arms over the bolsters and your head on your arms or on the bolster. Make sure your back and neck are not strained. If so, you may choose to rest your head on the seat of a chair or a low table with ample support.

◇ **Breath Assessment:**

Come into the posture and begin to release any past or future thoughts. Relax and surrender more and more with every breath. Notice your breathing pattern without trying to change anything. Notice the rise and fall of the belly and chest. Observe the length of the breath. Is it flowing naturally helping you to become calmer or does it feel rapid or shallow creating tension? Just observe for 3-5 minutes. Now count your inhales and exhales. Extend the exhales to assist your body in coming to a deeper state of relaxation, activating the parasympathetic nervous system (rest and digest). Allow your body and mind to surrender to the present moment and just be.

Remain here or you may sit up in a cross-legged meditation position and move into the practice of pratyahara; withdrawing of the senses (Technique #1). This practice helps with non-attachment or non-grasping. It is the practice of observing what is.

3. Technique #1: Pratyahara - Withdrawal of the Senses

Pratyahara, the fifth of Patanjali's eight limbs of yoga, is the practice of detaching or withdrawing from the five senses. When we let go of attachment to experiencing the outer world through our senses, we can come to a state of deep relaxation. It frees the mind of old habits and increases clarity so we may reduce the mind clutter and find inspiration and creativity. Pratyahara provides the foundation for the higher practices of yoga and is the basis for meditation. Proprioception is the awareness of the space around us. It helps us with balance and coordination. Interoception is the awareness of sensations inside the body like our heart beat, the breath and even the subtle energies of our nervous system related to emotions.

In the Bhagavad Gita (an ancient spiritual text), Shri Krishna explains in Chapter 2.58: "Just as the tortoise withdraws its limbs, so when a man withdraws his senses from the sense objects, his wisdom becomes steady." If we detect that an object, person or situation is about to disturb our equanimity, Krishna advises us to turn to our intellect, and completely withdraw our attention from that object, person or situation. You may be thinking *but how do we let go of our senses? We use them daily to navigate our world. It's impossible to shut them off completely, isn't it?* We can begin by focusing all of our attention on just one of the senses at a time in a non-attachment, non-grasping way. This will help us to focus on what is or isn't in need of our attention in times of stress or overwhelm.

I enjoy practicing pratyahara on the yoga mat. A fun practice is to blindfold yourself or just close your eyes as you move through yoga postures. It may feel strange but pretty soon you will begin to draw your awareness inward more and focus less on the outside world where we can become attached to all sorts of distractions. Your other senses will become heightened as you rely on your own inner intuition and sensations to guide you through the movements. This kind of practice helps me to trust in my inner guidance system as I navigate the world around me.

Let's Practice:
5 Five Steps to Pratyahara

Begin by sitting or lying down and becoming very still. Focus your attention on the five senses one at a time.

1. *Sight/Eyes*. Lightly close your eyes and then lift the upper eyelid slightly. When you lift the upper eyelid don't tense the forehead. You can slightly lift the outer edges of the eye toward the temple to avoid tensing. With the eyes closed, roll the pupils down. No straining. Notice shapes, colors or movement.

2. *Taste/Tongue*. Relax the jaw. Let the tongue drop away from the palate. Rest the tip of the tongue behind the lower teeth. Notice any taste in the mouth.

3. ***Nose/Smell.*** Bring your attention to the bridge of the nose. Feel the sensation of air entering and exiting the nostrils. Notice any scents in the air.

4. ***Ears/Sound.*** Relax the inner ear by allowing the cheekbones to release down towards the earlobe. Notice any sounds you hear in the environment.

5. ***Skin/Touch.*** Relax the face. Relax the body. Notice the sensation of the body sitting or lying down. Notice how the chair or floor feels where your body touches it. Notice your clothes touching your skin and the air passing over it.

Without focusing on any one of these remain quiet and still in the mind and body. Enjoy the total non-attachment to any thought, sensation or emotion and just be.

4. Yoga Asana: Drishti

Your drishti (pronounced dristi) relates to the fifth limb of yoga, pratyahara, withdrawing of the senses and the sixth limb of yoga, dharana, concentration. It is a soft, focused gaze on an object or image. In this yoga practice softly gaze at one spot as you move through the postures. See how still your mind can become when you focus on one spot. Choose something that is not moving. As you steady your gaze your mind and body will follow. This will help your asana routine become a moving meditation.

Let's Practice:

• Begin by sitting tall in staff pose (dansasana), with your legs outstretched. If your hamstrings are tight, elevate your hips on a folded blanket, or bend the knees slightly and use a strap around the feet. These modifications will allow the body to safely release into the pose. Spiral the thighs inward, point the toes upward, and extend through your heels.

- Softly gaze toward your toes as if you are looking through them. Your body will naturally move in the direction of your toes. With each inhalation allow the spine to elongate in the direction of the drishti. On each exhalation, allow the body to soften and surrender into the stretch while maintaining an open heart. Notice how the awareness of the body increases when you steady your gaze and eliminate distractions.

Gradually you'll begin to witness the dialogue of your mind–simply watching distracting thoughts as they come and go–as you begin to settle into a peaceful meditative version of the pose.

Ashtanga Yoga (by Sri K. Pattabhi Jois) offers nine focal points:
The tip of the nose- nasagram drishti
Between the eyebrows- ajna drishti
At the navel- nabhi drishti
At the hand- hastagram drishti
At the toes- Padayoragram drishti
Far to the right- parshva drishti
Far to the left- parshva drishti
At the thumbs- Angushtha ma dyai drishti
Up to the sky- Urdhva or antara drishti

Move through this yoga asana series focusing on different drishti spots.

Asana	Drishti
Seated side stretch - Reach the right hand up	The right hand
Seated side stretch - Reach the left hand up	The left hand
Seated Twist right and left	A spot in the distance
Table Top	A spot on the yoga mat
Downward Facing Dog	The navel
Forward Fold	Big Toes
Mountain	Tip of the nose
Tree Pose	Up to the sky
Warrior I - Reach up with palms together	The thumbs
Warrior II	The right or left hand
Mountain	Between the eyebrows (3rd eye)
Corpse pose (Savasana)	Eyes closed - third eye

5. Technique #2: Eden Energy: The Hook Up and Connecting Heaven and Earth (Edenenergymedicine.com)

The Hook Up - This Eden Energy Exercise[15] helps with balance and connection. The governing meridian runs up the back of the body from the root of the spine, up the back and neck, over the head, and down the face to the top lip. This is yang energy. The central meridian runs up the front of the body from the pubic bone to the bottom lip. This is yin energy.

Let's Practice:

To perform the hook up, place the middle finger of one hand on the center of the forehead and the middle finger of the other hand on the belly button. Lightly press in and then upward. Become very still. Visualize the two lines hooking up and see if you notice a shift.

Connecting Heaven and Earth - This Eden Energy Exercise also helps with balance and connection. By reaching up with one hand we are feeling a connection to the divine or source energy and by reaching one hand down we feel a connection with the earth and a sense of grounding and stability.

Let's Practice:

To perform connecting heaven and earth, stand tall in mountain pose with the palms together at your heart center. Reach the left hand up to the sky and the right hand down to the earth. Gaze up and feel the connection you are making to heaven and look down to feel a connection with the earth. Repeat with the left hand down and the right hand up. Repeat several times if you wish and then bring the hands back to your heart. Feel ease and balance.

---

15 www.edenenergymedicine.com

6. Restorative Asana #2: Leaning Tower with Incline legs and Happiness Bubble Visualization (Technique #2)

Essential Oil Suggestion: Tea Tree

Set-up: Place a bolster or rolled blanket against two blocks (one on the highest level and the other on the medium level). Lie back with your legs on the bolster and place a strap around the bolster and the legs so they feel supported. Listen to the Happiness Bubble visualization described in Technique #2.

EO: You may place *Tea Tree* essential oil on your wrists or diffuse it in the air. Breathe in the essential oils to open up the passageways in the nostrils and the whole body. Take long, deep, calming breaths. Play relaxing spa music, theta music, Tibetan singing bowl sounds or nature sounds. Rest and relax.

While in this restorative posture practice technique #2, the Happiness Bubble Visualization.

7. Technique #3: The Happiness Bubble Visualization

Let's Practice:

Come into the restorative posture and begin to surrender and let go of any tension. Feel the support of the ground and the props. Feel the blood moving back to your head and heart. We are going to imagine a relaxing place called your happiness bubble. This is a place where you can go in your mind and body when you are feeling overwhelmed, anxious, nervous, stressed or just need some space and time for yourself.

Imagine a relaxing place where you can go to feel safe. It can be a place in your home or a place you went to on vacation that you can visualize. It can be any imaginary place where you feel safe and relaxed. Envision all of the details. What is the weather and temperature? What do you see and hear? Are you out in nature? Relaxing on a beach? On a mountain top? In the tropics? Are you inside or outside? What does it smell like? Breathe in the fresh healing air and relax. Now, picture a large bubble or dome around you, like a fortress of solitude. This is a safe space. Rain comes down in the form of thoughts, stress, worry and just rolls down the sides of the bubble. In the bubble all is well and happy. All you feel here is peace and love.

Knowing that this is a place of comfort for you, notice how your body and mind feel. Scan your whole body for any tension and then surrender and let go. Allow your body to relax. You are safe. This is your sacred place. You can come here in your mind whenever you need a little solace. Stay here for as long as you like until you feel calm and happy and then stay here some more.

8. Restorative Yoga Asana #3: Lounge Chair Savasana with Bound Angle

Essential Oil Suggestion: Jasmine

Set-up: Place two blocks next to each other; one on the highest level and the other on the medium level or one on the medium level and one on the lowest level. Lean a bolster or a tightly rolled blanket against it. Lie down with your bottom close to the bottom edge of the bolster and recline back. Use rolled blankets or pillows under your arms for arm rest support. Bend your knees and walk your feet together. Allow your knees to fall out to the side into bound angle pose. Place blocks or blankets under the outer thighs near the knees so the legs are fully supported. Place an eye pillow on your eyes.

EO: You may place *Jasmine* essential oil on your wrists or diffuse it in the air. Breathe in the essential oils to open up the passageways in the nostrils and the whole body. Take long, deep, calming breaths. Play relaxing spa music, theta music, Tibetan singing bowl sounds or nature sounds. Rest and relax.

9. Closing. Burning or Dissolving Ritual

◇ **Letting Go.**

Get a lighter and a heat resistant bowl or a bowl filled with room temperature or warm water. Take the paper with the answer to the letting go question and say the following out loud:

> *"Dear Universe–I no longer need these thoughts, feelings, or circumstances that do not serve my highest and best good. I vow to be open to the lessons presented to me in order to create positive habits and improve my outlook on life."*

Now light the paper on fire and place it in the bowl and watch it burn or take the special dissolving paper and place it in the water and watch it dissolve. Let it go.

◇ **Inviting in.**

Read one of the following quotes of inspiration below or choose
your own. You may choose to print it on a paper or sticky note to
post where you will see it. Say the following out loud: "*Dear Universe–I invite this message of inspiration into my life at this time to
serve my highest and best good. I promise to be more present and
kinder to myself every day.*"

What will you invite into your life today?

Statement of gratitude to the Universe:

> "*Thank you universe for giving me the courage and strength
> to move forward everyday with faith that everything is
> as it is supposed to be for my highest and best good.*"

Quotes of inspiration:

> "*Every day brings a choice to practice stress or
> to practice peace.*" ~Joan Borysenko

> "*As far as I can tell, it's just about letting the universe
> know what you want and then working toward it while
> letting go of how it comes to pass.*" ~Jim Carrey

Story #6. I'm on the Edge of my Emotions!
(Ride the wave)

Do you ever feel like your emotions are right on the edge and at any moment you could cry, laugh, yell or lash out in some way? I have felt like that many times. I'm hovering on the edge and then someone says something. Anything. And here it comes. I can feel an emotional surge rising up to the surface.

One day I was sitting in front of a woman at the bank in the customer service office to close out an account. She didn't even say anything and I started crying and telling her what was going on in my life. I was emotionally overwhelmed. She was kind and listened and offered comfort. Then later the same day I was simply talking on the phone to the contact lens woman from the eye doctor's office and whoosh, another flood of emotion. It was good that I could let out what was bottled inside but not so good that I just burst out crying in front of these strangers. On the other hand, who's to say if it was good or not so good, it just happened. These incidences happened from pain I was holding in when my husband left me. I was carrying around sorrow and it just popped up in a moment.

Other times in the past, I would cry for different reasons. I remember once when I was living in Florida and I was not used to opening the kitchen drawer to get a spoon and seeing a gang of cockroaches scurrying away. Yikes and Yuck! When I saw my landlord in the hallway, I asked him to spray the apartment right away. He said "I will do it at the end of the week." I could feel the tears welling up and I started to cry and say "It's so gross! I need you to do it right now!" I remember the look of shock on his face seeing me cry over this. I was a bit embarrassed but, guess what? He got his exterminating spray out right away and began to spray the apartment. I have explored this other on-the-edge-of-my-emotions habit and I know exactly where it comes from. When I was a little girl, I used to ask my parents for something like a new toy or a cookie or to go to a friend's house and they would say "No." Next I would begin to beg, "Please can I? Why not? Come on" and they would keep saying, "No." Then I would turn on the waterworks and that worked every time. When I cried, they would give in and say "Yes." So, what did I learn from this? Crying gets you what you want; sympathy, a gift, attention. As an adult it is embarrassing to notice this ingrained thought process and pattern that when things aren't going my way, I can cry to get what I want. I realized that I had a difficult time with disappointment and the word no. When I heard it I felt I was being rejected. I have worked through this by noticing where it came from and why it worked for me as a child. It doesn't work so well as an adult and so I don't use crying to sway people anymore.

These are just two examples of my being on the edge of emotion and letting them take over. I have learned as I live and experience life and all of its ups and downs that emotions make good navigators but not good drivers. They are a guide to pay attention to what is happening within us. I can pause and look at the present moment and at the situation for what it is and not let my emotions take the driver's seat.

Gary Zukav, in his book "The Seat of the Soul," talks about how our emotions are there to reveal to us hurting or splintered parts of our personality that need nurturing. He says "The road to your soul is through your heart." I am much better at listening to what my emotions are trying to tell me and when I feel them arise, which is all the time, I become an observer and figure out the messages they are trying to convey. I look within and not outside to blame others or the world around me. When we learn to transform our emotions into positive energy we can align with the soul through the heart, in other words, we can LOVE!

Emotions make better navigators than drivers

Energy

I've always been a super energetic person! I love being involved in many things like singing, and dancing, riding my bike, teaching aerobics, zumba, bootcamp and step classes, waitressing, camping, and every active thing. All of these require lots of high vibrational energy and movement! Today I continue to be involved in lots of activities. My current home sits right in the middle of nature so I get out often to connect to the best energy booster there is. I stand in the creek and bask in the sun or even hug a tree The more I explore, practice, and teach yoga the more I am reminded that everything is energy! Air, water, earth, fire, space, your body, your environment, sounds, thoughts, words, everything! Your body is made up of water and atoms that are in a constant state of motion so you are vibrating all the time. Emotions are energy in motion. When we are in a high vibration state of love, kindness, compassion, gratitude, and generosity our body and mind experience optimal health and harmony. When we reside in a low vibrational state of fear, anger, sadness, jealousy and resentment it can lead to imbalance in our emotional state and in our body creating disease. When we live in a state of joy our intuition and spirituality are heightened. The more we feel connected to the universe and invite in joy and happiness the more we vibrate in wonderful, healing ways. In this section you will explore the energy that resides within and around you with practices of raising your vibrations, working with the chakras, and creating your reality through visualizations and chanting.

Let's Practice:

Sit tall or lie down in a comfortable position. Open your hands with your palms up. Remain very still. Now bring all of your awareness to your right hand. Keep your focus solely on the right hand without moving it. Can you begin to feel a tingling sensation in your hand? Thoughts are energy and when you bring all of your focus onto one thing, like your hand, energy goes there and you can feel it. Where attention goes, energy flows. Now shift your attention to the other hand and observe the flow of energy and sensation. Enjoy exploring your energy. Notice that what you focus your energy on you will find so practice focusing on what you wish to show up in your life and then notice what happens. See if you experience a change in your physical body and in your emotional energy states.

127

YES for Energy #1

1. Opening

◇ Letting Go

Questions of the day. On a piece of paper, that you will burn or dissolve at the end, write your answer to the question(s) below about what you wish to let go:

1. *What state of mind or activity can I let go of that drains me of my energy?*

2. *What low vibration emotion or attachment can I begin to release?*

◇ Hand on Heart Affirmations

"Gratitude brings me into a harmonious relationship with the good in everyone and everything that surrounds me."

"I choose to focus my time, energy and conversation around people who inspire, support and help me to grow into my happiest, strongest and wisest self."

"I see the positive possibilities all around me. I redirect the substantial energy of my frustration and turn it into positive, effective, unstoppable determination."

◇ Personal Mantra

Choose a mantra of your own that speaks to you today. Begin with "I am," and say it in the present moment as if it already exists! Your personal mantra should be something you truly believe. Say it out loud with energy, emotion, vigor, enthusiasm, and intention to grow these positive seeds within you!

Example Mantra: *"I am powerful, strong and loving and I use these strengths for good to contribute to the world and serve others!"*

◇ **Gratitude and Energy**

Say to yourself or out loud what you are grateful for and what positive energy you wish to invite into your life today! You may also choose an angel card with a word or a message of inspiration for the day.

2. Restorative Yoga Asana #1 and Breath Assessment: Basic Relaxation Pose

Set-up: Lie down on the floor or on a yoga mat with a blanket or pillow under your head. Place a rolled-up blanket or bolster under your knees. You may also place blankets under your arms. You may place an eye pillow over your eyes. Make sure you feel fully supported and relaxed.

◇ **Breath Assessment:**

Come into the posture and begin to release any past or future thoughts. Relax and surrender more and more with every breath. Notice your breathing pattern without trying to change anything. Notice the rise and fall of the belly and chest. Observe the length of the breath. Is it flowing naturally helping you to become calmer or does it feel rapid or shallow creating stress and tension? Just observe for 3-5 minutes. Now count your inhales and exhales. Extend the exhales to assist your body in coming to a deeper state of relaxation, activating the parasympathetic nervous system (rest and digest).

Allow your body and mind to surrender to the present moment and just be.

3. Lesson #1: Prana, Chakra, Vayus, Nadis: Energy and Emotions

Everything is energy. Our physical bodies could not exist without the spiritual life force that constantly supports it. When this energy leaves the body, our physical body dies and begins to break down. Our soul is our consciousness; the connection between our physical body and our spirit, and provides communication between the two.

Prana is the Sanskrit word for energy or life force. Our energy is vital to our well-being. It can be open, stuck, balanced, sluggish, closed, blocked and so on. As we explore our energy systems we may discover areas that are emotionally blocked or stuck. We hold emotions in our energetic bodies and if we don't process them they will remain stuck and eventually turn into disease.

Understanding and working with our energy systems can improve our physical, mental, emotional, and spiritual well-being. Emotional awareness is paying attention and being aware of your emotions all the time. A release of energy from our energy systems in fear will create pain and dysfunctions in the body. Physical symptoms will appear as an end result after a long time of holding onto emotional pain. A release of energy from our energy systems in love produces vitality, health and wellbeing. It produces joy and fulfillment. We can work with the energy in our bodies to notice where we may be holding on to something in our lives from the past, present, or future that is causing us to get stuck or that blocks free-flowing energy. The types of energy systems in the body are prana, chakras, vayus, and nadis. Other forms of energy are meridians (energy channels in the body) and acupressure points that stimulate and balance the flow of energy. After reading about these energy systems, you may be able to identify emotionally and/or physically stuck areas in your body. Then move to the yoga asana practices to help release the energy so it may flow more freely, bringing balance and ease to your physical and emotional body.

Prana, Chakra, Vayus, Nadis: Explanation

Prana = Life force or energy. When prana/energy flows freely we experience optimal health and well-being.

Chakra = Wheel. Chakras are energy centers that receive and express prana. There are seven main chakras that correspond to branches of the nervous system. These can be energized and vital or blocked and dim. Each chakra has an associated color, petaled lotus flower, and a seed (bija) sound and tone. {Details below}

Vayus = Wind or that which flows. This refers to the *way* in which prana moves through the body. There are five main Prana Vayus or currents of energy. {Details below}

Nadis = Channel. These are energy pathways or channels that carry prana. The three main ones are the ida, the pingala and the sushumna. {Details below}

Chakra, Vayus, Nadis: Details of Each
Chakras:

Root Chakra- Muladhara-. Located at the base of the spine. Color: red. Seed sound: Lam. Note: "C." Nature element: Earth . The root chakra represents the qualities of our foundation and a feeling of being grounded.

Sacral Chakra- Swadhisthana – Located at the lower abdomen/sexual organs. Color: orange. Seed sound: Vam. Note: "D." Nature element: Water. The sacral chakra represents the qualities of pleasure, desire, and security.

Solar Plexus Chakra-Manipura – Located at the navel area. Color: yellow. Seed sound: Ram. Note: "E." Nature element: Fire. The solar plexus chakra represents personal power, self-esteem, personality, identity, and ego.

Heart Chakra–Anahta - Located at the heart. Color: green. Seed sound: Yam. Note: "F." Nature element: Air or wind. The heart chakra represents love, compassion, care, and peace.

Throat Chakra Vishuddha – Located at the area of the throat. Color: blue. Seed sound: Ham. Note: "G." Nature element: Ether (space). The throat chakra represents communication, expression, and creativity.

Third Eye- Ajna - Located between the eyebrows. Color: indigo or purple. Seed sound: Om. Note: "A." Nature element: Light. The third eye represents intuition and psychic knowing.

Crown Chakra- Sahasrara – Located at top of the head. Color: purple or white. Seed sound: Om or none. Note: "B." Nature element: pure consciousness. The crown chakra represents consciousness and awareness, spiritual connection, oneness with the divine.

Vayus:

Prana Vayu – governs the region from the throat to the bottom of the heart, is associated with the element of air, and has an upward and forward motion associated with the inhalation.

Apana Vayu – governs the region of the lower body from the navel down through the legs, is associated with the element of earth, and has a downward moving force associated with exhalation and elimination, including waste as well as reproduction and childbirth.

Samana Vayu – governs the region of the solar plexus and abdominal organs, is associated with the element of fire, and has inward movement associated with digestive fire and metabolism. It is harmonizing and balancing for body, mind and emotions.

Udana Vayu – governs the region of the throat and head, is associated with the element of ether, and expels air upward through speech and sound.

Vyana Vayu – pervades the whole body and moves from the center outward, is associated with the element of water. It governs circulation on all levels.

Nadis:

The Ida is associated with the feminine, the left nostril, and right brain activity. It corresponds to the tamasic quality of nature (dull, inert, and still).

The Pingala is associated with the masculine, the right nostril, and left brain activity. It corresponds to the rajasic quality of nature (activity).

The Sushumna is the central energy/prana channel of the body. It corresponds with the sattva quality of nature (balanced, stable, and pure). The ida nerve channel runs up the left side of the sushumna and the pingala nerve channel runs up the right side in which vital air passes through.

Let's Practice:
How is your Energy?

Now that you know more about energy, notice where you may need more energy to flow. Take out a paper and pen and on the left side write down each area, one below the other: Chakras, Vayus, and Nadis. Then review the information you just read as well as the information to follow to identify the areas in your energetic body that may be stuck and in need of more energy. There will be some crossover in each of the three areas. Next, move on to the Yoga Asanas section for a yoga practice that will assist in allowing the energy to flow more freely, energizing your whole system for balance and homeostasis. This will not be a one-time practice. Our energies change every day according to our physical, mental, emotional and spiritual states. Check in with yourself daily to see how you are feeling energetically. Choose a practice to help to improve the flow of energy and your mental and physical well being!

{Visit www.Y4ES.com for sample yoga practices}

Chakra, Vayus, Nadis: Find your Energy Flow
Strong, Balanced, and Flowing OR Weak, Imbalanced, and Stuck

The Chakras:

Root- Muladhara

Balanced: When we feel confident and able to handle challenges

Unbalanced: When we feel threatened, as if we're standing on unstable ground.

Sacral- Swadhisthana

Balanced: When we feel abundance and confidence and have a sense of belonging, well-being and pleasure. We easily connect with others.

Unbalanced: When we experience imbalances in our physical body and our sense of security is diminished. We feel a lack of passion and repressed emotions. Sexually frustrated.

Solar Plexus - Manipura

Balanced: When we feel confident and capable

Unbalanced: When we experience low self-esteem, stress and anxiety.

Heart - Anahata

Balanced: When we are capable of giving and receiving love and developing spirituality

Unbalanced: When we lose our sense of connection with others and ourselves

Throat - Vishuddha

Balanced: When we can easily express the creative and life-affirming aspects of ourselves with confidence.

Unbalanced: When we experience ear, nose, and throat problems along with not being able to express ourselves or speak as our authentic self.

Third Eye - Ajna

Balanced: When we see things clearly as they are without being colored by opinions, perception or ego.

Unbalanced: When we experience confusion or clouded thoughts. We may experience headaches and dizziness.

Crown - Sahasrara

Balanced: When we feel peace, joy, serenity, positivity and balance in life.

Unbalanced: When we experience spiritual distrust or negativity about life and a disconnection from the body.

The Vayus (Wind):[16]

Prana Vayu- life force

Strong: When you add silence in the day and time for inward focus

Weak: When listening to loud music or watching violence on tv or negative news or any sensory overload. You experience excess worry, anxiety, low energy, and difficulty meditating.

Apana Vayu- downward breath

Strong: When elimination is regular and you possess the ability to let go of difficult thoughts or memories by processing it and releasing it while maintaining hope and positivity.

Weak: When there are elimination issues of any type and if you have difficulty letting go or experiencing constant worry. You may have a feeling of being ungrounded.

Samana Vayu- inward breath

Strong: When you are able to process/digest well. You have healthy physical digestion and you are also able to digest information well. You take in what is useful and eliminate information or thoughts that are not needed or are weighing you down.

Weak: When you have problems with digestion or you experience a feeling of depletion. You have the inability to think and talk about difficult experiences. Poor judgement, low confidence and lack of motivation.

Udana Vayu- upward breath

Strong: When you are willing to reach beyond limits by accepting challenges and making changes in life for personal growth.

16 https://yogainternational.com/article/view/how-to-work-with-the-5-prana-vayus-in-practice

Weak: When you may be stagnant in your career, personal growth or yoga practice. You may lack enthusiasm and communication skills. You don't speak up for yourself. You experience shortness of breath.

Vyana Vayu- whole body breath

Strong: When your emotions and ideas are able to flow freely. You are outgoing and social, and able to express yourself in loving ways

Weak: When you are limited in your ability to express and feel thoughts and emotions. You experience separation and isolation and have poor circulation.

The Nadis:

Ida

Open: When the air is flowing freely through the left nostril and there is a cool, freshness and quietness to the mind and body. Yin energy is activated.

Closed: When the air is not flowing freely through the left nostril leading to diminished right brain function of creativity. Creative and intuitive thinking is foggy.

Pingala

Open: When the air is flowing freely through the right nostril and there is a warm, active feeling. Yang energy is activated.

Closed: When the air is not flowing freely through the right nostril leading to diminished left-brain function of logical thinking. Detailed and analytical thinking is foggy.

Sushumna

Open: When the air is flowing freely in both Ida and Pingala there is a balance of energy through this central channel increasing physical and mental health.

Closed: When the air is not flowing freely in either or both Ida and Pingala, clear thinking and energy is diminished.

4. Yoga Asanas: Chakras, Vayus, Nadis

Let's Practice:

For your yoga asanas, choose the areas where you wish to open or find more balance for the Chakras, Vayus and Nadis and then perform the accompanying yoga poses.

Chakras:

Root Chakra -Muladhara - Mountain Pose

The Root Chakra is associated with grounding energy from the earth to help us feel connected and safe.

Mountain Pose (Tadasana) - Begin by standing with your feet slightly apart. Press your feet firmly into the mat. Activate your core, relax your shoulders, and reach the top of your head skyward. Bring your palms together. Visualize your Root Chakra as a bright red light shining out from the end of your tailbone.

Sacral Chakra Swadhisthana - Revolved Triangle Pose
The Sacral Chakra is associated with our creative center and is home to our self-expression, emotions, and pleasure.

Revolved Triangle Pose (Parivrtta Trikonasana) - Begin standing with your right foot forward and your hips square to the front of your mat. Place a yoga block inside your right foot and place your left hand on the block. Bring your right hand to your hip crease, thigh or low back and gently guide the hip back so your hips are in line. Slowly twist your torso to the right. You may extend your right arm to the sky so your right shoulder stacks on top of your left. Hold for a few breaths and release back to center. Repeat on the opposite side.

Solar Plexus Chakra -Manipura - Boat Pose
The Manipura chakra is associated with our self-esteem, sense of purpose, personal identity, individual will, digestion, and metabolism.

Boat Pose (Navasana) - Begin seated with your knees bent and your feet on the mat. Place your hands behind your hips, lift your chest, and lengthen your spine. To activate your core, slowly lean back and keep your heart lifted. Extend your arms forward and lift your shins so they are parallel with the mat. Focus on the core engagement. Hold 10-30 seconds.

Heart Chakra Anahata - Low or High Lunge Pose
The Anahata Chakra is associated with compassion, generosity, respect, and a connection with others. To be fulfilled we need to express unconditional love and compassion.

Low or High Lunge (Anjaneyasana) - Begin in Downward Facing Dog. Step your right foot forward between your hands and lower your left knee to the ground. Keep your hips square to the front of the mat. Shift your weight forward into your right foot to allow your hips to release and to stretch the front of your left hip. Reach your arms up to open the heart area and stretch the front body. Hold for a few breaths, then slowly release. Repeat on the opposite side.

Throat Chakra Vishuddha - Easy Seat Pose
The Vishuddha Chakra is associated with communication and authenticity and even having the confidence to speak in public.

Easy Seat (Sukhasana) with Chanting - Begin seated on your mat in easy seat pose with legs crossed and hands in Gyana Mudhra (index finger touching thumb and remaining fingers extended). Rest the back of the hand on your knees. Inhale as you lengthen your spine. Exhale and relax your shoulders. Now chant the mantra "Ong Namo Guru Dev Namo." This means "I bow to the creative energy of the infinite; I bow to the divine channel of wisdom." As you chant, visualize a blue light near your throat as it removes any doubt you may have regarding your truth. Continue chanting for three minutes or more.

Third Eye Chakra -Ajna - Dolphin Pose

The Ajna Chakra is associated with our intuition and inner guidance to help us on our path. It is our *sixth sense*.

Dolphin Pose (Ardha Pincha Mayurasana) - Begin on all 4's. Place your forearms on the ground. Be sure to stack your shoulders above your elbows. Now straighten your legs into Dolphin pose. Visualize energy connecting your Third Eye. Hold here for three or more breaths and then release to Child's Pose.

Crown Chakra -Sahasrara - Balancing Butterfly Pose

The Sahasrara Chakra is associated with devotion and is the seat of our consciousness that connects to the infinite. It varies from the other chakras because it is not a wheel but rather an opening.

Balancing Butterfly Pose (variation of Malasana & Baddha Konasana) - Begin kneeling on your mat with your toes tucked under. Now lift your knees and come onto the balls of your feet. Keep your heels together under your sit bones and open your knees as wide as possible. Once you feel stable, slowly bring your hands to your heart center. For more intensity, raise your hands overhead and hold. Hold for 5 to 10 breaths, then slowly release. (The image is of Bound Angle or butterfly)

Vayus:

Prana Vayu

Directing prana upward through Prana Vayu

Inhale: Allow the breath to flow in through your nose and imagine fresh oxygenated breath filling your lungs fully.

Exhale: Allow prana to linger as you slowly exhale and imagine the breath moving through all parts of the lungs.

Apply this breath-work as you practice the yoga poses.

Yoga Poses:

Backbends: Camel, Cobra, Sphinx, Locust, Bow Pose, Dancer, Bridge pose, Mountain pose and Extended Mountain Pose (arms overhead), Upper backbend, Warrior I, Chair pose, Savasana (corpse pose) and Meditation

Apana Vayu

Directing prana downward through Apana Vayu

Inhale: Feel the breath flow to the base of the spine/pelvic floor

Exhale: Move the breath down the legs and
out through the feet to the earth

Apply this breathwork as you practice the yoga poses.

Yoga Poses:

Standing poses: Mountain, Warrior I, Warrior II, Triangle, Revolved
Triangle, Standing or Seated forward folds and Seated Twists

Samana Vayu

Directing prana inward through Samana Vayu

Inhale: Let the breath move in through the nose and fill the whole body evenly: front, sides, and back of the torso

Exhale: Move the breath deeper inward to the center of the body

Apply this breathwork as you practice the yoga poses.

Yoga Poses:

Twists: standing, seated, and supine (on the back)
Core work: Supine (on the back): Bent knee Abdominal Crunches and Twists, Plank and Chaturanga Dandasana (Plank push up)
Forward fold: Standing and seated
Arm balances: Supported Headstand,
Crow pose, Firefly, Handstand

Udana Vayu

Directing prana upward through Udana Vayu

Inhale: Imagine the breath moving up from the earth into the soles of the feet and up the legs, through the spine, and up to the chest.

Exhale: Continue imagining the flow of energy in an upward moving flow through the crown of your head.

For inverted postures:

Inhale: Imagine that the breath begins at the hands and/or arms, whichever is in contact with the floor. Let it continue moving up the arms and torso as you lengthen your inhale.

Exhale: Move the breath through the legs and out through the soles of the feet.

Yoga Poses:

Inversions: Downward Facing Dog, Handstand, Legs up the Wall, and other inversions, Warrior I, Chair pose, Eagle pose, Seated forward folds, Bridge or Wheel Pose

Vyana Vayu

Directing prana all through Vyana Vayu

Inhale: Imagine the breath moving from the nose to the heart, and even to the back of the heart.

Exhale: Imagine the breath moving out through the arms and legs and through the length of the torso and through every pore in the body.

Yoga Poses:

Sun Salutations, Backbends and side bends, Savasana (corpse pose)

When we are aligned with good intentions, love and kindness and non-harming (ahimsa), we can do whatever we want with this energy, feeling our lives flourish in harmony with nature and one another.

5. Technique #2: Eden Energy Medicine; Daily Routine[17]

These practices are called energy medicine. To learn more, see Donna Eden's work. I took a course in her work and learned the following practices. I really enjoy feeling the movement of my energy and experiencing the benefits that go along with them. You may explore these further by reading her books or taking her training.

17 edenenergymedicine.com

Let's Practice:

1st: **4 Grounding Taps/Thumps.** Tap in these areas on your body as you take three deep breaths for each.

1) Cheekbones - helps digestion, 2) Under the Collarbone - helps with reducing toxins, 3) Center of the chest -Thymus - helps boost the immune system, 4) Sides of the body by the rib cage – Spleen - helps metabolism

2nd: **Cross over Shoulder Pull.** This will help with energy and clarity. Take one hand to the opposite shoulder and sweep across the body to the opposite hip. Repeat on the other side and alternate side to side six or more times.

3rd: **Cross Crawl.** This helps the brain to work well and energies in the body to flow and harmonize better. Sit or stand. March with high knees. Now sweep the opposite arm up and around to touch the opposite thigh. Repeat for 1 minute or up to 24 times.

4th: **The Wayne Cook.** This helps with clarity and balancing your emotional state. Sit in a chair and take the right ankle across the left thigh. Take the left hand to hold the right ankle and the right hand across and onto the bottom of the foot. Take deep breaths in while holding this. Switch to the other side. End by placing all fingertips and thumbs together and form a triangle. Place the thumbs on the forehead at the third eye. Take 3 deep breaths.

5th: **Crown Pull.** This relaxes the prefrontal cortex and helps circulate blood flow and energy in the skull. Take the fingertips of both hands and place them at the center of the forehead and sweep across the brow to the temples. Then move up to the top of the head and keep pressing in and pulling downward and also forward as you move along the skull to the back of the head. When you get to the neck pull forward at the back of the neck and rest the hands on the top of the shoulders

6th: **Connecting Heaven and Earth.** This makes space in the body to help the energy to move and travel. Rub hands together and then place them on the thighs. Then sweep them up in a circle and to prayer hands at the heart. Then inhale and press one hand up to the sky and the other towards the ground. Reaching out from the shoulders, stretch in both directions with palms flat. Hold the breath. Bring hands to heart and then repeat to the other side. Do this 2 more times. Then exhale and hang reaching the hands for the earth. Make figure 8's in the air as you stand.

7th: **The Zip up.** This helps to reduce negative energy and encourages strength. Trace the central meridian by taking both hands to the pubic bone and draw a line straight up the front of the body, like zipping a zipper, all the way to the bottom lip. Then pretend you are locking it up and throwing away the key.

8th: **The Hook Up.** This helps to connect the central meridian in the front of the body from the pubic bone up to the bottom lip, and the governing meridian in the back of the body from the tailbone all the way up the back body, over the head and to the top lip. Place one finger in the belly button and one on the center of the forehead at the third eye. Push in lightly and draw up. This connects the two meridians to create a strong force and helps every other energy system.

6. Restorative Yoga Asana #2: Deer Pose with Chest on a Low Bolster

Essential Oil Suggestion: Lemon

Set-up: Place a bolster or rolled up blanket on the floor or propped up with low blocks, blanket or firm pillow. Sit with your left hip at the end of the bolster and both knees facing to the left. Place the sole of your left foot on the inner right thigh in Deer Pose. Rotate your torso towards the bolster and rest your chest down on it. You may wish to have another blanket or pillow under your head. Turn your face towards your knees.

EO: You may place *Lemon* essential oil on your wrists or diffuse it in the air. Breathe in the essential oils to open up the passageways in the nostrils and the whole body. Take long, deep relaxing breaths. Play relaxing spa music, theta music or Tibetan singing bowl sounds with or without nature sounds. Rest and Relax.

7. Technique #3: Raise Your Vibrational Frequency Lesson from Teal Swan[18]

How to Raise your Frequency and Increase your Vibration

Thoughts >>>> Emotion >>>> Energy/Vibration >>> Light

Low vibrational frequency= Decreased state of consciousness. Your perception is limited, and the flow of love, life force and intuition are restricted.

Higher vibrational frequency= Increased state of consciousness. Your life force and perception are high. You radiate love and it raises the consciousness of all you encounter. When your vibrations are negative (low) or positive (high) - you will know because... Negative---> doesn't feel good and Positive---> feels good

Let's Practice:

To increase your vibrations, choose thoughts that are positive and any of the practices below.

Whatever your most dominant thought is and what you are focusing on is what you will manifest. Observe thoughts without judge-

---

18 https://tealswan.com/

ment. Allow your feelings to come out. Write, cry, punch a pillow or anything that will discharge energy.

Ways to increase your vibrations:

- Make conscious positive changes: in your lifestyle, beliefs, fears and judgements
- *Music:* choose music that makes you feel good
- Spend time near people, places and things that hold a high frequency: friends, animals, nature
- Choose anything inspiring: books, movies, spiritual teachers
- Exercise: stimulate endorphins and the brain. Something you like
- Aromatherapy or color therapy
- Write in a positive aspects or gratitude journal. Look for things in life that help you feel good and positive
- Spend time in water: Light is pure source energy. Water is second. Take a shower or bath or be near or in a body of water. It's vibrationally cleansing
- Practice random acts of kindness. When you project and radiate love outwards you increase your vibration
- Inquiry: Get to know yourself. The more you do the easier it becomes to hold a high frequency
- Laugh and smile. Anything you do, say, think will automatically increase your vibration

Dedicate yourself to happiness and prioritize it above all. You can't afford the luxury of a negative thought. If you do have one though, just accept where you are, express it and move into the direction of positive emotions.

8. Restorative Yoga Pose #3: Lounge Chair Savasana with Chakra Meditation and Seed Sounds

Essential Oil Suggestion: Juniper Berry

Set-up: Place two blocks next to each other; one on the highest level and the other on the medium level or one on the medium level and one on the lowest level. Lean a bolster or a tightly rolled blanket against it. Lie down with your bottom close to the bottom edge of the bolster and recline back. Use rolled blankets or pillows under your arms for arm rest support. Place a rolled blanket or bolster under your knees if you wish. Place an eye pillow on your eyes.

EO: You may place *Juniper Berry* essential oil on your wrists or diffuse it in the air. Breathe in the essential oils to open up the passageways in the nostrils and the whole body. Take long, deep relaxing breaths. Play relaxing spa music, theta music or Tibetan singing bowl sounds with or without nature sounds. Rest and Relax.

Chakra Balancing Meditation: (create a recording of your own from the script below or use the recording from www.Y4ES.com)

In this guided meditation, we will focus on your energy centers or the seven chakras. The seed sounds are associated with each chakra and are meant to active the energy in them.

Begin in a fully supported and relaxed posture. Remove any distractions. Feel the space in the room; the walls, the ceiling and the floor. Notice your body lying on the floor and let go of any thoughts or worries. Take a long full deep breath in through your nose and sigh it out through your mouth. Continue to take relaxed breaths, in through your nose and out through your nose. Feel your belly expand as you breathe in and contract as you breathe out. Breath in. Breathe out. Relax every muscle in your forehead and eyes. Allow your jaw to relax fully and notice a warm sensation of ease spreading down your neck and your chest. Release any tension. Now the warm relaxing feeling moves down your shoulders and arms and all the way to your fingers. Release any tension in your spine and back. Feel the flow of comfort spread down your torso, hips and legs and all the way to your feet and toes. Return to a focus on the breath and focus on the oxygen moving through your whole body carrying energy and light.

Trust the process of this chakra meditation and release everything that no longer serves you. As we move through the chakras bring your full awareness to the area of the body and the associated color and meaning of each. The intention is to feel a sense of openness and balance in the whole body. When you direct your energy towards your chakras you can unblock them. You enable them to function in a supportive and balanced way. Your loving energy can unblock them. We will imagine a swirling light energy guiding each one to open and heal.

Begin by bringing your awareness to the first chakra, the root or Muladhara, located at the base of the spine. Picture the color red in this area. This chakra represents stability and safety. It is your foundation and support in life. Imagine the red light moving in a swirling shape to offer a sense of grounding stability to your whole being. Say the seed sound "Lam" silently to yourself three times.

Now move your awareness to the second chakra, the sacral or Swadhisthana located below your navel or pelvis area. Picture the color orange in this area. This chakra represents abundance, well-being, and pleasure. Imagine the color orange swirling around and offering you a sense of well-being and peace. Say the seed sound "Vam" silently to yourself three times.

Next, move your awareness to the third chakra, the solar plexus or Manipura located at your upper abdomen in the center of the torso. Picture the color yellow in this area. This chakra represents your sense

YES

of self. It is home to self-confidence, courage and power. Imagine that yellow color as a ball of energy swirling around freely and offering you a feeling of high self-esteem and kindness to yourself. Say the seed sound "Ram" silently to yourself three times.

Now move your awareness to the fourth chakra, the heart or Anahata located at your heart. Picture the color green in this area. This chakra represents all forms of love, care, and compassion towards yourself and others. Imagine the color green as a swirling ball carrying healing energy and a sense of love for all beings. Say the seed sound "Yam" silently to yourself three times.

Next, move your awareness to the fifth chakra, the throat or Vishuddha located at the throat. Picture the color blue in this area. This chakra represents communication and the ability to speak, express and be your authentic self in a non-harming way to yourself and others. Imagine a swirl of blue energy focused here giving you a sense of confidence and truth in your speech. Say the seed sound "Ham" silently to yourself three times.

Now shift your awareness to the sixth chakra, the third eye or Ajna located on your forehead between your eyebrows at the third eye. Picture an indigo or purple color in this area. This chakra represents our intuition and ability to see clearly. It guides your imagination and wisdom. Imagine that purple light glowing and swirling at the center of your head directly behind the spot on your forehead offering you the wisdom and guidance you need to create the life you desire. Say the seed sound "Aum" silently to yourself three times.

Now move your awareness to the seventh chakra, the crown or Sahasrara located at the top of the head. Picture the color violet or white in and above this area. This chakra represents our spirituality, higher consciousness, and connection to the divine, universe, or higher power. Picture a swirling bright white light beginning at the crown and rising up above your head to offer a feeling of oneness and connection to all that is. There is no seed sound for this chakra. Bring awareness to the silence.

Now, picture white or gold healing light and energy moving up from the earth beginning with your feet and flowing through your whole body all the way to the crown and beyond. Every part of your body is charged with the energy of self-love and acceptance.

This meditation was designed to help release any stuck energy and cleanse your chakras. Begin to bring your awareness back into the space, noticing the energy in and around you as you bring some movement back to your body. Slowly open your eyes and take a long deep breath in and sigh it out. Notice how you feel.

9. Closing. Burning or Dissolving Ritual

◇ **Letting Go:**

Get a lighter and a heat resistant bowl (for the burning ritual) or a bowl filled with room temperature or warm water (for the dissolving ritual). Take the paper with the answer to the letting go question and say the following out loud:

> *"Dear Universe–I no longer need these thoughts, feelings, or circumstances that do not serve my highest and best good. I vow to be open to the lessons presented to me in order to create positive habits and improve my outlook on life."*

Now light the paper on fire and place it in the bowl and watch it burn or take the special dissolving paper and place it in the water and watch it dissolve. Let it go.

◇ **Inviting In:**

Read one of the following quotes of inspiration below or choose your own. You may choose to print it on a paper or sticky note to post where you will see it. Say the following out loud: *"Dear Universe–I invite this message of inspiration into my life at this time to serve my highest and best good. I promise to be more present and kinder to myself every day."*

What will you invite into your life today?
Statement of gratitude to the Universe:

> *"Thank you universe for the great amounts of positive focus and energy that help me to manifest what I desire into my life."*

Two quotes of inspiration:
Here's a little background on the first quote by Wayne Dyer. As he spoke in front of an audience he asked them "What comes out of an orange when you squeeze it?" The answer is, of course, orange juice. He said "Yes. Orange juice. Not apple juice or grapefruit juice; orange, because that's what's inside."

> *"What comes out when life squeezes you? When someone hurts or offends you? If anger, pain and fear come out of you, it's because that's what's inside." ~Wayne Dyer*

> *"Take chances, make mistakes. That's how you grow. Pain nourishes your courage. You have to fail in order to practice being brave." ~Mary Tyler Moore*

Story #7. Release the Pain with a 'Crack!'

(Listen to your body)

"I experienced a lot of emotional pain over a divorce that blindsided me, holding that emotional pain inside for many months until it led to physical pain. I learned to use the word 'experienced' instead of 'had' so I remember it is just something passing through, not something I need to identify with or own."

Likewise, physical pain can lead to emotional pain. The divorce was an uprooting which led to feelings of loss of security and stability. I was uprooted not only by his leaving but by having to sell the house on my own, move out and find a place to live, and re-figure my finances. I noticed that during this difficult time while teaching yoga classes my whole pelvic area began to shake violently. It freaked me out but I knew that it was a manifestation of instability in my root and sacral chakras; energy centers where our sense of safety, security, stability, creativity, and sexuality live. They were way off balance! I was experiencing such pelvic and low back pain that I had trouble standing, lying down, walking and sitting. I practiced yoga postures, chanted the chakra seed sounds, used essential oils, shook out the area and visualized positive healing. These all worked somewhat but pain still remained. Things were really stuck! My friend, Erin, suggested I go to the chiropractor. I took her advice and when I met with the chiropractor I told her that I knew the pain was emotional. She did an assessment and then began making some adjustments. When she got to the adjustment on my lower back and sacrum she positioned me on one side, leaned over poised to push down and said to take a deep breath in. When I exhaled and she pushed down a huge crack resounded and I felt a sudden rush of energy and emotion. A flood of tears just poured out of me! I knew that was the release I needed.

Physical and emotional pains can come from a variety of sources and can bring our energy systems, specifically our chakras, out of balance as well as our thoughts and the accompanying emotions. "Our experiences and the associated emotions are only experiences until we judge them based on our perceptions or beliefs", author and visionary, Gregg Braden, explains. "Healing comes from allowing ourselves to feel whatever the world gives us to feel. Negative feelings are indications that something is inviting us to take a look. The only time negative emotions become a problem is when we ignore them and they are unresolved. Then we continually mask our pain, rage, jealousy or fear. When we don't look at these feelings or when we try to push them away, then we begin to have problems. The feeling itself is not the problem. Taking a look and seeing what the feelings are telling us is the key to resolving them and moving towards understanding and joy."

I have felt the feelings of abandonment, loss, anger, resentment, betrayal, and fear. I processed them by feeling them, forgiving, and embracing the lessons I learned. I am grateful for the marriage I had and for the insights I gained from the divorce. It has actually made me a stronger, more resilient, understanding, and caring person. The message here is to pay attention to the signals our body gives us. These messages may start as a whisper with a slight twinge or pain but if we ignore it the signals will get louder until we are forced to pay attention. Nurture your body and emotions with care and attention every day.

YES for Energy #2

1. Opening

◇ **Letting Go**

Questions of the day. On a piece of paper, that you will burn or dissolve at the end, write your answer to the question(s) below about what you wish to let go.

- *What painful or difficult situation is like an arrow that hit me hard?*
- *When things get overwhelming and I respond from fear I tend to...*

◇ **Hand on Heart Affirmations**

"I tune in and listen to my body so I know exactly what I need."

"I have abundant energy and vitality which contributes to my well-being."

"I choose to be happy because I know how smoothly my life flows when I am joyful."

◇ **Personal Mantra**

Choose a mantra of your own that speaks to you today. Begin with "I am," and say it in the present moment as if it already exists! Your personal mantra should be something you truly believe. Say it out loud with energy, emotion, vigor, enthusiasm, and intention to grow these positive seeds within you!

Example Mantra: *"I use my personal power and energy for good! I invite joy, positivity and abundant energy into my life today!"*

◇ **Gratitude and Energy**

Say to yourself or out loud what you are grateful for and what positive energy you wish to invite into your life today! You may also choose an angel card with a word or a message of inspiration for the day.

2. Restorative Yoga Asana #1 and Breath Assessment: Legs up the Wall

Set-up: Choose a plain wall in your home and place your yoga mat or a long blanket on the floor extending from the wall into the room, to lie on. You may also have a folded blanket to place near the wall to go under your hips and a blanket or pillow under your head. An eye pillow for your eyes is nice too and helps with deep relaxation. Another prop that you may choose to try is a sandbag or rolled blanket to place on the bottom of your feet (assistance from another person is helpful). Come close to the wall and scootch (it's a word) your hips close to the wall, extend your legs up and rest your hips on the floor or on a blanket. Another way to extend your legs up the wall is to sit next to the yoga mat or blanket with your back against the wall and legs extended forward. Then roll onto the mat or blanket by placing your shoulder down and swinging your legs up the wall. This method works well to get your bottom as close to the wall as possible. You may place a sandbag or blanket on your feet for a grounding sensation. Legs up the wall is also a great option for the end of your practice.

◇ **Breath Assessment:**

Come into the posture and begin to release any past or future thoughts. Relax and surrender more and more with every breath. Notice your breathing pattern without trying to change anything. Notice the rise and fall of the belly and chest. Observe the length of the breath. Is it flowing naturally helping you to become calmer or does it feel rapid or shallow creating tension? Just observe for 3-5 minutes. Now count your inhales and exhales. Extend the exhales to assist your body in experiencing a deeper state of relaxation, activating the parasympathetic nervous system (rest and digest). Allow your body and mind to surrender to the present moment and just be.

3. Technique #1: Qi Gong. The 5 Animal Frolics.

Qi Gong uses energy to find balance and calm in these meditative movements based on the way animals move. These are called the 5 Animal Frolics. Begin Standing for each one. Repeat the movements for each one 8 to 10 times.

Let's Practice:

Monkey: Stand with arms to the side of the body and the palms facing forward. Slowly move the hands to the center of the body with elbows bent out to the side. Point the fingers towards each other with palms facing down and make a quick grasping movement so the finger-tips touch the thumb and fingers point down. Lift the wrists up with the back of the hands directly under the chin with elbows pointing down and shrug the shoulders as you rise to the balls of the feet. Hold. Look left, right, center. Lower back down to starting position.

Tiger: Stand with arms to the side of the body and the palms facing forward. Slowly move the hands to the center of the body with elbows bent out to the side. Point turn the fingers towards each other with palms facing down. Spiral fingers in from pinky to make a fist. Extend arms straight up the center of the body to the sky. Open the hands with palms up and fingers pointing towards each other. Spiral fingers in towards each other again and make fists. Lower arms back down the center to start.

Crane: Bend from the waist, lean forward, and press the backs of the hands together with elbows slightly bent out. Rise up to stand as you lift the arms up the center of the body and then out to the side of the body like you are drying your wings as you touch the right foot forward, without shifting the weight forward. Step the foot back and bend forward once again touching the backs of the hands together. Rise up again spreading the arms up and out and touch the left foot forward.

Bear: Stand firm with knees bent and move the arms around the body in a sway movement rotating from the waist. Next, step the right foot forward and alternating reaching right arm and then left with a shoulder roll forward and a grasping motion 4 times. Then step back to standing. Step the left foot forward and repeat.

Deer: Stand with the arms by the side of the body. Reach both arms to the right with the right arm at shoulder height and the left arm below that with "antler" hands (tuck in the middle two fingers in and hold with the thumb and keep pinky and index finger out). Look in that direction. Step the left foot forward and then sweep the arms across the center of the body with the left arm high and the right arm low by the waist with a bent elbow. Look over the left shoulder. Hold. Sweep the arms up in a circle over the head around to the right and back to start with a small pause. Now sweep the arms to the left and repeat to the left side, reversing the arm positions.

4. Yoga Asanas:
Mountain Visualization and Energy Rich Asana

I first learned this mountain visualization in a workshop and loved the idea of visualizing myself as a mountain; tall and stable, firm and confident. It helped me to realize there is always strength within me. I just need to tap into it in times of difficulty or overwhelm.

Let's Practice:

Mountain Pose. Guided Mountain Visualization: Close your eyes and Imagine that you are a mountain. Picture what type of mountain you are. Are you very tall? Do you have snow caps? Are you covered with grass? Picture yourself as the mountain, stable and strong. Proud and unmoving. Now imagine what is all around you in the environment. Trees? Grass? People picnicking on you? Goats roaming? Imagine your surroundings and how it makes you feel to *be* a mountain. What words come to mind to describe the way you feel as a mountain. Proud. Majestic. Strong. Capable. Courageous. Vulnerable. Notice your physical body and how you may be standing taller as you imagine the stability and power you feel as a mountain. Carry this feeling throughout your yoga practice today and remember it on and off of the mat in the face of any fear, worry or emotional upset. You can stand proud and strong. Now take some full deep breaths in through the nose and out through the nose. Open your eyes and take in the environment with a renewed sense of self.

Energy Rich Asanas

Sun Salutation - Surya Namaskar. Sun Salutation is yang
and solar energy; a fiery, active and energizing flow. It
warms the body. Repeat as many times as you like.

Let's Practice:
Sun Salutation Flow:

1. Mountain Pose (Tadasana) - Stand tall with proper alignment .

2. Extended Mountain Pose (Utthita
    Tadasana) - Reach arms to the sky.

3. Forward Fold - (Uttanasana) - Bend from
    the waist and reach for the ground.

4. Lunge Right (Anjaneyasana) - Step the right
    leg back to a low lunge or high lunge.

5. Downward Facing Dog (Adho Mukha Svanasana) - Step
    left leg back and lift the hips into Downward Dog. Hands
    and feet are firm on the floor. Body is in a "V" shape.

6. Plank (Phalakasana) - Move forward from Down
    Dog to plank with a "wave" action, drawing in and
    up through the belly to lengthen out - shoulders
    stacked over wrists. Body in one long line.

7. Four limb Staff Pose (Chaturanga) to Cobra - Bend
    the elbow straight back about 6 inches right near your
    ribs. Lower to the floor with the knees down.

8. Cobra (Bhujangasana) - Press your hands to
    the floor near your ribs and lift the chest. Keep
    the chin down and gaze forward OR

9. Move to Upward Facing Dog (Urdhva Mukha
    Svanasana). Arms straight, chest open, legs off of
    the floor, and the tops of the feet on the floor.

10. Downward Facing Dog (Adho Mukha Svanasana)- Draw the navel in and lift the hips back to Downward Facing Dog.

11. Lunge Right (Anjaneyasana) - Step the right food forward into a low unge or high lunge.

12. Forward Fold (Uttanasana)- Let your body release into a forward fold.

13. Extended Mountain Pose (Utthita Tadasana). Rise up to standing and reach the arms.

14. Mountain Pose (Tadasana)- Lower arms to the side back to Mountain Pose.

Moon Salutation- Chandra Namaskar. Moon Salutation is yin and lunar energy; calming, relaxing, and a slower meditative flow. It cools and relaxes the body. Repeat as many times as you like.

Let's Practice:

Moon Salutation Flow:

Turn sideways to the mat and stand at the right end.

1. Mountain Pose (Tadasana) - Stand tall with proper alignment.

2. Side Stretch Right (Parsva Urdhva Hastasana) - Reach arms up and bend to the right.

3. Side Stretch Left (Parsva Urdhva Hastasana) - Lift back to center and bend to the left.

4. Wide Leg Pose (Prasarita) - Step wide to the left and reach the arms out from your shoulders.

5. Warrior II (Virabhadrasana II) - Turn the left toes out to the left side and bend the left knee.

6. Triangle (Trikonasana) - Straighten the left leg and reach the left hand for the leg and the right hand to the sky.

7. Intense side stretch (Parsvottanasana) - Rotate your hips towards the left leg and fold forward bringing your head towards your knee.

8. Low lunge (Anjaneyasana) - Lunge with the right knee up or down.

9. Left Side Lunge (Skandasana) - Turn to the right with the right knee up, so you are facing the long edge of the mat. Bend your left knee and lunge to the left.

10. Right Side Lunge (Skandasana) - Now lunge to the right side.

11. Low lunge (Anjaneyasana) - Rotate hips to the side and lunge with the left knee up or down.

12. Intense side stretch (Parsvottanasana) - Straighten the right leg and fold forward bringing your head towards your knee.

13. Triangle (Trikonasana) -Keep the right leg straight and place the right hand on the leg and reach the left hand to the sky.

14. Warrior II (Virabhadrasana II) - Bend the right knee
    and lift the body. Reach the arms to the side.

15. Wide Leg Pose (Prasarita) - With wide
    legs turn your feet to face forward.

16. Mountain Pose (Tadasana) - Step the right foot to meet the left.

17. Side Stretch Right (Parsva Urdhva Hastasana)
    - Reach arms and bend to the right.

18. Side Stretch Left (Parsva Urdhva Hastasana) -
    Reach arms and bend to the left. Bring hands to
    prayer. Repeat the whole sequence again.

5. Technique #2: Lesson:
The Cure for Fear by Albert Brooks[19]

Everyone feels fear. I am writing this part of the book during the Coronavirus. Most people are experiencing fear right now; Fear of losing their job or if they did lose their job of not finding another, fear of catching the virus, fear of their loved ones catching it and dying, fear of going outside. Before the virus there was still plenty of fear. Our lives are filled with fear in one form or another. What is the opposite of love? Many people think the opposite of love is hate or indifference. It is fear. Arthur Brooks, an author, a professor at the Harvard Kennedy school, a French horn player and jazz musician for many years, and teacher of happiness, says in his podcast 'The Art of Happiness' that courage is feeling fear and doing it anyway. In the podcast he asks "What are some of your fears?" Here are a few common ones he names:

Fear of loss: a relationship, job, health, friendship, prestige

Fear of failure: The remedy for the fear of failure is FAILING

Phobias: Fear of spiders, snakes, heights,
flying, closed spaces, germs, shots etc.

When fear becomes persistent and a part of our everyday lives it can lead to anxiety disorder and freeze us on our journey. Practices

19 Content from 'The Art of Happiness' podcast by Arthur Brooks. Article in "The Atlantic" 'Love is Medicine for Fear' July 16, 2020

from Arthur Brooks can help us to find the courage to move through them, reduce anxiety and feel courageous in our lives.

Let's Practice:
Arthur suggests trying the following to reduce or even eliminate fear:

1) *Think of small fears* that you are currently experienced or have experienced in life and face them therapeutically. Expose yourself to them on purpose. Albert says this is called "stress inoculation" and is a form of Cognitive Behavior Therapy. Essentially the goal is to help reduce the level of fear and anxiety connected with certain reminders, thereby also reducing avoidance. You confront the fears without avoiding them.

2) *Envision your fears.* Sit with them, meditate on them and imagine yourself being courageous! Courage is not the absence of fear but feeling the fear and moving forward anyway.

3) *Love.* The ultimate prescription for fear is LOVE! Love neutralizes fear. Through love there is no fear. Don't address the fear, cultivate more love! Love is the medicine for fear. Arthur says "Our society has a fear epidemic and a love defect."

My personal mantra is "Love what is." Circumstances are going to show up in life that may bring about fear. In each of these moments we always have three choices. We can change the circumstances if possible, remove ourselves from the situation, or accept it as it is. In the moment decide what is best for you and do that. If you find yourself running from every situation take a look at that too and see if facing the fear, looking at its cause, and infusing it with love will help inspire more peace and less anxiety.

6. Restorative Yoga Asana #2: End to End Bolsters with Guided Nature Visualization

Essential Oil Suggestion: Rosemary

Set-up: Place two bolsters or long firm pillows end to end. Place two blocks or firm pillows at the end of the bolsters where your feet will be (optional). Rest your whole back along the bolsters and rest your calves on the blocks or pillows.

EO: You may place *Rosemary* essential oil on your wrists or diffuse it in the air. Breathe in the essential oils to open up the passageways in the nostrils and the whole body. Take long, deep, calming breaths. Play relaxing spa music, theta music, Tibetan singing bowl sounds or nature sounds. Rest and Relax.

Guided Stream Visualization: (you may record yourself saying this or listen to the recording on www.Y4ES.com)

Close your eyes and relax. Bring your attention to your breathing. Notice the natural flow of the breath without trying to control it. Now imagine that you are going for a morning walk in the woods near a stream. It's a cool, crisp day and the sun is just beginning to rise. You see the sun beams peeking through the trees. As you walk through the woods you breathe in the fresh air and the scent of forest and pine all around you. You hear the leaves crunching beneath your feet. Now you begin to walk towards the stream and hear the gentle trickling sounds of water passing over rocks. A leaf releases from a tree above and you watch as it floats on the air down to the water and lands in the trickling stream. It navigates its way along and as you walk near the water you are mesmerized by the way it floats, gliding over the rocks and branches. A gentle breeze comes and you take a deep breath in, enjoying the fresh morning air. Now the leaf meets with the larger creek and gracefully floats away. You lift your gaze to view the beauty around you: trees, sky, water and the sandy banks of the creek. A deep wave of relaxation washes over you as you take in all of nature's wonders. As the birds wake up to the morning you pause to listen and appreciate their sweet songs carried on the breeze. The trees sway and gratitude fills your whole being. You are grateful to be alive, experiencing such beauty. You feel a deep connection with nature and the positive flow of energy that engulfs you. As you turn to walk back home you marvel at how just walking in nature brings a sense of peace and calm to your being.

7. Technique #3: Mantra Purusha with RY #3

(Recording can be found on www.Y4ES.com)
Mantra Purusha is the marriage of Mantras and Marma Therapy[20]

The combination of mantra (a Sanskrit word meaning mind tool) and marma (a Sanskrit word referring to any open, exposed, weak, or sensitive part of the body, infused with prana or life force energy) holds the potential to heal the physical body, alter the frequency of the subtle body, and eliminate negative thought patterns.

Mantra Purusha, an Ayurvedic tool for healing, utilizes marma points, each containing the energies of Vata, Pitta, and Kapha. In total, there are 108 marmas distributed across various regions of the body: 37 on the head and neck, 22 on the arms, 22 on the lower extremities, 14 on the back, and 12 on the chest and stomach. Notably, the mind itself is considered the 108th marma point.

Mantras put the mind into a state to become a conduit for higher flowing energy and grace. It provides focus, strength, adaptability, and plasticity for the mind by forming new synaptic connections in the brain.

20 https://www.coloradoayurveda.org/articles/mantra-purusha-the-marriage-of-mantra-and-marma-therapy

The energy of mantras can be deciphered from several factors: the sound factor, pranic factor, and mental factor. The sound factor acts upon the body, the pranic factor acts upon the prana vayus, and the mental factor acts upon the mind and heart.

The Sanskrit language is the only language that transmits meaning through sound. It is a vibrational language and therefore it can awaken Kundalini and transform us. There are 50 sounds and each sound relates to a place on the body or a marma. The 16 vowels relate to the head and senses, the first 20 consonants relate to the main joints on arms and legs, the last 5 consonants relate to the abdominal region, the 9 semi-vowels relate to the tissues, mind, and soul. Experience Mantra Purusha as you relax in Savasana in the next section. (See the Mantra Purusha chart below. Enjoy the chanted sound experience during RY #3)

8. Restorative Yoga Asana #3: Lounge Chair Savasana with Mantra Purusha

Essential Oil Suggestion: Lime

Set-up: Place two blocks next to each other; one on the highest level and the other on the medium level or one on the medium level and one on the lowest level. Lean a bolster or a tightly rolled blanket against it. Lie down with your bottom close to the bottom edge of the bolster and recline back. Use rolled blankets or pillows under your arms for arm rest support. Place a rolled blanket or bolster under your knees if you wish. Place an eye pillow on your eyes. You may also lie flat on your back in Savasana with no props.

EO: You may place *Lime* essential oil on your wrists or diffuse it in the air. Breathe in the essential oils to open up the passageways in the nostrils and the whole body. Take long, deep relaxing breaths. Play relaxing spa music, theta music or Tibetan singing bowl sounds with or without nature sounds. Rest and Relax.

Mantra Purusha - Primal Sounds

Once you are comfortable allow yourself to set an intention for healing. Allow yourself to be accessible to love of the divine and to your whole self. Through this practice you will hear the names of a part of the body. You should bring your awareness to that part of the body as the primal Sanskrit sounds are chanted three times for that part of the body. Don't try too hard but try not to fall asleep. Don't expect anything to happen. Just notice how you feel through the process. Breathing in and breathing out bring your awareness to the top of your head.

Head

Am (Ahhhm)	Top of head	Am (Open Aaaam)	Forehead
Im (Im)	Right eye	Im (Eeem)	Left Eye
Um (Ohm)	Right ear	Um (Ooooom)	Left ear
Rm (Rim)	Right nostril	Rm (Reem)	Left nostril
Lm (Lim)	Right cheek	Lm (Leem)	Left cheek
Em (Iem)	Upper lip	Aim (I-eeem) (I'm)	Lower lip
Om (Om)	Upper teeth	Aum (Ahhoom)	Lower teeth
Am (Am)	Upper palate	Ah (Ah-ha)	Lower palate
	Arms		
Kam (Cum)	Right shoulder	Cam (Cham)	Left shoulder
Kham (Kah-hum)	Right elbow	Cham (Ch-hum)	Left elbow
Gam (Gum)	Right wrist	Jam (Jyam)	Left wrist
Gham (Ga-hum)	Right base of fingers	Jham (Jah-hum)	Left base of fingers
Nam (Nnnam)	Right fingertips	Nam (Nyam)	Left finger tips
	Legs		
Tam (Tom)	Right leg	Tam (Tahm)	Left leg
Tham (Ta-ham)	Right knee	Tham (Curl tongue)	Left knee

Dam (Dahm)	Right ankle	Dam (Daaam)	Left ankle
Dham (Da-hum)	Right base of toes	Dham (Curl Tongue)	Left base of toes
Nam (Nahm)	Right tips of toes	Nam (Nnnahm)	Left tips of toes

Abdomen

Pam (Pom)	Right abdomen
Pham (Phhham)	Left abdomen
Bam (Bahhm)	Lower back
Bham (Ba-ham)	Navel
Mam (Mum)	Lower abdomen

Tissues

Yam (Yaahm)	Plasma	Ram (Rahm)	Blood
Lam (Llllam)	Muscle	Vam (Vahm)	Fat
Sam (Sh-ahm)	Bone	Sam (Curl Tongue)	Nerve Tissue
Sam (Sahm)	Reproductive tissue	Ham (Hahm)	Prana
Ksam (Ksham)	Mind		

ALL of the sounds are now said in pairs and the last ones (Tissues) are said one after another followed by a long pause. Begin to deepen your breath. Move your toes and fingers. Turn your head gently from side to side. Roll to one side and make your way to a seated position with a short contemplation practice.

9. Closing. Burning or Dissolving Ritual

◇ **Letting Go.**

Get a lighter and a heat resistant bowl (for the burning ritual) or a bowl filled with room temperature or warm water (for the dissolving ritual). Take the paper with the answer to the letting go question and say the following out loud:

"Dear Universe–I no longer need these thoughts, feelings, or circumstances that do not serve my highest and best good. I vow to be open to the lessons presented to me in order to create positive habits and improve my outlook on life."

Now light the paper on fire and place it in the bowl and watch it burn or take the special dissolving paper and place it in the water and watch it dissolve. Let it go.

◇ Inviting In.

Read one of the following quotes of inspiration below or choose your own. You may choose to print it on a paper or sticky note to post where you will see it. Say the following out loud: *"Dear Universe–I invite this message of inspiration into my life at this time to serve my highest and best good. I promise to be more present and kinder to myself every day."*

What will you invite into your life today?

1. Statement of gratitude to the universe
   about what you wish for today:

   "Thank you, Universe, for infusing my body and mind with great amounts of energy and love to guide me on my life's journey"

2. Two quotes of inspiration

   "Death is not the greatest loss in life. The greatest loss is what dies inside us while we live." ~Norman Cousins

   "Holding on to anger is like grasping a hot coal with the intent of throwing it at someone else; you are the one who gets burned." ~Buddha

Story #8. Don't Let the Rat's Ruin Your Life
(Don't sweat the small stuff)

I am a big fan of the TV show *Friends*. My family and friends can tell you that I love it so much that I can quote any episode. Ok, so I'm not so proud of that fact but I will say that there are some good life lessons in the show and, when life shows them to me, I say, "That reminds me of a *Friends* episode!" One of my favorites is the episode about Phoebe, played by Lisa Kudrow, and the rat babies! She rescues rat babies after their mom, Bob, dies. She puts them in a shoebox and is taking care of them as her boyfriend, Mike, played by Paul Rudd, looks on with mixed emotions. In one scene Mike tells her that the rats are going to multiply and then she will have many more rats to take care of. She begins to freak out over the responsibility and Mike says, "I know this is going to sound crazy but we could not let the box of rats ruin our lives." Ha, ha, ha! I love it.

In our daily lives we can get so caught up in worrying over the "What ifs" that we aren't able to handle the present moment as it currently is. Some of this worry comes from the ego and what it naturally wants to grasp onto. Some of it comes from our past programming and trauma. Some of it from our over scheduled lives or feeling like we have to do for others, all the while forgetting about taking care of ourselves.

So, let's not let the "rats," a metaphor for all of the worry and stuff we place on ourselves, ruin our lives because that's exactly what they can do. Unless we can catch ourselves going to that place of upset, worry, fear, doubt, shame, blame, or the 'I'm not good enough' feeling we may begin to spiral out and create a problem that is worse than the one we are currently facing. We can easily let things snowball by thinking of the worst case scenario.

Phoebe comes up with a solution after her boyfriend reminds her that the situation is not that serious and decides to give the rats away to good homes. There is always a solution to the problems and sometimes it takes a friend to help us to see the light. We can pause, take a deep breath, find the solution in the moment and not let the rats (life stuff) ruin our lives! In these moments we can learn to ask "What do I need to do to take care of me?" and then, with a little help from your friends (or the support of YES sessions and community) you learn and practice doing just that.

In any situation, you always have three approaches that will keep you in positivity: ACCEPT, ENJOY OR ENTHUSE!

YES for Energy #3

1. Opening

◇ **Letting Go**

Questions of the day. On a piece of paper, that you will burn or dissolve at the end, write your answer to the question(s) below about what you wish to let go:

1. *What can I let go of today that keeps me from enjoying the present?*

2. *What critical thoughts of myself, people or things do I wish to let go of so I can return to peace within?*

◇ **Hand on Heart Affirmations**

"I am vibrant and full of passion and energy about everything I do."

"I connect to the energy within me and all around me so I can be my best self and create the life I love."

"I choose to spend time around water and in nature to raise my positive energy vibrations."

◇ **Personal Mantra**

Choose a mantra of your own that speaks to you today. Begin with "I am," and say it in the present moment as if it already exists! Your personal mantra should be something you truly believe. Say it out loud with energy, emotion, vigor, enthusiasm, and intention to grow these positive seeds within you!

Example Mantra: *"I am in control of my emotions and can choose to raise my vibrations and positive thoughts and feelings in an instant!"*

◇ **Gratitude and Energy**

Say to yourself or out loud what you are grateful for and what positive energy you wish to invite into your life today! You may also choose an angel card with a word or a message of inspiration for the day.

2. Restorative Yoga Asana #1 and Breath Assessment: Supported Torso

Set-up: Lie down on the floor or mat with a blanket or pillow under your back and a blanket or pillow under your head. Place a rolled-up blanket or bolster under your knees. You may also place blankets under your arms. Come into a restful, supportive position.

◇ **Breath Assessment:**

Come into the posture and begin to release any past or future thoughts. Relax and surrender more and more with every breath. Notice your breathing pattern without trying to change anything. Notice the rise and fall of the belly and chest. Observe the length of the breath. Is it flowing naturally helping you to become calmer or does it feel rapid or shallow creating tension? Just observe for 3-5 minutes. Now count your inhales and exhales. Extend the exhales to assist your body in coming to a deeper state of relaxation, activating the parasympathetic nervous system (rest and digest). Allow your body and mind to surrender to the present moment and just be.

3. Technique #1: Acupressure

Acupressure is a traditional Japanese and Chinese medicine practice of applying pressure to specific points on the body to relieve physical and emotional tension and pain in the body. It can be applied to one's self and to others. Pressure is placed on local and distal points. A local point is where the pain is felt. A distal point is a point far away from the local point of pain. With regular practice of holding points you will feel a sense of joy and well-being, a sharper mind, increased energy and balanced emotions. As you move through the acupressure points bring to mind images of appreciation, acceptance, and love. Imagine how you wish an area of the body or emotion to feel, like "relaxed, free, loose" not "pain free" which will invite in the idea and therefore the energy of pain. For each acupressure point listed, press and hold it as you breathe deeply allowing your thoughts and the area to soften and relax. Section 4 guides you to practicing the yoga postures listed for each body part and emotion. You may search on the web for the exact point locations indicated by the number.

Let's Practice:

Begin with a body Assessment. Notice where there is discomfort. Place a hand on that area. Now ask it how you would like it to feel. Instead of "No pain" or "Not stiff," choose how you want it to feel like "relaxed, loose, at ease." Simply saying the words and shifting your perception makes a shift in the body. Now notice the areas that feel relaxed and comfortable. Continue to breath and expand the breath through the whole body.

The following chart will guide you to release a stuck emotion or pain. You may search online for more about acupressure to relieve physical or emotional pain.

Acupressure and Yoga

Emotion	Body Part	Acupressure and Yoga to Heal
Joy/Heart-ache	Heart	**Acupressure:** (Ht7)Hand. Press on the right hand below the junction of pinky and ring finger at the crease of the wrist and below heel of the hand. You may also place the thumb of the right hand at the throat and the fingers on the heart and pulse/tap the chest. **Yoga:** 9 hearts. Inviting heaven in. Breath of Joy. Cobra, Camel
Anger	Liver	**Acupressure:** (Lr3) Center of the foot. Press 1-2" down between the big toe and second toe. **Yoga:** Revolved chair, Revolved side angle, Revolved Triangle, Seated Twist, Bridge pose.
Grief/Anx-iety/Depres-sion	Lungs	**Acupressure:** (Lu9)Wrist. Press just below the thumb side on the wrist crease in a circular motion. (Lu7) Arm. Press on a spot about 2" down the arm on the thumb side. **Yoga:** sandbag, diaphragm, and/or three-part breath
Fear	Kidneys	**Acupressure:** (Kl3) Ankle. press and hold on the depression just on the inside of the ankle. **Yoga:** Cup hands onto low back and gently pat. Then rub up and down. Bring hands to belly and breathe deeply. Sphinx pose, sphinx w/1 knee bent at a time, supported heroes pose, bound angle with head bowed down.
Melan-choly	Spleen	**Acupressure:** (Sp6) Leg. Press on a point 3" up from the ankle on the inside of the leg. **Yoga:** Lie supine (on your back). Dead bug: arms and legs extend to the sky. Extend opposite arm and leg. Twist: Right knee to chest and cross over the body. Repeat left
Worry	Stomach	**Acupressure:** (P6 - Pericardium 6) Wrist. Press below the wrist, 2 finger widths down the arm. **Yoga:** Seated - circle torso one way and the other. Seated Twist. On back - Bring 1 knee into the chest at a time with the nose towards the knee.
Stress & Worry	Heart & Brain	**Acupressure:** (Ht5) Arm. Press on the underside of the arm. A finger width below the wrist crease just inside the tendon that runs along the pinky finger side. **Yoga:** Meditation. Index finger to thumb in Gyan mudra. Chant the mantra Sat Nam= True self. Practice deep breathing exercises.

4. Yoga Asanas and Emotions

One of my favorite spiritual teachers, Caroline Myss[21], is an author and speaker in the field of medical intuition. She developed the field of Energy Anatomy, a science that correlates specific emotional/psychological/physical/spiritual stress patterns with diseases. I loved her book *Anatomy of the Spirit* and gained much insight on the body's power to heal when we look deeply at resolving our emotional wounds. Practicing yoga postures can assist in our healing.

See Technique #1 Acupressure and Yoga table above for the following yoga postures to relieve stuck emotions.

{Not all listed postures are pictured}

Let's Practice:

Heartache: 9 hearts. Inviting heaven in. Breath of joy, cobra, camel, sphinx

---

21 https://www.myss.com/

Anger: revolved chair, revolved side angle, revolved triangle, seated twist, bridge

Grief: Sandbag, diaphragm breathing and/or three-part breathing

Fear: Cup hands onto low back and gently pat. Then rub up and down. Bring hands to belly and breathe deeply. Sphinx pose, sphinx w/1 knee bent at a time, supported heroes pose, bound angle with head bowed down.

Melancholy: Lie supine (on your back). Dead bug: Arms and legs extend to the sky. Extend opposite arm and leg. Twist: Draw the right knee to chest and cross it over the body. Repeat left

Worry: Seated - circle torso one way and the other. Seated twist-Right and Left. Lie Supine (on back) Bring one knee into the chest. Nose towards the knee

Stress: Meditation. Fingers on wrist for centering. Mantra is Sat Nam= True self. Deep breathing exercises, child's pose.

5. Lesson #2 : Chanting Mantras

The word mantra is a Sanskrit word. Broken down "man" means mind and "tra" means release. A mantra is a mind tool for release. We chant mantras to free the mind of chatter, calm the nervous system, and rearrange the molecules in the mind and body with the chants' vibrational energy. Each mantra has a message for a specific purpose. Japa is a type of meditation facilitated by chanting mantras. Japa means to chant a mantra more than one time. After chanting the mantra, you then sit quietly to meditate. There are three ways you may chant for Japa meditation:

1. Manasika Japa is chanting the Mantra in your mind.

2. Upamshu Japa is chanting in a low voice or a whisper.

3. Vaikhara is chanting the mantra out loud.

Kirtan is another way of chanting mantras. Kirtan means narrating or reciting. The mantras are chanted or sung with the use of musical instruments.

Mantras can be chanted at any time throughout the day. As you chant you may count the number of repetitions using mala beads. Typically, malas, meaning garland or necklace, have 108 (a sacred number) beads. You may chant 108 times or as many as you like. (See www. Y4ES to hear and practice chanting)

Let's Practice:

To begin chanting the mantras, come to a seated position in a comfortable chair or on a cushion. Sit up tall and chant the following mantra 10 to 108 times. You may choose one or two to chant. Come back to this section to find new mantras to chant. There are ten here for you to choose from and there are so many more wonderful mantras to chant for anything you wish to let go of, invite in, or heal. I experienced a retinal detachment and found an eye healing mantra online to chant while I recovered. You may search for more online or attend some local in person or virtual chanting or kirtan sessions.

1. Ganesha Mantra:

Chanting this mantra helps to remove obstacles in your life. Ganesha or Ganapati is a Hindu god with a human body and an elephant head. He is considered the remover of obstacles. The Yoga for Emotional Support logo is an elephant head symbolizing removing obstacles that stand in our way in life with the letters YES depicted in the head.

"Om Gum Ganapataye Namaha"

Om: Represents the birth of the universe and the connection between all living beings.

Gam: The sound of the root chakra to awaken energy at the base of the spine.

Ganapataye: Another name for Ganesha, the deity who removes obstacles.

Namaha: A salutation, similar to namaste and often translated as "I bow"

2. Another Ganesha Mantra is:

"Om Shree Vakra-Tunndda Maha-Kaaya Suurya-Kotti Samaprabha Nirvighnam Kuru Me Deva Sarva-Kaaryessu Sarvadaa"

1st line: Salutations to Sri Ganesha who has a curved trunk, a large body and whose splendor is similar to a million suns.

2nd line: O Deva, please make my undertakings free of obstacles, by extending your blessings in all my works, always.

3. Lakshmi Mantra:

Chanting this mantra invites abundance into your life. Lakshmi is a Hindu goddess symbolizing prosperity or abundance. Lakshya means "aim" or "goal." Lakshmi represents all that brings good fortune, prosperity, and beauty. After removing obstacles with the Ganesha mantra you may invite in prosperity or abundance with this mantra.

"Om Shreem Maha Lakshmiyei Namaha"

Om: the cosmic sound of the universe

Shreem: the *bija* mantra of Lakshmi and
the sound vibration of prosperity

Maha: the Sanskrit word meaning "great"

Lakshmiyei: the energy that represents
Lakshmi, goddess of abundance

Namaha: A salutation, similar to namaste
and often translated as "I bow"

4. Ong So hung Mantra:

Chanting this mantra stimulates and opens the heart chakra. It is a beautiful recognition that each of us is a part of the creative consciousness of the universe.

"Ong Sohung"

Ong: The Creative Consciousness of the Universe

Sohung: I am that!

5. The Health mantra:

Chanting this mantra brings good health to all the systems of the body.

"Sama dosha sama agnischa sama dhatu mala kriyaaha Prasanna atma indriya manaha swastha iti abhidheeyate"

One is in perfect health when the three doshas (vata, pitta and kapha), the digestive fire (digestion, assimilation and metabolism) all the body tissues and components (dhatus: plasma, blood, muscle, fat, bone, nerves, reproductive system), all the excretory functions, are in perfect order with a pleasantly disposed and contented mind, senses and spirit.

6. Gayatri Mantra:

Chanting this mantra invites more love and light into your being. This is a popular universal healing mantra that can be used for healing headaches, chronic fatigue, depression, and neuroses. Its cleansing power is strong, and it treats even viral diseases like the flu or severe cold. It disinfects the energy field around the person.

{This mantra also has mudras (hand gestures) that go along with it. You may find many YouTube videos describing how to perform the series of mudras. My favorite is by Richard Miller.}

**"om bhur bhuvah svaha tat savitur varenyam
bhargo devasya dhīmahi dhiyo yo nah prachodayat"**

Om: the cosmic sound of the universe Bhur: embodiment of vital spiritual energy (prana); Bhuva: destroyer of sufferings; Swaha: embodiment of happiness; Tat: that; Savitur: bright like the sun; Varenyam: best choices; Bhargo: destroyer of sins; Devasya: divine; Dhimah: may absorb; Dhiyo means intellect; Yo: who; Nah: our; Prachodayat: may inspire

We meditate on the transcendental glory of the supreme deity, who is inside the heart of the earth, within the life of the sky and inside the soul of heaven.

7. Hare Krishna or the Maha Mantra (the great chant):

Chanting this mantra is said to raise our consciousness to the highest level. It invites in happiness, self-discovery and love and most importantly a connection to God or the divine. It paves the way to inner peace and freedom (moksha).

"Hare Krishna Hare Krishna Krishna Krishna Hare Hare Hare Rama Hare Rama Rama Rama Hare Hare"

It consists of three Sanskrit names of the Supreme Being; "Hare, he who is energy," "Krishna, he who is attractive" and "Rama, he who is a reservoir of pleasure."

8. Peace Mantra:

Chanting this mantra is helpful before classes in school or any-time you are working with a group. It helps to create an atmosphere of peace as you all work together. It also helps to remove obstacles and invite in positivity. You can recite this mantra to initiate yourself into aligning with your higher self. It ignites your inner healer and teacher. It creates a sanctuary of support and protection in the present moment but especially on the journey you are about to embark on.

"Om Saha navavatu Saha nau bhunaktu Saha viryam karava vahai Tejasvi navadhitamastu Ma vidvisavahai Om Shanti, shanti, shanti"

Om, may we all be protected

May we all be nourished

May we work together with great energy

May our intellect be sharpened (may our study be effected)

Let there be no animosity among us

Om, peace (in me), peace (in nature), peace (in divine forces)

9. Another Peace Mantra:

Chanting this peace mantra leads to pure knowledge of oneself.

**"Om asatoma sadgamaya Tamasoma jyotirgamaya
Mrityorma amritam gamaya"**

Gamaya: lead me from
Take us from the false to the truth
From darkness to light
From death to eternal life

10. Love Mantra:

Chanting this brings the vibrational energy of love into your life.

"Aham prema"

I am love.
May the love that I am radiate into the world

6. Restorative Yoga Asana #2:
Side lying Pose with Bolster at the back

Essential Oil Suggestion: Lemongrass

Set-up: Place a bolster or rolled up blanket on one side of your mat and another one on the other side. Lie down on your side and sandwich the front bolster or blanket between your legs. Rest your head on a blanket or pillow to support your head and to keep pressure off of your shoulder. Rest your back on the other bolster or on a rolled blanket that is behind you.

EO: You may place *Lemongrass* essential oil on your wrists or diffuse it in the air. Breathe in the essential oils to open up the passageways in the nostrils and the whole body. Take long, deep relaxing breaths. Play relaxing spa music, theta music or Tibetan singing bowl sounds with or without nature sounds. Rest and Relax.

7. Lesson & Technique #3: Create your Reality - Eckhardt Tolle, Shakti Gwain, Abraham (Esther) Hicks, Joe Dispenza

The more I live this life the more I understand the great amount of potential we all possess to create anything we desire. I have been studying the law of attraction and ways to manifest what we desire into our lives since the movie "The Secret" came out in 2006. The law of attraction states that you will attract into your life, whether wanted or unwanted, whatever you give your energy, focus, and attention to. There is a bit more to it than that. After you put your energy forth in the form of thoughts and energy, then you must also step into action to see those desires realized. I've often observed that after setting a clear intention and directing all my energy towards it, I entrust the rest to the universe and witness the manifestation unfold. The manner in which it materializes is consistently a delightful surprise!

Eckhart Tolle[22], author of "The Power of Now," "A New Earth," and "Silence Speaks", has offered countless teachings on practicing presence. Focusing on the present moment is the place to begin creating your reality. He says when we are present we can notice our thoughts and how they serve us or defeat us.

Shakti Gawain[23] is another influential teacher who taught about the power of our thoughts. I began exploring her teachings just about 6 months before she died in November 2018. She is the author of many books. Her most popular book is "Creative Visualization" where she

22 https://eckharttolle.com/
23 http://shaktigawain.com/

describes using our mental energy to improve our health, prosperity, relationships, and desires. She spoke of not only trusting in but relying on our intuition to guide us in life.

Esther Hicks[24] shares profound insights from the teachings of Abraham, focusing on the Law of Attraction which states, 'what you think about, you bring about'. The law encourages you to align your thoughts and emotions with your desires, guiding you toward the realization of your true self.

Paying attention to your feelings and thoughts and directing your focus towards what you desire, sets a vibrational frequency to attract your desired outcomes. One of my favorite Abraham Hicks quotes is "Worry is using your imagination to create something you don't want." This emphasizes the importance of staying present and minimizing stress about the future.

In her teachings and in one of my favorite books "The Vortex", she shares ways to come into alignment with who you really are by becoming a vibrational match to what you desire and the person you aspire to be.

Joe Dispenza[25], renowned author, speaker and healer of himself imparts step-by- step processes in his books "You are the Placebo" and "Breaking the Habit of Being Yourself" to guide individuals in shaping their own realities. A key message he shares is the vital role of envisioning our desires with a clear intention and an elevated emotion. By vividly picturing every detail of what we wish to create, engaging our emotions and senses in the process, we embark on a journey to manifesting our aspirations.

Joe Dispenza as well as Gregg Braden[26]; scientist, author, educator and pioneer, explore the profound capabilities of the pineal gland. Nestled in the center of the brain, this gland is associated with the third

24 https://www.abraham-hicks.com/
25 https://drjoedispenza.com/
26 https://greggbraden.com/

eye, located between the eyebrows at the bridge of the nose serving as a connection between the physical and spiritual realms. Aligned with the sixth chakra it is often referred to as our sixth sense. Trusting in this sixth sense or intuition, become a powerful practice for manifesting our desires. Both Joe and Gregg advocate envisioning our desires as if they are already here and happening in the present moment. What you desire is no longer a vision of what you wish to happen in some future time but it already exists in the here and now. Picture that you *are* the author, or the successful business owner. You *have* the partner you desire by your side. You *are* financially secure feeling abundance in all areas of life. You *feel* happy, content, peaceful, and free. Practice the visualizations below and discover more about manifestation and connecting to your intuition, pineal gland, third eye, sixth sense, and the profound art of manifestation to unlock the key to your true potential.

There are so many other teachers like Wayne Dyer, Deepak Chopra, Stuart Wilde, Napoleon Hill, Louise Hay, Jim Rohn, Tony Robbins, and Bob Proctor, who teach these practices. You may purchase their books or find their teachings online.

'Universe every day' is my term for staying in a high vibrational state and manifesting what I desire with creative visualization and the law of attraction. I've observed that when I am in a peak state of positive thoughts and emotion about what I desire, amazing things show up in my life in surprising ways that I never could have predicted. Conversely, hen I find myself in a low vibrational state nothing new seems to materialize.

Here is a technique to try right now to kickstart your journey to creating your reality and manifesting your desires. I've found that making this a daily practice, especially in the morning, sets the tone for the day and helps maintain the vibrational energy. Give it a try and see the positive shift it can bring into your life.

Create Your Reality
Visualization Option #1

Let's Practice:

Begin by setting a clear intention of what you wish to manifest in your life. Focus on one specific area, such as career, family, relationships, finances, or friendships. Take a moment to either write it down or get very clear in your mind about what you intend to manifest in your life. Envision your desire as if it has already happened, emphasizing the importance of saying 'yes' to what you want rather than dwelling on what you don't want. Wherever you put your energy and focus the law of attraction will align it for you. Activate your thoughts and create your reality. Let's begin the visualization.

Sit in a chair in an upright posture. Feel your body sitting tall and notice the sensations of being grounded. Also notice sensations of expansiveness. Be present with all the sensations that arise in you without judgement.

Now, place your hands on your heart inviting one sacred breath in through your nose, allowing it to travel through your body, and exhaling with thoughts and feelings of gratitude, compassion and love, creating an inner environment of high emotional vibrations. Now as you enter the time to manifest what you desire, choose a scene from your future life and picture it vividly with a clear intention and an elevated emotions as if it has already manifested.

Imagine all of the details - receiving an award, being with your ideal partner, living in the home of your dreams, achieving your ideal weight, being fit, healthy and happy. Visualize where you are, who is there, what they are saying and doing, as well as your own actions and words. Engage all your senses- sights, sounds, smells, tastes, and physical sensations. Feel every nuance. As you immerse yourself in the details remember the more vividly you imagine, the better chance of creating your desired life. Feel the vibrational energy of your vision recognizing the self worth and power you bring as the leader, partner, author, friend, and teacher.

When thoughts of doubt attempt to creep in, redirect your focus back to the scene you've created- the exact manifestation you've attracted into your life. Take a moment to assess your feelings in that envisioned reality. Hold onto the positive emotions and make this exercise a part of your daily routine to shape the person you desire to be.

Do you know the best way to predict the future? By what you are doing today. How are you showing up today? Are you thinking positive thoughts? Are you engaging in positive actions? If so, then you are paving the way to a future filled with more of the same. Embrace the mindset that you are already the person you've envisioned. You will transition from thinking to doing to being that person.

Creative Visualization by Shakti Gwain
Visualization Option #2

Shakti Gwain, a wonderful author, speaker, counselor, and teacher had a similar take on visualizing what you desire in your life. Here are her steps.

Let's Practice:

1) Set your goal.
Decide on something you would like to have, work toward, realize, or create.

Your desire can be on any level – a job, a house, a relationship, a change in yourself, increased prosperity, a happier state of mind, improved health, beauty, a better physical condition, solving a problem in your family or community, or whatever.

First, choose goals that are fairly easy for you to believe in, that you feel are possible to realize in the fairly near future. That way you won't have to deal with too much negative resistance in yourself, and you can maximize your feelings of success as you are learning creative visualization.

2) Create a clear idea or picture

Create an idea, a mental picture, or a feeling of the object or situation exactly as you want it. You should think of it in the present tense as already existing the way you want it to be. Imagine yourself in the situation as you desire it, now. Include as many details as you can.

3) Focus on it often

Bring your idea or mental picture to mind often, both in quiet meditation periods, and also casually throughout the day, when you happen to think of it. This way it becomes an integrated part of your life, and becomes more of a reality for you. Focus on it clearly, yet in a light, relaxed way.

4) Give it positive energy

Make strong positive statements to yourself. Affirm that it exists now. See yourself receiving or achieving your idea. While using affirmations, temporarily suspend any doubts or disbelief you may have, at least for the moment, and practice getting the feeling that what you desire is very real and possible.

Continue to work with this process until you achieve your goal. Remember that goals often change before they are realized, which is a perfectly natural part of the human process of change and growth. So don't try to prolong it any longer than you have energy for it. If you lose interest, it may mean that it's time for a new look at what you want.

If you find that a goal has changed for you, be sure to acknowledge that to yourself. Get clear in your mind the fact that you are no longer focusing on your previous goal. End the cycle of the old, and begin the cycle of the new. This helps you avoid getting confused, or feeling that you've "failed" when you have simply changed.

When you achieve a goal, be sure to acknowledge consciously to yourself that it has been completed. Often we achieve things that we have been desiring and visualizing, and we forget to even notice that we have succeeded! So, give congratulate yourself and be sure to thank the universe for fulfilling your requests.

8. Restorative Yoga Asana #3: Lounge Chair Savasana with a Visualization

Essential Oil Suggestion: Melissa

Set-up: Place two blocks next to each other: one on the highest level and the other on the medium level or one on the medium level and one on the lowest level. Lean a bolster or a tightly rolled blanket against it. Lie down with your bottom close to the bottom edge of the bolster and recline back. Use rolled blankets or pillows under your arms for arm rest support. Place a rolled blanket or bolster under your knees if you wish. Place an eye pillow on your eyes.

EO: You may place *Melissa* essential oil on your wrists or diffuse it in the air. Breathe in the essential oils to open up the passageways in the nostrils and the whole body. Take long, deep relaxing breaths. Play relaxing spa music, theta music or Tibetan singing bowl sounds with or without nature sounds. Rest and Relax.

Guided Nature Visualization
Visualization Option #3

Let's Practice:

Relax completely in a comfortable position. Visualize yourself in any place in nature. Picture strolling in a green meadow, or by the sea with the ocean sounds and the sand beneath your feet. Visualize a journey to the top of a mountain, near a waterfall or lake, or surrounded by trees in a forest. Take time to create a picture in your mind of a familiar place in nature or one that you create in your imagination in the moment with all of the glorious sights and sounds, scents and associated feelings. Wander and explore and notice a calm, peaceful and serene sense of well-being wash over you. When you create a nature visualization that gives you a peaceful feeling you can return to it anytime you wish.

{You may listen to guided visualizations at www.Y4ES.com}

Guided Healing Visualization
Visualization Option #4

Let's Practice:

Every health problem originates from some disruption of the energy frequencies in our bodies. Sickness or pain in the body indicates that something is off an important gift for you to learn and grow. When you heal the emotional body, you will heal the physical body. Trapped or stuck emotions will always manifest somewhere in the body as pain or disease. You can heal yourself by addressing the underlying cause of your emotional pain and with positive energy and focus visualizations. Our bodies are self-healing mechanisms. Relax into a comfortable position and bring your awareness to the body and breath. Where our thoughts go energy flows. Direct your thoughts and energy to that area with an intention of healing. Use your intuition to think of healing words. Use your imagination to visualize shapes or colors moving to the area and healing the

pain of the headache, tumor, broken bone, cyst, or whatever you are experiencing. Drop into a deep level of consciousness and receive the nourishing you need. Feel the energy, light and healing travel to all of the cells in your body. Envision your body healthy, healed and whole.

9. Closing. Burning or Dissolving Ritual

◇ **Letting Go:**

Get a lighter and a heat resistant bowl (for the burning ritual) or a bowl filled with room temperature or warm water (for the dissolving ritual). Take the paper with the answer to the letting go question and say the following out loud:

"Dear Universe–I no longer need these thoughts, feelings, or circumstances that do not serve my highest and best good. I vow to be open to the lessons presented to me in order to create positive habits and improve my outlook on life."

Now light the paper on fire and place it in the bowl and watch it burn or take the special dissolving paper and place it in the water and watch it dissolve. Let it go.

◇ **Inviting In:**

Invite in inspiration with a statement of gratitude. Then read one of the following quotes of inspiration below or choose your own from a favorite book. I recommend printing it out on paper or writing it on a sticky note to post where you will see it. Say the following out loud: *"Dear Universe–I invite this message of inspiration into my life at this time to serve my highest and best good. I promise to be more present and kinder to myself every day."*

What will you invite into your life today?

1. Statement of gratitude to the universe
    about what you wish for today:

    *"Thank you Universe, for reminding me that my thoughts
    are energy. Where energy flows attention goes"*

2. Two quotes of inspiration

    *"Nobody can hurt me without my
    permission"* *~Mahatma Gandhi*

    *"Energy is contagious, positive and negative
    alike. I will forever be mindful of what and who
    I am allowing into my space."* *~Alex Elle*

Story #9. The Yo-Yo Day! It's all OK
(Experience the gamut of emotions)

Wow! What a day. It began like any other day with a delightful morning walk with my dog at my new home, surrounded by thousands of acres of wooded trails. The walk in the woods was refreshing, relaxing, renewing, and inspiring -a perfect start to the day.

Next, it was time for breakfast and off to work. Working at the desk at the yoga studio, I greeted students with smiles, engaging in conversation and asking questions. Then I taught a vinyasa yoga class where our focus was on flow and movement, breath and strength. Keeping the energy positive, I transitioned to a chair yoga class, changing gears to accommodate a different group and their abilities in seated postures.

Then it was time for lunch but...uh oh, my plans took and unexpected turn when I received a call from my daughter that she was in a car accident! My heart raced and I rushed to check on her and the kids she was babysitting. After ensuring everyone was ok, except for her totaled car, I proceeded to a follow-up eye appointment for a retinal detachment I experienced several months before. I was nervous and anxious wondering if it was healing alright since my eye had remained dilated. Luckily, all was healing well.

A late lunch and a walk with the dog lifted my spirits, followed by a quick call to resolve an accidental charge to my credit card. Finally, I returned to the studio for two private sessions with clients who each had specific needs. I had to be present and listen to their concerns and assist in yoga breathing, meditations and postures.

The day continued with two more yoga classes at the studio- a Yoga for Emotional Support class focusing on self-care techniques, restorative postures and meditations, followed by a more active FLY! Vinyasa class. Whew! What a day.

As I reflected back on my day, I realized that such days can make me feel like a yo-yo with my energy and emotions-shining between low-key activities like a calm and pleasant walk to high-energy moments like solving problems that require more mental, physical and emotional stamina.

So, how do I manage this yo-yo effect? I practice what I have learned through yoga and teach in *YES* classes- I become the observer. Walking through each moment, I stay present, observing situations, emotions, thoughts, interactions, and activities without getting too attached. I remind myself that 'this too shall pass.' In the past I would react out of fear leading to stress and tension. My breathing would be rapid and my body felt tense and tight. This created tension and a feeling of upset. Since I wasn't observing my physical, mental, and emotional experience I didn't understand what was wrong. Now, as I move from one task to the next I respond with love for myself, avoiding the yo-yo effect and approaching things with balance and harmony. Sometimes the *yo-yo* does an 'around the world' move and I know that I lost touch with the present for a moment. I come back and 'walk the dog' and everything feels calm again!

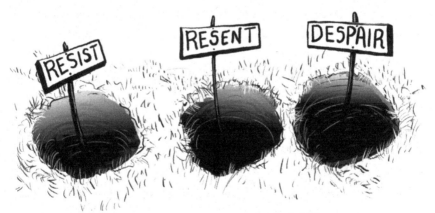

IN ANY SITUATION, YOU ALWAYS HAVE THREE APPROACHES THAT WILL KEEP YOU IN NEGATIVITY:

Heart Opening

As long as I can remember, I've had a deep desire to help others and see the best in all people. One vivid memory from my childhood stands out: at a wedding when I was six or seven, when it came time for the bride to throw the bouquet, she threw it way over everyone's head and it unexpectedly landed at my feet. I picked it up and handed it back so she could try again and a roar of laughter filled the room. Today I know they were just laughing because I was only seven. Not quite ready for marriage yet!

Throughout my life I have continued to open my heart to support my sisters, friends, partners, kids, and even strangers. A recent and cherished memory involves my daughter who made me my most treasured gift- a small wooden box adorned with orange tiles glued all around it and a small clasp to hold it shut. Inside there are a variety of small papers with different images or patterns on them and a heartfelt message or memory. One of my favorites is the one that said 'You see the beauty and best in everyone. You make everyone feel special and wanted.' I am so grateful for this gift and the time she put into it to open her heart and share her impressions of me.

Opening our heart to people and possibilities is both amazing and fulfilling, yet it can also be painful and challenging. It's a delicate balance. Vulnerability accompanies and open heart, bringing the risk of hurt, but the alternative- closing our hearts- feels far worse. With an open heart we cultivate deep and meaningful relationships, trust, authenticity and love. I am drawn to love, evident in my T-shirts that say 'love.' Some of my favorites are the one from Hershey Park with a Hershey's kiss for the "o" in LOVE, the Cirque du Soleil "Beatles Love", and one that says "Love is the Answer" with curly 70's style writing. They all remind me to love openly and unconditionally.

In this section enjoy yoga heart opener postures like cobra, sphinx, camel, bow pose, and dancer. They allow us to lift the heart and stretch this part of our bodies that arc usually held in a contracted and hunched position. A personal favorite heart opener pose is stargazer. As we all open our hearts to the sky I'm inspired to sing a note, "Ahhh-hhh!," lifting my voice to the heavens. I invite you to enjoy lifting your voice, heart, and spirits as you discover wonderful ways to invite more joy into your life.

Let's Practice:

Heart opening ideas:

1. Place your right hand on your heart and your left hand over top. Invite in a feeling of gratitude, care and compassion. Do this anytime throughout your day. Notice how you feel.

2. Create a heartfelt list of activities and experiences that serve as a catalyst for opening your heart and inviting more love and joy into your days.

3. Start a gratitude journal or a positive aspects journal. Each day write things that you are grateful for or that brought you a feeling of inspiration, wonder or awe

4. Each night before bed, take a moment to intentionally choose what you wish to reflect upon while you sleep. This is an opportunity to focus on positive and uplifting aspects of your life

YES for Heart Opening #1

1. Opening

Letting Go

Questions of the day. On a piece of paper, that you will burn or dissolve at the end, write your answer to the question(s) below as what you wish to let go:

1. *What thoughts of feelings hold me back from being caring and compassionate towards others?*
2. *Who or what (situation) do I wish to forgive?*

◇ **Hand on Heart Affirmations**

"When I follow my heart I always find my way."

"I have unconditional love and compassion for myself and others."

"The more I give love the more I receive love."

◇ **Personal Mantra**

Choose a mantra of your own that speaks to you today. Begin with "I am," and say it in the present moment as if it already exists! Your personal mantra should be something you truly believe. Say it out loud with energy, emotion, vigor, enthusiasm, and intention to grow these positive seeds within you!

Example Mantra: *"I am love and light! I feel its radiant energy shining from me, through me and all around me. It shines brightly out into the world to everyone and everything in my path today."*

◇ **Gratitude and Energy**

Say to yourself or out loud what you are grateful for and what positive energy you would like to invite into your life today!

2. Restorative Yoga Asana #1 and Breath Assessment: Basic Relaxation Pose

Set-up: Lie down on the floor or on a yoga mat with a blanket or pillow under your head. Place a rolled-up blanket or bolster under your knees. You may also place blankets under your back. You may place an eye pillow over your eyes. Make sure you feel fully supported and relaxed.

◇ **Breath Assessment:**

Come into the posture and begin to release any past or future thoughts. Relax and surrender more with every breath. Notice your breathing pattern without trying to change anything. Notice the rise and fall of the belly and chest. Observe the length of the breath. Is it flowing naturally helping you to become calmer or does it feel rapid or shallow creating tension? Just observe. Next, count your inhales and exhales. Cultivate longer exhales. Allow your body to surrender to the present moment and just be.

3. Technique #1: Positive Affirmations

One of my daily go-to techniques is the practice of positive affirmations, a tool I've been using since the beginning of my yoga journey and even prior, unknowingly. What are affirmations? They are the thoughts or words we repeatedly say or think. The fascinating thing is we can affirm what we don't want, unintentionally inviting negative aspects into our lives.

If we repeatedly think or say things like 'I'm not good enough,' 'nobody cares about me,' 'I don't matter,' then we will invite more of these sentiments to manifest. We may even actively seek proof to validate these beliefs, further reinforcing their presence into our lives. It's a self-fulfilling prophecy- whatever we expect to find , we will find.

Positive affirmations, on the other hand, are thoughts or words that we actively choose to welcome into our lives. When spoken with a clear intention and elevated emotion they will begin to show up into our lives. When creating your affirmations it's crucial to frame them in the here and now, such as 'I am filled with abundant energy and kindness', 'I stay true to myself in word and deed every day.' 'I invite opportunities for continued growth and loving relationships.' If expressed as a future wishes like 'I will be in a loving relationship,' 'Someday I will get the job of my dreams,' or 'I hope I will find peace and joy soon,' they tend to remain as a future wish.

I have sticky notes all over the place: on the kitchen cabinets, on the bathroom mirror, on my bedroom wall, in the car, and on my computer to serve as constant reminders that my thoughts hold power and influence my reality.

I draw inspiration from my favorite spiritual teachers such as Shakti Gawain, Lois Hay and Esther Hicks who have imparted valuable insights on positive affirmations in their teachings and books. Below are just a few ways to add affirmations into your life.

Let's Practice:
Sticky Note Affirmations:
Take a moment to think of some limiting beliefs or even some negative affirmations you are currently saying to yourself. List them so you can really see and then feel the energy that they elicit. It probably doesn't feel very good. Now throw those away! Next take time to think of some positive affirmations that you truly believe and you wish

to invite into your life. If you need a little help, here are some example affirmations:

- Every day in every way I'm getting better and better.
- Everything I need is coming to me easily and effortlessly
- I have everything I need to enjoy my here and now
- I love and appreciate myself just as I am.
- I accept all my feelings as part of me.
- The more I love myself, the more love I have to give to others.
- My relationship with _____ is growing happier every day.
- I enjoy relaxing and having fun.
- I communicate clearly and effectively.
- This is an abundant universe and there's plenty for everyone.
- A mindset of abundance and joy is my natural state of being.
- It's okay for me to have fun and enjoy myself, and I do!
- I am healthy and beautiful!
- _____ is coming to me, easily and effortlessly.
- The light within me is creating miracles in my life here and now.
- I give thanks for my life of health, happiness and self-expression.

Take time to jot down the positive affirmations that resonate with you today on sticky notes. Place these notes strategically around your home, workplace or frequented space where they catch your eye. These will act as daily reminders of the affirmations you wish to embrace, inviting positivity into your life.

Bonus: Song of Affirmation

My sister, Linda, is a wonderful piano player and artist (She contributed her artistic flair to the book by creating all the illustrations that follow each story, beautifully capturing the emotions expressed in our narratives.) She is also great at putting new words to a familiar tune. She wrote the following "Song of Affirmation" sung to the tune of "Angels from the Realms of Glory" (See www.Y4ES. com to hear it sung by Christine). Another great way to remind yourself of what you wish to affirm each day is to sing it. I love to sing this to invite in the vibrational energy of singing and the accompanying message.

Song of Affirmation:
I am healthy, I am wealthy, I'm successful and have time.
I am loved by pets and people; my hearts filled with art and rhyme.
Nature, laughter, peace and safety, happiness and love are mine.

4. Yoga Asanas: Heart Opening Flow

A heart opening yoga flow offers physical and psychological benefits. It strengthens the upper back, relieves tension in the neck and shoulders, improves the posture and increases lung capacity and blood circulation. It allows an openness in the chest and therefore the heart so we can be open to opportunities, love and kindness.

In this series be sure to flow, one breath, one movement or hold postures for many breaths if you wish.

Let's Practice:

- Begin on all 4's. Move into cow and cat
- Downward Facing Dog
- Right Lunge - Right foot forward to a lunge with left knee down or up. Reach up
- Goal post arm position and lift the sternum to the sky
- Return to Down Dog
- Lung the left foot forward with right knee down or up. Reach up
- Goal post arm position and lift the sternum to the sky

- Mountain Pose w/fingers interlaced behind your back
- Forward fold
- All 4's
- Camel pose
- Bridge - lie on your back. Bend your knees and lift the hips
- Windshield wiper knees - knees side to side
- Savasana

5. Technique #2: The Octopus Technique[27] (by Teal Swan)

Teal Swan, spiritual teacher and author, created the octopus technique designed to help us to have compassion for others and see their perspective. Here is her explanation of the process: "We perceive other people through our own filters. It becomes very hard to relate to people who are different to us. We begin to project our own perspective onto them. When we are practicing empathy, instead of stepping out of our perspective and *into* their shoes, we take our perspective into their shoes. And so, even though we may see solutions they don't see, we don't accurately see or feel them.

In order to exit our own reality so as to enter theirs, and by doing so completely attune to them, I want to teach the octopus technique." We are source consciousness manifesting physically. To conceptualize this, imagine an octopus. The head of the octopus represents the source. A united oneness. Sort of a blank slate of potential energy. The legs of the octopus represent aspects of that united oneness extending down into a human body. Use this symbolic image to get into someone else's perspective. Close your eyes and observe your breathing. Feel your thoughts bouncing around and just let them do that until they slow down. When you feel ready, imagine your consciousness or soul retracting back up your leg of the octopus and returning to source consciousness (the head of the octopus). As you do this, imagine leaving your identity in this life behind. See yourself leaving the story of your life, the people in it, your beliefs, your likes and dislikes, your past experiences all behind. Feel yourself stripping free of them so as to return to source. Then when you are ready, think of someone whose perspective you would like to see. Hold them as your focus and imagine finding the leg that extends from the octopus head you are in (source) down into their embodiment.

---

27 Teal Swan https://tealswan.com/resources/articles/the-octopus-technique-r203

Imagine, sense, or feel yourself going down the octopus's leg into their perspective completely, having left yourself behind so all you are now is the consciousness who is feeling through their body, seeing through their eyes. Imagine opening your eyes AS them. Imagine smelling as them and tasting as them and most of all, feeling the emotions they are experiencing. How does it feel to be in their body? What are you thinking in their body? See if you can feel their past experiences and how those experiences are shaping their current perspective. If you are wanting to understand exactly how they experience a specific situation, let yourself live or relive that experience *as* them. Feel and see the difference between how they experience life and how you used to experience life when you were you.

Spend as much time completely immersing yourself in their perspective as deeply as you can. If you experience emotional reactions as a result of it, surrender and let it happen. Gain as much understanding and awareness as you can. Be them until you feel a sense of emotional and mental and physical comprehension. And then when you are ready, imagine retracting once again back up the octopus's leg into the head of the octopus (source). But this time take your comprehension of the person whose perspective you went into, with you. Carry that comprehension and experience back down the octopus's leg that extends to your perspective in this life. Feel yourself carrying that full awareness and understanding as you come back to your own life. And when you are ready, slowly open your eyes.

All you need to know about the other person and about what to do relative to them will be revealed as a result of doing this exercise. Your awareness will multiply and your perspective on so many things will change. So be brave enough to leave yourself behind. The more often you do this exercise, the better you will get at dis identifying with yourself so as to identify with someone else's perspective. And soon, it may not be a visualization. It may in fact graduate to a full blown out of body experience.

6. Restorative Yoga Asana #2: Mountain Stream

Essential Oil Suggestion: Rose (or a rose blend)

Set-up: Place a bolster or rolled blanket under the knees. Place a rolled blanket under your shoulder blades. Your shoulders will rest on the floor. Rest your head on a pillow or blanket.

EO: You may place *Rose* essential oil on your wrists or palms or diffuse it in the air. Breathe in the essential oils to open up the passageways in the nostrils and the whole body. Take long, deep relaxing breaths. Play relaxing spa music, theta music or Tibetan singing bowl sounds with or without nature sounds. Rest and Relax.

7. Technique #3: The Five Kleshas

The Kleshas, found in 'The Yoga Sutras of Patanjali; 2.3-2.9,' are the five afflictions or obstacles to fulfilling the goals of our lives. The goals are work, wealth, pleasure and freedom. The practice of yoga can reduce these afflictions and lead to a state of calm.

The five kleshas are: *Avidya* (ignorance), *asmita* (ego), *rāga* (attachment), *dvesha* (aversion), and *abhinivesha* (fear of death)

The Five Kleshas:

1. **Avidya - Ignorance:** This is lack of wisdom and not seeing things as they are or ignoring the truth. Making the impermanent permanent. Being with the way things are and accepting, not denying, what is in front of us will free us from this affliction.

Let's Practice:

How do we see the truth? We can use something called Neti Neti. Neti means no or not that. When we feel emotions rising to the surface we can remind ourselves "I am not that", Neti Neti. Then we can ask ourselves what is really happening here? Who am I in this situation or thought? Who do I think I am? Find an answer that is harmless. If it is coming from a place of anger or hate then take a few breaths and allow it to come from someplace else. The more we do this the more we can come from a place of love by changing our responses to things. This will happen over time as you practice, not immediately.

2. **Ashmita - Egoism:** This is the story of 'me' or identifying with a self-image that we believe is us but it is not. We all may notice at times when we are only consumed with ourselves and not giving much thought to others. The created self begins to dominate over the true self. Who I think I am is just the ego. Who is the true self? Realizing that we are consciousness and not this body or mind will free us from this affliction.

Let's Practice:

Take a look at how you express yourself in the world and ask "Is this really who I am?" If it is not me then how can I learn to be more compassionate, calm, softer and present? Move through each situation, conversation and experience in this way to really reflect on the way you show up in thoughts, words and deeds. See what changes you can make today.

3. **Raga - Attachment:** This is when we look outside of ourselves for contentment. We think "I enjoyed this experience and want to have it again" and then we keep trying to recreate all the highs that we have. We also look at what people can give us and do not take them for who they really are. When the pleasurable experience is over we start searching for the next

one. We begin to see people by the tools by which we can achieve what we want rather than the spiritual beings they are. We attach to people and things for security and pleasure. Moderation and balance will free us from this affliction.

Let's Practice:

The opposite of attachment is non-attachment. Non-attachment doesn't mean detaching from the world but rather taking a look at what you find yourself attached to. Self-study, or Svadhyaya, will help you to notice when you are attaching to something. Ask yourself, "Do I actually need this or is it just a craving?"

4. **Dvesha/Dukha - Aversion:** This is what we don't want. It's the opposite of raga. Let's say you meet a new person and you get along and enjoy each other's company. After a while you see some things you don't like in them and you run away or push them away because you think you are avoiding suffering. You may say, "I don't want to know you anymore because you are not who I thought you were." Actually they are not who you wanted them to be and you don't even know what that is. We can see pleasure and pain, dukkha and sukha, in the same experience. Facing uncomfortable situations rather than avoiding them will free us from this affliction.

Let's Practice:

Practicing vipassana meditation and presence will help you to see clearly when you are allowing yourself to get caught in the grip of suffering. An inward journey will help you to find freedom (moksha).

5. **Abhinivesha-Clinging to Life:** This is fear of death or clinging to life. When we cling to life that stops us from living. This fear of death can be little deaths like fear of change, not getting what we want, or worrying about what others will think of us. It can be the fear of the end of our lives or others. When

we are caught in the grip of the fear of death we forget to live, breathe and be. Living each day as if it were your last and being kind to yourself and others will free us from this affliction.

Let's Practice:

What death are you afraid of? Identify this fear and sit with it. The answer lies within. Practice deep breathing and meditation to release the fear. (Also, see Energy #2, T#2: Cure for Fear)

Be sure to observe the Kleshas as they arise and remind yourself that as humans, all experience these afflictions or obstacles to living our best life. Simply notice when they arise and then, without judgement, take steps to overcome these influences.

8. Restorative Yoga Asana #3: Lounge Chair Savasana

Essential Oil Suggestion: Orange

Set-up: Place two blocks next to each other; one on the highest level and the other on the medium level or one on the medium level and one on the lowest level. Lean a bolster or a tightly rolled blanket against it. Lie down with your bottom close to the bottom edge of the bolster and recline back. Use rolled blankets or pillows under your arms for arm rest support. Place a rolled blanket or bolster under your knees if you wish. Place an eye pillow on your eyes.

EO: You may place *Orange* essential oil on your wrists or palms or diffuse it in the air. Breathe in the essential oils to open up the passageways in the nostrils and the whole body. Take long, deep relaxing breaths. Play relaxing spa music, theta music or Tibetan singing bowl sounds with or without nature sounds. Rest and Relax.

9. Closing. Burning or Dissolving Ritual

◇ **Letting Go.**

Get a lighter and a heat resistant bowl or a bowl filled with room temperature or warm water. Take the paper with the answer to the letting go question and say the following out loud:

"Dear Universe–I no longer need these thoughts, feelings, or circumstances that do not serve my highest and best good. I vow to be open to the lessons presented to me in order to create positive habits and improve my outlook on life."

Now light the paper on fire and place it in the bowl and watch it burn or take the special dissolving paper and place it in the water and watch it dissolve. Let it go.

◇ **Inviting In.**

Read one of the following quotes of inspiration below or choose your own. You may choose to print it on a paper or sticky note to post where you will see it. Say the following out loud: *"Dear Universe–I invite this message of inspiration into my life at this time to serve my highest and best good. I promise to be more present and kinder to myself every day."*

What will you invite into your life today?

1. Statement of gratitude to the universe
    about what you wish for today:

    "Thank you, universe, for all of the kindness, love and caring that shines from me to others and reflects back to me from them."

2. Two quotes of inspiration

"We don't set out to save the world; we set out to wonder how other people are doing and to reflect on how our actions affect other people's hearts." ~ *Pema Chodron*

"If you change the way you look at things, the things you look at change." ~*Wayne Dyer*

Story #10 – What Someone Else is Doing is Affecting Me!
(non-judgement)

As I sat in the office awaiting my hair appointment I overheard two women talking. As I eavesdropped (it was pretty hard not to) it quickly became apparent that their little corner of the waiting room was gossip central. Their exchange was filed with 'can you believe that?' and 'get this...' and 'you wouldn't believe what he said next' as they shared the latest negative complaints about others. My first response was to block it out and distract myself with a book or my phone and then a realization struck me- *what someone else is doing or saying is affecting me*. Of course, this is true for every human being. Our lives are woven with countless interactions, each leaving an imprint on our emotions and reactions.

Curious about this dynamic, a Google search revealed an interesting insight; that when we allow others to have an effect on us we essentially surrender our power- our energy. This can either empower us or drain us of our energy depending on the influence. Negative behaviors such as excessive drinking, rude remarks, hurtful online posts or anything we think others "should not" do can elevate stress and anxiety. Positive actions like receiving compliments, experiencing acts of kindness, or anything we think others "should" do contribute to increased joy and happiness.

Since relationships and connections are so important, we all want approval for who we are and what we do. We want to feel loved and accepted. So that we are not tossed around emotionally by everything that happens around us in our immediate circumstances and environment we can reclaim our power and thus increase our energy and positivity.

To take back your power and energy here are some great ideas that my google search produced:

- Don't allow someone's opinion of you to dictate your self-worth

Be true to yourself

- Don't give in to guilt trips

Be your authentic self

- Do what you wish to do and not what others tell you to do

Say "yes" only to what you truly wish to do

- Don't hold grudges

Let it go

- Don't invest time in gossiping

Be impeccable with your word

- Work hard to avoid complaining or criticizing

Be kind

- Stick to your goals. Don't change them because they were not accepted by someone

Decide, commit, succeed, and never give up

- Don't set out to be right or prove someone wrong

Be compassionate. There is no right or wrong

- Let others bring out your best, not your worst

Always do your best and be happy

When we give away our power to another person it affects our emotional state. Take your power back by becoming the driver of your life. Make a conscious effort to stay in control of how you feel, think and act so you can reach your greatest potential.

So, the next time you catch yourself being affected by what someone else is doing, notice your thoughts, feelings and actions and take your power and energy back. Focus on your own self-care and self-love. Do what brings you a peaceful feeling instead of an underlying sense of anxiety. At the hair salon I simply put my earplugs in and played some of my favorite 80's music while I waited.

YES for Heart Opening #2

1. Opening

◇ Letting Go

Questions of the day. On a piece of paper, that you will burn or dissolve at the end, write your answer to the question(s) below about what you wish to let go:

1. *What heartache am I holding on to from the past or present?*
2. *What actions of another person or situation am I holding on to that it's time to release?*

◇ Hand on Heart Affirmations

"When I listen to my heart I know what to do."

"I am fully open to giving and receiving love."

"May I be filled with compassion & gratitude for all beings."

◇ Personal Mantra

Choose a mantra of your own that speaks to you today. Begin with "I am," and say it in the present moment as if it already exists! Your personal mantra should be something you truly believe. Say it out loud with energy, emotion, vigor, enthusiasm, and intention to grow these positive seeds within you!

Example Mantra: *"I feel with great enthusiasm all of the love that surrounds me every day and I look for opportunities to love and give to others without draining my energy."*

◇ **Gratitude and Energy**

Say to yourself or out loud what you are grateful for and what positive energy you wish to invite into your life today! You may also choose an angel card with a word or a message of inspiration for the day.

2. Restorative Yoga Asana #1 and Breath Assessment: Basic Heart Opener

Set-up: Roll a blanket and place it on the floor or mat horizontally or vertically. If the blanket is horizontal then lie down with your shoulder blades on the blanket. If the blanket is vertical then lie with the blanket down the full length of your spine. Place a blanket or pillow under your head. You may place a rolled-up blanket or bolster under your knees and you may also place blankets under your arms. Come into a restful, supportive position.

◇ **Breath Assessment:**

Come into the posture and begin to release any past or future thoughts. Relax and surrender more and more with every breath. Notice your breathing pattern without trying to change anything. Notice the rise and fall of the belly and chest. Observe the length of the breath. Is it flowing naturally helping you to become calmer or does it feel rapid or shallow creating tension? Just observe for 3-5 minutes. Now count your inhales and exhales. Extend the exhales to assist your body in coming to a deeper state of relaxation, activating the parasympathetic nervous system (rest and digest). Allow your body and mind to surrender to the present moment and just be.

3. Technique #1: Tendency to Judge

Judgements. We all have them. We judge ourselves and others. We condemn and put down. It is an ego reaction. Our ego wants to be right or wrong, superior or inferior to help us to feel secure. What do you do when you find yourself judging? I asked my teenage daughter this question once and she said "I ask myself 'What does that have to do with me?' " I love this answer. To me this statement carries a duel meaning. First, it asks us to consider what relevance another person's behavior, appearance, attitude, or background has to our own lives. They are just living their lives and there's no need for it to impact our personal journey.

Second, it encourages introspection, offering the opportunity to turn the question inward: What does this judgement reveal about me? Often, the roots of our judgements lie in learned behaviors or aspects within ourselves that we find challenging. Exploring our internal landscape allows us to unravel the conditioning that fuels these judgements and paves the way for more acceptance of others and ourselves.

If another person is acting in a harmful way (physical or mental abuse) we don't have to accept this behavior and can hold our boundaries by saying something to elicit a change, if possible, or reducing or eliminating interactions with them. But first ask yourself if their behavior is truly harming or is it a story we have created based on our limiting beliefs or past programming. By navigating this self-discovery, we can cultivate a greater sense of joy and acceptance into our lives.

Let's Practice:
When finding yourself judging another:

1. Step back and observe. Monitor your thoughts. Catch yourself when you start to judge.

2. Avoid Stereotyping

3. Soften your heart. Look for the positive. What good can you find in someone or something?

4. Focus on yourself and your positive attributes. Don't judge yourself either.

We are all on our own path to awakening. It's part of the process. Nobody or nothing is better or worse than anyone or anything else. Be your authentic self and always practice ahimsa - non-harming.

Next, try this practice:

Place a rose blend of essential oils on your hands and take in a long deep breath of the oil. Now, gently place your hands on your heart, feeling a deep connection to this center. Allow love and kindness to fill your heart, picturing a time when you felt unconditionally loved and cared for by someone. Feel all of the emotions and body sensations that go along with that memory. Feel it resonate in your heart and radiate throughout your whole being.

4. Yoga Asanas: Heart Openers and Counter Poses

What happens when we open our heart? We can feel ready to receive any opportunities or gifts that present themselves to us. We feel a physical expansion in the chest and a release and dropping down of the shoulder blades in back. We may feel a sense of vulnerability by exposing our heart and lifting the sternum. In these heart opening postures, pay attention to any physical or emotional sensations and be open to experiencing them all. After these heart opening postures a counter pose is added to provide balance. For the postures that require it, remember to repeat them on the other side.

Let's Practice:

Heart Opening Pose	Counter Pose
Side Stretch. Cross leg seated side stretch with top hand behind your head	**Twist and Bend.** Cross the top elbow over towards the opposite knee
Cow and Tiger. All 4's with back arched. Extend right arm and left leg. Reach back and hold your left ankle with your right hand.	**Cat and Downward Dog.** Round the back into a cat stretch and then straighten your legs for Downward facing dog.
Sphinx. Come to forearm plank and lower your hips. Open your heart. Chin in.	**Forearm Plank or Plank.** Extend your legs straight into plank on your forearms
Bow Pose. Come to rest on your stomach and reach your arms back to hold onto your ankles and lift your chest.	**Prone Savasana.** Rest on your belly with your forehead on stacked hands or with your head to the side and arms by your side
Camel. Come up onto your knees and place your fists or palms on your sacrum or low back	**Rabbit.** Sit back onto your heels. Place your hands on the floor next to your hips and begin to fold forward, drawing the navel in and your forehead towards your knees
Reverse Table. Come to a seated position with your knees bent and your hands behind your hips with fingers pointing forward. Lift the hips and hold and lower.	**Forward Fold.** Sit in a staff pose with your legs extended straight out and hands by your hips. Begin to hinge from the hips for a forward fold.
Star Gazer. Sit with your legs a little wider than your hips. Take your right foot and place it on the inside of your left thigh. Place your right hand next to your hip and reach the left hand out to the left. Now swing that arm forward and up so that you are up on your right knee and the left leg is straight.	**Twist.** Come down from Star Gazer and twist your upper body towards your left leg with your right arms on the outside of your left thigh and your left arm behind your back for support.
Bridge. Roll to your back and bend your knees. Keep your knees drawing in and slowly lift your hips up into bridge pose.	**Savasana.** Rest into corpse pose with arms and legs straight or add support with blankets or pillows.

5. Technique #2: The Work by Byron Katie[28]

Have you found yourself passing judgement? Judging defined as 'forming an opinion or conclusion about someone or something,' is something I find myself making doing more often than I care to admit. In these moments, I try to turn inward to explore the origins of these impressions. I remind myself of my commitment to remaining content and happy and then I delve deeper to decide if the judgement is causing harm, either to me or someone else. When I discovered the teachings of Byron Katie, I learn ways to work with my judgements to process the 'shoulds' I wrestle with. Her method involves asking four questions and then using the 'turn around' to shift perspective, fostering healthier relationships with others. Here's a glimpse into her process:

'The work' is a powerful and useful tool when your thoughts create stories about people and situations in your life. It is a process of inquiry. When you find yourself "judging your neighbor", pause and ask these four questions about the thoughts you have.

1. Is it true?
2. Can you absolutely know it is true?
3. How do you react, what happens, when you believe that thought?
4. Who would you be without that thought?

From Byron Katie's Website: "As we do 'The Work' of Byron Katie, not only do we remain alert to our stressful thoughts–the ones that cause all the anger, sadness, and frustration in our world–but we question them, and through that questioning the thoughts lose their power over us. Great spiritual texts describe the what; what it means to be free. 'The Work' is the how. It shows you exactly how to identify and question any thought that would keep you from that freedom."

---

28 https://thework.com/

Let's Practice:

Think of a situation in your life where you are judging another. Then ask The Four Questions:

1. **Is it true?** The answer is either yes or no. Be still and find your honest answer. If you answered yes, move to question number 2. If no then move to question number 3.

2. **Can you absolutely know that it's true?** If you answered yes to question number 1, take the time to look again and see if you can truly say yes

3. **How do you react/what happens when you believe that thought?** Close your eyes and witness what you are feeling and thinking and what emotions arise when you believe that thought. How do you treat the other person? How do you treat yourself?

4. **Who would you be without that thought?** Close your eyes and take time to observe the situation again and reflect on how you see that person now. Drop all judgements.

The Turnarounds:

After asking and processing these four questions you may then proceed to the Turnarounds. This is the process of finding the opposites of the original statement.

> *Byron Katie's Example:* Original Statement:
> Paul doesn't listen to me
>
> The turnarounds: Paul does listen to me
> OR I don't listen to myself
> OR I don't listen to Paul.

There are many wonderful resources on Byron Katie's website so that you may further explore this technique. {www.thework.com}

6. Restorative Yoga Asana #2:
Pillow Fest or Bridge w/Block

Essential Oil Suggestion: Bergamot

Set-up: For Pillow Fest, get as many pillows as you have from your bed or couch. Stack and lean them up against each other to lie back on. Place more pillows or folded blankets under the arms. For bridge with block pose, lie all the way down on your back and then lift the hips into bridge pose. Slide a block on the low or medium level or a rolled blanket under the hips.

EO: You may place *Bergamot* essential oil on your wrists or palms or diffuse it in the air. Breathe in the essential oils to open up the passageways in the nostrils and the whole body. Take long, deep relaxing breaths. Play relaxing spa music, theta music or Tibetan singing bowl sounds with or without nature sounds. Rest and Relax.

7. Reading #3: Heart Coherence Meditation[29]

Heart - Brain Connection or Heart Coherence
Three Steps to Compassion

We have 40,000 specialized cells that are like brain cells but not in the brain. These are called sensory neurites. They exist in the heart. They can learn, think, remember and communicate with us independently from the neurons in the brain in a language we may or may not recognize because we are conditioned to communicate only with our brain.

When we harmonize the heart and the brain we can experience our deepest empathy, compassion and intuition. Some of the benefits of communicating with our heart are:

- We can process information quickly because we don't go thru the logic and ego brain
- Our affirmations are especially potent when we communicate through the heart
- Healing and intuition are more readily available

Let's Practice:
3 Steps to Harmonize the Heart and the Brain.
Sit quietly and place your hands over your heart.

1. **Slow your breathing.** Take a five-count inhale and a six or seven count exhale. This sends a signal to the body to relax. This frees your body to let go of the stress hormones and the feelings of stress and awakens the healing chemistry in your body. You are giving your body the opportunity for healing. Breathe a little slower from the heart space.

---

29 This concept is from the heart math institute called the quick coherence technique www.heartmath.org

2. **Shift your awareness from the thinking mind to the heart.** Shift your attention from the mind to the heart and notice all of your focus go to your heart.

3. **Feel into your heart.** Feel one or a combination of one of the following four emotions: care, appreciation, gratitude, compassion. Imagine someone or something for whom you feel care, appreciation, gratitude, or compassion. Research has found that these four key words will activate the connection between our heart and our brain.

Take one more deep breath and as you release that breath know that this act is the key to the deepest truth of who you are as an individual in this world. When you are working to solve a problem, write, create, add something new in your life, improve your heart and immune health, it all comes from this simple act of heart-brain connection and compassion.

8. Restorative Yoga Asana #3: Lounge Chair Savasana with Snake Blanket and Bound Angle

Essential Oil Suggestion: Sage

Set-up: Place two blocks next to each other; one on the highest level and the other on the medium level or one on the medium level and one on the lowest level. Lean a bolster or a tightly rolled blanket against it. Lie down with your bottom close to the bottom edge of the bolster and recline back. Use rolled blankets or pillows under your arms for arm rest support. Open a yoga blanket all the way. Roll it lengthwise to form a long snake blanket. Place your feet together and knees out in bound angle pose. Wrap the snake blanket over the top of your feet and then under each thigh for support (Snake blanket not shown in the image). Place an eye pillow on your eyes.

EO: You may place *Sage* essential oil on your wrists or diffuse it in the air. Breathe in the essential oils to open up the passageways in the nostrils and the whole body. Take long, deep relaxing breaths. Play relaxing spa music, theta music or Tibetan singing bowl sounds with or without nature sounds. Rest and Relax.

9. Closing. Burning or Dissolving Ritual

◇ **Letting Go:**

Get a lighter and a heat resistant bowl (for the burning ritual) or a bowl filled with room temperature or warm water (for the dissolving ritual). Take the paper with the answer to the letting go question and say the following out loud:

*"Dear Universe–I no longer need these thoughts, feelings, or circumstances that do not serve my highest and best good.
I vow to be open to the lessons presented to me in order to create positive habits and improve my outlook on life."*

Now light the paper on fire and place it in the bowl and watch it burn or take the special dissolving paper and place it in the water and watch it dissolve. Let it go.

◇ **Inviting In**

Read one of the following quotes of inspiration below or choose your own. You may choose to print it on a paper or sticky note to post where you will see it. Say the following out loud: *"Dear Universe–I invite this message of inspiration into my life at this time to serve my highest and best good. I promise to be more present and kinder to myself every day."*

What will you invite into your life today?

1. Statement of gratitude to the universe
   about what you wish for today:

   *"Thank you Universe for giving me everything
   I need to enjoy my here and now."*

2. Two quotes of inspiration

   *"In order to heal themselves, people must recognize
   first, that they have an inner guidance deep within and
   second, that they can trust it."* ~Shakti Gawain

   *"Yoga is a light, which once lit, will never dim. The better
   your practice, the brighter the flame."* ~B.K.S. Iyengar

Story #11. I'm Disappointed (in you)

(What am I responsible for?)

"I am disappointed in you!" Has anyone ever said this to you? The definition of disappointment is– Sadness or displeasure caused by the non-fulfillment of one's hopes or expectations. Therefore, if someone says to you, 'I'm disappointed in you,' that is telling you that you are not fulfilling *their* hopes and expectations of *you*. Who are they to cause you bad feelings for not fulfilling their expectations?

I remember a story that my mom told me once. I was about 14 or 15 and a good friend of hers was over at our house and my mom said to me that she was disappointed in me. Her friend suggested that saying that was not helpful and makes her child feel like they need to seek approval rather than acting from a sense of self-worth. My mom told me this story many years later and still remembers her friend's advice, emphasizing the importance of mindful language.

Recently, my friend Dawn, confided that she carries guilt for 'disappointing' her sister, Amy. Amy harbors resentments and criticisms about what Dawn did or did not do in the past. Every time they spend time together or have conversations Amy brings up her disappointments in Dawn. This constant rehashing has strained their relationship, leaving Dawn with feelings of guilt, shame, and blame.

This cycle often begins in childhood when parents resort to expressions like 'We want you to develop independent thinking but of you don't meet our standards we will express our disappointment in you.' Such declarations can lead to self-disappointment rather than nurture understanding.

None of us wish to let someone down. We hate to disappoint our family and friends and the people who trust in us. We especially hate disappointing ourselves. But we all will disappoint others and ourselves many times in life because we are human.

If someone says, 'I'm disappointed in you,' it signals their inability to get past those feelings. It's not your responsibility to take care of their disappointments. Blaming others for how you are feeling is never a way to contentment and loving relationships. It is natural to feel disappointed. When these feelings arise, whether they are about another person or ourselves, we can sit with them and say out loud, 'I am feeling or experiencing disappointment.' Observe how that disappointment manifests and feels but don't blame anyone or anything for it. Avoid making others responsible for your feelings. Avoid saying, 'I'm disappointed in you.' If someone says this to you, you can simply say, "I'm sorry you feel that way," and allow them to take responsibility for their own emotions.

To be truly happy in all of the moments of your life, be proud of yourself now. Be proud of what you have accomplished and take the focus off of life's disappointments. My friend Dawn shared with me that she sat with her feelings and was able to look clearly at what she is and is not responsible for in her own life. She could be proud of this moment without looking back with regrets or guilty feelings that she let someone down. She can also allow Amy to be responsible for her own feelings, disappointments, and joys.

The Uphill Battle. Navigating personal growth can be like riding a bike uphill on gravel. Each time we learn and practice a new skill, like noticing when a trigger elicits an unwanted response and then changing it to a new habit, it can feel like we are stuck or even sliding backwards. At first the friction or resistance is great because we haven't created momentum yet but once we practice and keep going we gain momentum and begin to grow confident in our skills. Then, just like riding a bike, our tires find traction, grip the ground, and move us forward. Soon we gain more and more momentum and confidence and we rise to the top of the hill and then effortlessly coast downhill.

As Newton's first law of motion states, "A body in motion stays in motion unless acted upon by a force." It also states "A body at rest tends to stay at rest." Be the body in motion, even if it's just one small step at a time. Soon, with practice, the momentum will build along with your confidence and you will soar to new heights.

YES for Heart Opening #3

1. Opening

◇ **Letting Go**

Questions of the day. On a piece of paper, that you will burn or dissolve at the end, write your answer to the question(s) below about what you wish to let go:

1. *When the ego is loud what self-defeating or self-important things does it say?*

2. *What blame or shame do I project onto others so I will feel better?*

◇ **Hand on Heart Affirmations**

"I choose positive loving thoughts and am open to love."

"I deeply and completely love and accept myself and I nurture my inner child."

"I love and accept myself exactly as I am."

"I am courageous and confident in all I do."

◇ **Personal Mantra**

Choose a mantra of your own that speaks to you today. Begin with "I am," and say it in the present moment as if it already exists! Your personal mantra should be something you truly believe. Say it out loud with energy, emotion, vigor, enthusiasm, and intention to grow these positive seeds within you!

Example Mantra: *"I am a warrior of kindness and positivity. I approach life and each moment knowing that all is happening just as it is supposed to because it's happening!"*

◇ **Gratitude and Energy**

Say to yourself or out loud what you are grateful for and what positive energy you wish to invite into your life today! You may also choose an angel card with a word or a message of inspiration for the day.

2. Restorative Yoga Asana #1 and Breath Assessment: Flying Flapping Fish

Set-up: Lie down on the floor or mat with a blanket under your back and a blanket or pillow under your head. Place blankets or blocks for support near your upper back. Roll to your side and place a bolster or rolled blanket between your legs. Now open the top arm all the way so your back is resting on the ground or props that you placed there as your lower body remains in twist. Combine the two images below: side lying twist with the lower body and a heart opener with the upper body. Come into a restful, supportive position.

◇ **Breath Assessment:**

Come into the posture and begin to release any past or future thoughts. Relax and surrender more and more with every breath. Notice your breathing pattern without trying to change anything. Notice the rise and fall of the belly and chest. Observe the length of the breath. Is it flowing naturally helping you to become calmer or does it feel rapid or shallow creating tension? Just observe for 3-5 minutes. Now count your inhales and exhales. Extend the exhales to assist your body in coming to a deeper state of relaxation, activating the parasympathetic nervous system (rest and digest). Allow your body and mind to surrender to the present moment and be.

3. Technique #1: Patanjali's Eight Limbs of Yoga

1. **Yamas:** Restraints. External Ethics.

    a. Ahimsa - non-harming

    b. Satya - truthfulness

    c. Asteya - non-stealing

    d. Brahmacharya - non-excess or right use of energy

    e. Aparigraha - non-possessiveness or non-attachment

2. **Niyamas:** Observances. Internal Ethics

    a. Saucha - purity or cleanliness

    b. Santosha - contentment

    c. Tapas - self discipline

    d. Svadhyaya - self-study

    e. Ishvara Pranidhana - surrender to the divine or higher being

3. **Asanas:** Physical postures
4. **Pranayama:** Breathing exercises, and control of prana
5. **Pratyahara:** Withdrawal of the senses
6. **Dharana:** Concentration and cultivating inner awareness
7. **Dhyana:** Meditation
8. **Samadhi:** Union with the Divine. Enlightenment or Bliss

The true benefits of yoga come from expanding beyond the physical practice on the mat into life. The Yoga Sutras of Pananjali describe these eight limbs as a way to live a passionate life filled with integrity and kindness. One where we are looking more and more inward to understand ourselves and outward to understand and appreciate our connection to everything and everyone.

Friends of mine, Charles and Rachel, who I met at Kula Kamala Ashram in Pennsylvania, showed me their identical tattoos. They each had the first Yama, Ahimsa, written in Sanskrit on the inside of their wrists. They told me they plan to focus on the first and second limb; each of the Yamas and Niyamas, one each year, until they are incorporating them into their lives as much as they can. I love this idea.

We humans, of course, have our faults and may not practice the yamas and niyamas flawlessly all the time but the reminder to live our lives following these moral disciplines and personal observances offers a guide to live a purposeful life. The third limb is asana, moving our bodies in and out of postures. The first three limbs are an outward focus and the next five progressively draw our awareness inward to focus on breathing, withdrawing from or non-attachment to the senses, concentration, meditation, and finally to a state of total bliss or a sense of oneness with all things where nothing disturbs our state of mind, body, and spirit.

Let's Practice:

Reflect on the Eight Limbs and explore ways to incorporate them in your life. Personally, I find a daily practice or ritual to be effective. When I wake up each morning I incorporate many of these practices that set the tone for my day. Each morning I start by expressing gratitude out loud. I then choose an angel card for inspiration and set an intention for the day. In my meditation room, I light a candle and declare my affirmation with vigor and purpose such as, 'Thank you universe for the abundance and focus in my life today.' I then engage in a five minute meditation followed by five to thirty minutes of yoga asana. Throughout the day I consciously practice non-harming, non-stealing, and truthfulness. While some aspects like managing my energy expenditure and practicing non-attachment to things, people or even emotions, present challenges, I continue integrating them into my daily routine.

Consider writing down, saying out loud, or even tattooing on your wrist an area you wish to focus on. Honor yourself by infusing this intention into your day through each interaction, thought and action you perform.

4. Yoga Asanas: Heart Focus

This practice is a focus on asanas with 'heart', representing a flow that you create from your very soul. Personally, I love to move through my own personal practice and wing it based on how I'm feeling that day. Rather than planning a sequence of postures in advance, I simply begin moving and allow my body to guide the way. I might incorporate a twist, a kick, a standing split or a gentle series of postures where I never come to a standing position at all. The practice could revolve around balances, sun salutations, or anything that feels right in the moment, lasting anywhere from 5 to 75 minutes. Creativity and compassion are at the center of the sequence and I never know what to expect. Grant yourself permission to do what's best for you today. If you need guidance to create your own yoga sequence, try the following suggestions.

Let's Practice:
A flow practice:
Try a sequence where you begin seated, move to all 4's and add some postures, flow through sun salutations and/or warrior postures, throw in a balance or two and then move to some seated postures and finally onto your back for relaxing postures and savasana.

A stationary practice:
Think of some of your favorite yoga postures and move into them one after another holding each one for 1 to 6 breaths or longer. Bring focus, presence, and awarcncss to each one.

A flexibility practice:

Where could you use a bit more flexibility? In your neck and shoulders? Your back? Hamstrings? Hips? Choose postures that help you to find more flexibility by moving in and out of them 3-6 times and then holding for at least one minute. You may use a yoga strap around your feet in a seated or lying down position to assist in your stretches.

A relaxation practice:

Begin this practice in a seated or lying down posture and focus on breath awareness. Guide your attention to the gentle rise and fall of your breath to cultivate a serene mental state. With each breath you can incorporate this poem by Ticht Nhat Hanh:

Breathing in I calm my body
Breathing out I smile
Dwelling in the present moment
I know this is a wonderful moment

Choose a sequence of relaxing postures that feel easeful and restorative. Offer yourself kindness and care as you rest, move, relax, and draw your awareness inward.

5. Technique #2: Lesson: The 5 Invitations[30]

I was assigned to read the book "The Five Invitations: Discovering what Death can Teach us about Living Fully", while taking a Spiritual Leadership Certification with Swamini Shraddhananda Saraswati at Kula Kamala Ashram in PA. In the book, the author, Frank Ostaseski, shares his experience as co-founder of the Zen Hospice project, a place where he offers compassionate care to those who are at the end of life. The Five Invitations are reliable guides for being with the dying. And, as it turns out, they have a relevance for all of us in living a life

---

30 Book: The Five Invitations" by Frank Ostaseski
https://fiveinvitations.com/the-book/

of integrity, meaning and purpose. They guide us toward appreciating life's preciousness.

Here are the five invitations. I invite you to explore them and purchase the book to experience all of the wonderful stories and insights it holds about dying and living.

The Five Invitations:

1. **Don't wait:** Live life. Forgive everyone. Do not hold grudges. Forgiveness releases our hearts from anger and negativity and clears the way to love. Make peace (otherwise it's bondage), let go, apologize,

2. **Welcome everything and push nothing away.** No matter how comfortable or challenging it may be, welcome all experiences. Don't deny anything. If you are having difficult conversations with someone ask for clarity. Listen. Be. Don't deny suffering.

3. **Bring your whole self to the experience.** Your body is a colony of organs, systems, and emotions. Sometimes we only bring forward our fearful or prideful self or our sexual self or uncertain, courageous, weak, or scared self. Bring it all forward!

4. **Find a place of rest in the middle of things.** Picture the eye of the storm. Find the middle road. It will not cause you harm. Find a place of ease and comfort. Remain steadfast in the center and do not allow yourself to be pulled away by all the debris flying around. Don't go to the extremes of pleasure or anger and pain. We can hear what others have to say instead of making assumptions about what they mean.

5. **Cultivate a "Don't know" mind.** Be ok with not knowing. Keep inquiring. Each moment will change. Invite others to share with you so you can understand. We can't know 100 % of everything. Be open to learning.

6. Restorative Yoga Asana #2: Twist with Chest on Bolster.

Essential Oil Suggestion: Sweet Orange

Set-up: Place two blocks next to each other; one on the highest level and the other on the medium level or one on the medium level and one on the lowest level. Lean a bolster or a tightly rolled blanket against it. Place rolled blankets on either side of the bolster for arm rest support. Sit next to the bolster with your hip touching it. Place a bolster or rolled blanket between your legs. Now twist your chest to face the bolster and rest your chest on it. Turn your head in the direction of your knees.

EO: You may place *Sweet Orange* essential oil on your wrists or diffuse it in the air. Breathe in the essential oils to open up the passageways in the nostrils and the whole body. Take long, deep relaxing breaths. Play relaxing spa music, theta music or Tibetan singing bowl sounds with or without nature sounds. Rest and Relax.

7. Technique #3: Metta Meditation with RY#3

Metta Meditation: Metta means loving kindness. In this meditation you will be opening your heart to yourself and others and offering loving kindness to them all. Practice this meditation while in Restorative Yoga Asana #3 - Lounge Chair. You may ask someone to read this for you or find a recording on the website www. Y4ES.com

- Lie down in a restorative posture or you may choose to sit up
- Be comfortable and alert

- Focus on your breathing for a few moments to calm your mind.

- Place your attention on the area of your heart.

- Bring your focus to yourself. Imagine offering loving kindness to yourself.

- Say quietly in your mind "May I be well, healthy and strong. May I be happy. May I abide in peace, and love."

- Now bring someone to mind who is close to you or whom you respect like a partner, friend or family member.

- Say quietly in your mind "May you be well, healthy and strong. May you be happy. May you abide in peace, and love."

- Imagine the person happy.

- Imagine them sending love back to you.

- Next bring someone to mind who is a casual acquaintance or whom you have neutral feelings for. It could be the friend of a friend, someone you see in the neighborhood, or a person who works at a store that you frequent.

- Say quietly in your mind "May you be well, healthy and strong. May you be happy. May you abide in peace, and love."

- Imagine the person happy.

- Imagine them sending love back to you.

- Bring to mind someone you are angry with or someone who is difficult to get along with or who has hurt you.

- Say quietly in your mind "May you be well, healthy and strong. May you be happy. May you abide in peace, and love."

- Imagine the person happy.

- Imagine them sending love back to you.

- Next imagine all beings. Think of people in your hometown, state, and beyond to all the states and all of the countries and all beings in the whole world.

- Say quietly in your mind "May you be well, healthy and strong. May you be happy. May you abide in peace, and love."
- Imagine all beings happy.
- Imagine the whole world sending love back to you.
- Stay here with the feelings of loving kindness as long as you like and when you are ready rise up. Notice what has changed and how you feel in your mind, body and soul.

Loving kindness is about loving people, animals, and the world. It's about doing good deeds, thinking good thoughts and speaking good words. These are some of the most important qualities a person can possess.

8. Restorative Yoga Asana #3: Lounge Chair Savasana with Metta Meditation

Essential Oil Suggestion: Sweet Marjoram

Set-up: Place two blocks next to each other; one on the highest level and the other on the medium level or one on the medium level and one on the lowest level. Lean a bolster or a tightly rolled blanket against it. Lie down with your bottom close to the bottom edge of the bolster and recline back. Use rolled blankets or pillows under your arms for arm rest support. Place a rolled blanket or bolster under your knees if you wish. Place an eye pillow on your eyes.

EO: You may place *Sweet Marjoram* essential oil on your wrists or diffuse it in the air. Breathe in the essential oils to open up the passageways in the nostrils and the whole body. Take long, deep relaxing breaths. Play relaxing spa music, theta music or Tibetan singing bowl sounds with or without nature sounds. Rest and Relax.

9. Closing. Burning or Dissolving Ritual

◇ **Letting Go:**

Get a lighter and a heat resistant bowl (for the burning ritual) or a bowl filled with room temperature or warm water (for the dissolving ritual). Take the paper with the answer to the letting go question and say the following out loud:

"Dear Universe–I no longer need these thoughts, feelings, or circumstances that do not serve my highest and best good. I vow to be open to the lessons presented to me in order to create positive habits and improve my outlook on life."

Now light the paper on fire and place it in the bowl and watch it burn or take the special dissolving paper and place it in the water and watch it dissolve. Let it go.

◇ **Inviting In:**

Read one of the following quotes of inspiration below or choose your own. You may choose to print it on a paper or sticky note to post where you will see it. Say the following out loud: *"Dear Universe–I invite this message of inspiration into my life at this time to serve my highest and best good. I promise to be more present and kinder to myself every day."*

What will you invite into your life today?

1. Statement of gratitude to the universe
   about what you wish for today:

   "Thank you universe for guiding me in the ways of love."

2. Two quotes of inspiration

   *"To the ego, loving and wanting are the same, whereas
   true love has no wanting in it, no desire to possess
   or for your partner to change." ~Eckhart Tolle*

   *"The most beautiful moments in life are moments when you are
   expressing your joy, not when you are seeking it." ~Sadhguru*

Story #12. Sit with it
(This too shall pass)

Change. We all experience it and it ain't easy. Whether it's a fleeting moment or a prolonged period- lasting 10 seconds, 10 days, 10 months or 10 years- change arises, lingers, and eventually dissolves. Everything is impermanent, and yet acknowledging that 'this to shall pass' doesn't make it any less challenging. Life is full of transitions such as moving, changing jobs, illness, loss, injury, and, heartache, each accompanied by a flood of thoughts, sensations, and emotions that manifest in our body, mind and soul.

Ignoring these through distraction, denial or the facade that everything is ok, allows them to fester. Consequently, the positive changes you seek will become more difficult, potentially leading to a tailspin of despair and unhappiness.

Reflecting on my own life, I recall a childhood memory of a favorite pink velvety chair that spun around and brought me immense joy. One day my mom said it was time to let the chair go and I resisted this so much. "Noooo!" I said crying "I love that chair!" She reminded me that change is inevitable and we will experience lots of changes throughout our lives. I reluctantly let go of the chair understanding that nothing lasts forever, especially material things.

Childhood experiences of change and their associated emotions persist into adulthood. What matters is how we process them. When the waves of emotions associated with change and the physical manifestations emerge, we can choose to sit with them. Be with the emotions. Embrace them, acknowledge the thoughts and be present with your body. Here's what you can do:

"There's a lump in my throat."
Sit with it
"There's a tightness in my chest."
Sit with it

"There's an ache in my belly."

Sit with it

"There's confusion in my mind."

Sit with it

"There's a pain in my back."

Sit with it

"There's sadness, anger, fear, doubt, anxiety,
worry, blame in my whole being."

Sit with it

And know these two things:

1. Right now, this is how it is

and

2. "The primary cause of your unhappiness is never the situation but your thoughts about it." (A quote by Eckhart Tolle)

   It may not be easy to sit with your feelings, but incredibly, when you do the feelings diminish. So, after you sit with them and really feel them, take a moment to acknowledge their presence without judgement, and then consciously let them go. Here's what you can do next:

3. Change the thoughts.

   What you think creates how you feel, so sit with the feelings and then change the thoughts. The new positive energy thoughts might be:

   "This is a temporary state of being."

   "I am more than my thoughts."

   "I am capable of many wonderful things."

"This too shall pass."

Reinforce this shift by listing all of the things you have accomplished in your life, recognizing the people who love and support you and reflect on what you are grateful for. These positive thoughts will help guide you towards feeling better.

4. Take action.

    Use the emotions you feel to push you towards change and greatness. Focus on the positive in every situation. Know that whatever is happening is supposed to happen because it's happening! Then take charge of your life with action towards whatever you envision for you!

    "Emotion without action is irrelevant." ~ Jody Williams

5. Love.

    Love yourself, others, life situations, the present moment, choices, opportunities, fluidity, transitions, transformation and change. Love it all. Grow in love and light. Feel love towards yourself and then spread the love to others. Growth only happens through change!

Relaxation

Relax. We hear this advice all the time when we are feeling out of sorts or stressed from the day or anytime an emotion hits us. I know there have been times when I don't want someone to say "just relax" to me when I am feeling uptight, even though I know this is the best thing I can do. When we relax it puts our whole body into a state of rest and digest. Ah Ha! The good 'ol parasympathetic nervous system. Relaxing allows us to digest our food and ease our body and mind into a state where we are able to function more effectively. The opposite is a heightened state of fight or flight where we are not able to feel rested at all.

What are your favorite ways to relax? It might be helpful to write out a list and keep it someplace so the next time you feel overwhelmed and tension arising you can refer to the list to help yourself relax. Some of my favorite things are walking in nature, deep breathing, sitting still, slow flow yoga, restorative yoga, and listening to soothing music or nature sounds. Enjoy these relaxation sessions with techniques for letting go. I even have a vanity license plate that says 'YOGAAAH' - Yoga practices are my favorite way to relax.

Let's Practice:

Grab a paper and pen and jot down at least ten of your favorite ways to relax. Post this list in a visible place as a daily reminder to love yourself enough to incorporate these into your day. One of my favorite spiritual teachers, Teal Swan, says in any situation ask yourself "What would a person who loves themself do?" When faced with the choice of how to unwind and show self-love, simply refer to your list for some inspiration.

YES for Relaxation #1

1. Opening

◇ **Letting Go**

Questions of the day. On a piece of paper, that you will burn or dissolve at the end, write your answer to the question(s) below about what you wish to let go:

1. *What keeps me in my comfort zone that does not serve my best health and well-being?*

2. *When I am feeling stressed or anxious what do I utilize for comfort that does not support my physical and mental health and wellbeing?*

◇ **Hand on Heart Affirmations**

"I create a relaxing atmosphere in my life."

"I purposefully make time in my schedule for relaxation and stillness."

"I choose to take the time I need to relax fully with a walk in nature, a nap, massage, bath, or anything that allows me to rest and rejuvenate."

◇ **Personal Mantra**

Choose a mantra of your own that speaks to you today. Begin with "I am," and say it in the present moment as if it already exists! Your personal mantra should be something you truly believe. Say it out loud with energy, emotion, vigor, enthusiasm, and intention to grow these positive seeds within you!

Example Mantra: *"I have a choice every moment to feel relaxed or happy, stressed or joyful. Today I choose joy!"*

◇ **Gratitude and Energy**

Say to yourself or out loud what you are grateful for and what positive energy you wish to invite into your life today! You may also choose an angel card with a word or a message of inspiration for the day.

2. Restorative Yoga Asana #1 and Breath Assessment: Basic Relaxation Pose

Set-up: Lie down on the floor or on a yoga mat with a blanket or pillow under your head. Place a rolled-up blanket or bolster under your knees. You may also place blankets under your back. You may place an eye pillow over your eyes. Make sure you feel fully supported and relaxed.

◇ **Breath Assessment:**

Come into the posture and begin to release any past or future thoughts. Relax and surrender more and more with every breath. Notice your breathing pattern without trying to change anything. Notice the rise and fall of the belly and chest. Observe the length of the breath. Is it flowing naturally helping you to become calmer or does it feel rapid or shallow creating tension? Just observe for 3-5 minutes. Now count your inhales and exhales. Extend the exhales to assist your body in coming to a deeper state of relaxation, activating the parasympathetic nervous system (rest and digest). Allow your body and mind to surrender to the present moment and be.

3. Technique #1:
Singing "I Have Arrived" and other Songs[31]

Singing is a wonderful way to improve your mood, release stress, increase lung capacity and assist with deep breathing. It releases endorphins, improves your posture and raises your vibration. Singing songs with an inspirational message brings us hope and positivity.

Here are some of my favorite popular songs to sing.
Wonderful World (sung by Louis Armstrong)
Pure Imagination (sung by Gene Wilder)
I Can See Clearly Now (by Johnny Nash)
Across the Universe (by the Beatles)
I Have Arrived (by Ticht Nhat Hahn)

My sister and I wrote some uplifting and positive songs:

All is Well (by Christine Shaw)
All is well, all is well, in this moment all is well
All is well, all is well, in this moment all is well.

I am loving, I am joyful, I am filled with peace and harmony
Sun is shining all around me and I feel a wave of energy
When this world brings me down, present
moment's what I've found
It can heal what hurts me. Gratitude is all I see

I am happy, I am giving, I see so much love surrounding me
Nature, laughter, friends and kindness, all
these things are as they're meant to be
When my thoughts turn to good, all things happen as they should
When the universe answers me, all is well and I am free

All is well, all is well, in this moment all is well
All is well, I can tell, in this moment all is well.

31 For the tunes to the songs go to www.Y4ES.com

Take a Deep Breath (by Christine Shaw)

Take a deep breath and feel your body filled with energy.
You can heal yourself. Just breath, just breathe, just breathe.
Listen to your body, heal it with your soul.
Breathe life in, exhale pain out.
When you relax and tune in to intuition it helps.
Your mind is free to bring about anything you desire.

I am Consciousness (by Christine Shaw)
I am conscious-ness, using this body.
I am energy, using thoughts to create my reality
I am love and light, that's what I choose to be
and I know that there are infinite possibilities.
I am not my thoughts. All that I own is free.
I am this bright soul, a reflection of my personality.
I am stillness to see my inner self
and I know that love and kindness brings good health.
Strength and trust, hope and faith; these will guide me on my path.
Fearlessness, happiness; this is how I lead my life.

Song of Affirmation (by Linda Shaw)
I am healthy, I am wealthy, I'm successful and have time.
I am loved by pets and people; my heart
is filled with art and rhyme.
Nature, laughter, peace and safety, happiness and love are mine.

Glory Be to Me (by Linda Shaw)
Glory be to my powers and to my strength
and to my hopes and dreams.
When there's something I desire, I can always make it happen.
Until the end again and again.

You may find many of these songs on the website www.Y4ES.com

4. Yoga Asanas: The Granthis (knots)

See 5. Lesson #2: The 3 Granthis and the associated yoga asanas as remedies to untie the knots. Read more about the Granthis in the next section, then practice these asanas to release them

Let's Practice:

1. **Brahma Granthi:** Associated with the root chakra

    a. Tadasana - Mountain pose with long deep breaths

    b. Child's pose with a bolster

    c. Seated Postures: Dandasana - Staff pose with a forward fold, Seated twist, Bound angle, Side stretches

    d. Meditation

2. **Vishnu Granthi:** Associated with the heart chakra

   Heart Opening Postures:

   a. Cow / Cat

   b. Camel pose

   c. Sphinx pose

   d. Bow pose

3. **Rudra Granthi:** Associated with the throat and third eye chakras

   a. Fish pose

   b. Bridge pose

   c. Shoulder stand

5. Lesson #2: The 3 Granthis. Untie the Knots[32]

There are three granthis (psychic knots) in the physical body which are obstacles or doubts that are difficult to untie. They can prevent prana (breath) from moving through the body and rising up the sushumna (energy channel).

The granthis are called Brahma, Vishnu and Rudra, and they represent levels of awareness where the power of maya, ignorance and attachment to material things, is especially strong. Each person who aspires to make changes must transcend these barriers to release these knots. The granthis are also associated with the three Gunas or qualities of nature: tamas, rajas, and sattva.

Tamas is a state of darkness, inertia,
inactivity, materiality and ignorance.

Rajas is a state of energy, action, change, and movement.

Sattva is a state of harmony, balance, joy, and intelligence.

The Granthis:

Brahma granthi functions in the region of **mooladhara (root chakra)**. It implies attachment to physical pleasures, material objects, excessive selfishness, and instability. It is connected to **tamas**: negativity, lethargy and ignorance.

Remedy: Tadasana, Deep Pranayama, Child's pose with a bolster, Seated Postures, Meditation

Vishnu granthi operates in the region of **anahata (heart chakra)**. It is associated with the bondage of emotional attachment and attachment to people. A tight knot causes discomfort in breathing or heart palpitations and tightness in

---

32 https://www.theartofhealing.com.au/yoga-granthis.html

the sternum. It is difficult to give and receive. It is connected with **rajas**: passion, ambition, energy and assertiveness.

Remedy: Mudras, Gratitude, Metta Meditation (loving kindness), Heart opening postures. Mantra (mind tool): **So Hum** (I am - energy and life itself)

Rudra granthi functions in the region of **ajna (throat) up to Sahasrara (third eye) chakra.** It is connected with sattva - harmony, balance and intuition, tight throat, or trouble swallowing. One must surrender the sense of individual ego and transcend duality to make further spiritual progress.

Remedy: Fish pose, bridge pose or shoulder stand.

The granthis are housed along the central nerve channel within our body known as the Sushumna Nadi. This runs through the central axis of our body and is where energy either flows freely, or is blocked by the accumulation of our life stories, attachments, rejections, fears, and conditioning.

Each granthi represents an obstruction where we may feel physically stuck. Underneath the physical congestion is a strong attachment to emotional bondage and unconscious patterning.

Have you ever thought you dealt with an issue only to find yourself in a full -blown explosion when triggered? You thought the issue was resolved, but under the right circumstance the unresolved difficulty reappeared and took over.

If we don't get to know these blockages and if we push away the uncomfortable feelings we will continue to stay in a cycle of emotional bondage that keeps us under the veils of our excuses, justifications, misperceptions, confusion, and attachment. If we want to improve our overall well-being and live in a state of greater integration and alignment otherwise known as a state of yoga (or union) then it is worth taking steps to examine, process and ultimately untie these knots.

6. Restorative Yoga Asana #2: Forward Fold with a Bolster

Essential Oil Suggestion: Frankincense

Setup: Place two or three blocks along the mat and stack a bolster on top. Sit in front of the bolster with legs wide on either side. Place additional blankets or blocks to rest your head on. You may also rest your head on your folded arms on a low table or chair.

EO: You may place *Frankincense* essential oil on your wrists or diffuse it in the air. Breathe in the essential oils to open up the passageways in the nostrils and the whole body. Take long, deep relaxing breaths. Play relaxing spa music, theta music or Tibetan singing bowl sounds with or without nature sounds. Rest and Relax.

7. Technique #3: Buzzing Bee Breath

This breathing technique, Buzzing Bee (Bhramari pranayama), reduces stress, tones the nervous system and brings extreme calm to the body. Place fingers onto these points on the face: Thumbs in the ears, pinky fingers at the corners of the mouth, ring finger at the side of the nostrils, middle finger on the eyelids, and the index finger near the temple at the edge of the eyebrow. Alternately, you may just put your fingers in the ears if this feels better. Close the eyes and draw your awareness inward. Take a deep breath in and on the exhale, with lips slightly parted, make a buzzing sound like a bee. Repeat this five or more times to feel a sense of release and deep calm within.

8. Restorative Yoga Asana #3: Lounge Chair Savasana with A Visualization Treat for your Cells[33]

Essential Oil Suggestion: Spearmint

Set-up: Place two blocks next to each other: one on the highest level and the other on the medium level or one on the medium level and one on the lowest level. Lean a bolster or a tightly rolled blanket against it. Lie down with your bottom close to the bottom edge of the bolster and recline back. Use rolled blankets or pillows under your arms for arm rest support. Place a rolled blanket or bolster under your knees or if you wish, place feet together in bound angle pose with blocks supporting your legs. Place an eye pillow on your eyes.

33 Waller, P. (2010): *Holistic Anatomy; An Integrative Guide to the Human Body*; Berkeley, CA: North Atlantic Books page 43.

EO: You may place *Spearmint* essential oil on your wrists or diffuse it in the air. Breathe in the essential oils to open up the passageways in the nostrils and the whole body. Take long, deep relaxing breaths. Play relaxing spa music, theta music or Tibetan singing bowl sounds with or without nature sounds. Rest and Relax.

Reading during RY #3:

I read the book *Holistic Anatomy* by Pip Waller while studying Yoga Therapy at Kula Kamala Ashram. I love the information in the book and this guided visualization to imagine our cells with healing, relaxing energy. Here it is word for word from the book.

A Visualization Treat for your cells (from *Holistic Anatomy*)

"Find a quiet place to relax where nothing will disturb you for fifteen to thirty minutes. Sit comfortably or lie down and breathe gently for a few minutes, saying to yourself as you breathe in, "I breathe in healing, relaxing energy," and as you breathe out, "I breathe out all tension, anxiety, and negativity." Also try "Every time I breathe out, I become twice as relaxed." After a few minutes like this, imagine you are floating on a cloud of golden light, warm and safely enveloped. Begin to breathe in this healing light. As you breathe in, feel the warm, loving, golden energy filling your lungs. It begins to spread through your body, up into your head, neck, and shoulders, down into your arms and hands. It spreads down your back and into your belly. The warm golden healing light fills your pelvis and moves down your legs into your feet. Your whole body is filled with warm, healing, golden light.

Imagine the cells of your body, billion upon billion, each one filled with this healing golden glow. Imagine one of your cells, anywhere you like. See it, feel it, think it filled with warm, healing light energy. The cell is expanding, relaxing, happy and joyful as it bathes in the healing light. Every cell in your body is celebrating, enjoying the warm and golden healing light.

Your cells know what to do; your body knows what to do. We are completely as we are supposed to be, and our bodies, minds, and spirits are equipped with wonderful healing mechanisms. Allow yourself to enjoy this knowledge, allow the warm golden light to spread its glow throughout your body, and throughout your mind and spirit. All is well.

Afterwards, gently bring your attention back into the place you are in, and resume your daily activities, knowing you are filled with light and your cells are zinging with joy!"

9. Closing. Burning or Dissolving Ritual

◇ **Letting Go:**

Get a lighter and a heat resistant bowl (for the burning ritual) or a bowl filled with room temperature or warm water (for the dissolving ritual). Take the paper with the answer to the letting go question and say the following out loud:

"Dear Universe–I no longer need these thoughts, feelings, or circumstances that do not serve my highest and best good. I vow to be open to the lessons presented to me in order to create positive habits and improve my outlook on life."

Now light the paper on fire and place it in the bowl and watch it burn or take the special dissolving paper and place it in the water and watch it dissolve. Let it go.

◇ **Inviting In:**

Read one of the following quotes of inspiration below or choose your own. You may choose to print it on a paper or sticky note to post where you will see it. Say the following out loud: *"Dear Universe–I invite this message of inspiration into my life at this time to serve my highest and best good. I promise to be more present and kinder to myself every day."*

What will you invite into your life today?

1. Statement of gratitude to the universe about what you wish for today:

    "Thank you, Universe, for offering me all that I need to enjoy this precious present moment."

2. Two quotes of inspiration

    "Don't get so busy making a living that you forget to make a life." ~Dolly Parton

    "Children are happy because they don't have a file in their minds called All the Things That Could Go Wrong." ~Marianne Williamson

Story #13. The Female Brain
(Understanding our programming)

I was in the library and I set an intention to find a good movie with a message. As I perused the movie selection one jumped out at me. It was called <u>The Female Brain</u>.

I thought, 'I'm interested in that!' It didn't look like a documentary or a TED talk. From the DVD cover, it looked like a comedy. Sold! or, since it was from the library, borrowed! It looked a little odd but I gave it a try. To my surprise it was excellent! A neuroscientist studies the brain and how it functions. The movie follows three couples and their interactions. When the couples are having a discussion, the scene suddenly pauses and an image of the brain and its functions is drawn over the female or male brain. Arrows and words are added to explain why we respond to people and situations the way we do. We respond with our amygdala (the part responsible for processing emotions including fear and pleasure) or our prefrontal cortex (the executive functioning part responsible for decision making, planning and organizing thoughts). We activate the neurotransmitter dopamine (responsible for motivation and reward) and serotonin (responsible for feelings of well-being and happiness) when we are excited or things are going well.

One of my favorite scenes is when a couple, Lexi and Adam, who are dating and living together, are looking in the mirror and getting ready for the day. Lexi has lots of makeup and beautifully coiffed hair and is really put together. She looks at Adam and says he should straighten his hair and pop the zit on his back and other nit-picky things. He gets annoyed with this and later in the movie breaks up with her saying that he is happy the way he is and he doesn't want her to try to change him. When Lexi goes to her parent's house for a party her mom starts criticizing her dress, hair, and makeup which really annoys her.

In the final scene, Adam has moved out and Lexi goes to see him. He opens the door to her and she is standing there with messed up hair, no makeup, and looking very vulnerable. She pours out her heart saying she is so sorry for trying to change him and she realized that this is what she learned was love, from her mother. If she looked just "right" then her mom would love her. She begs him to give her another chance and he says, "I will but you have to promise not to try to change me and accept the demotion to 'just my girlfriend.'"

I loved this scene because so many of us are acting unconsciously from what we learned from our upbringing and our programmed brain. We act from the place of 'I wish to feel loved and cared for.' Then words are said or things happen that lead us to feeling unloved. By recognizing that it is our programming and accompanying thoughts about what is happening, we can relax and not respond from fear of not being loved.

Actress Whitney Cummings plays the lead character in "The Female Brain." After reading the book with the same title by Louann Brizendine, M.D., she really wanted to make a movie about it. You may find an interview with her and neuroscientist Moran Cerf on YouTube called "The Future of the Female Brain."[34] Whitney talks about her childhood trauma, epigenetic imprinting and how she has worked through it by understanding her brain.

YES focuses on recognizing the responses we have based on our programming. We can learn to work towards understanding these responses and ways to reprogram the effects from our past so we don't internalize or take things so personally. Then we can begin to live in a sea of serenity. We can enjoy relationships with others because we have a great one with ourselves!

34 You Tube video called The Future of the Female Brain: https://www.youtube.com/watch?v=nA626skVRpk&t=2405s

Ways to boost Dopamine and Serotonin

Exercise	Proper Nutrition
Nature	Massage
Meditation	Happy Memories
Gratitude	Yoga
Essential Oils	Therapy

Choosing which emotions you will or won't let in can be detrimental to your health. If we cling to the ones we do like and push down or bottle up the ones we don't then those that we bottle up will eventually demand to be examined and processed. They will show up as pain in the body and mind. Understand and accept all of your emotions as a part of being human.

YES for Relaxation #2

1. Opening

◇ Letting Go

Questions of the day. On a piece of paper, that you will burn or dissolve at the end, write your answer to the question(s) below as to what you wish to let go:

1. *What story am I telling myself about the future that prevents me from feeling joy today?*

2. *I have difficulty relaxing when...*

◇ Hand on Heart Affirmations

"My body and mind are relaxed and at peace."

"I effortlessly let go of any thoughts, concerns or worries."

"I enjoy nurturing myself with deep relaxation."

◇ Personal Mantras

Choose a mantra of your own that speaks to you today. Begin with "I am," and say it in the present moment as if it already exists. Your mantra should be something you truly believe. Say it out loud with emotion, vigor, enthusiasm, and energy with an intention to grow the positive seeds of that message within you!

Example Mantra: *"Before I speak I ask myself, is it kind, is it true, is it necessary and then I respond from a place of non-harming."*

◇ Gratitude and Energy

Say to yourself or out loud what you are grateful for and what positive energy you wish to invite into your life today! You may also choose an angel card with a word or message of inspiration for the day.

2. Restorative Yoga Asana #1 and Breath Assessment: Incline Legs

Set-up: Use two blocks. Place one on the highest level and the other on the medium level in front of it. Lean a bolster or a tightly rolled blanket against it. Lie down on the floor with your legs up on the bolster. Take a yoga strap or belt and wrap it around the bolster and your legs for support. Lie back with a pillow or blanket for your head. You may also choose to relax in legs up the wall pose.

◊ **Breath Assessment:**

Come into the posture and begin to release any past or future thoughts. Relax and surrender more with every breath. Notice your breathing pattern without trying to change anything. Notice the rise and fall of the belly and chest. Observe the length of the breath. Is it flowing naturally helping you to become calmer or does it feel rapid or shallow creating tension? Just observe. Next, count your inhales and exhales. Cultivate longer exhales. Allow your body to surrender to the present moment and just be.

3. Technique #1: The Joy of Letting Go

Think of the current voice that is telling you things that aren't true. When you notice these voices, you can begin to change them with positive optimistic mantras. Here are a few to try:

"I am capable. I choose to think thoughts that serve me well. I choose to reach for a better feeling. All is well in this moment. Even though I have pain I will not let it overcome me. My life is unfolding beautifully. I always observe before reacting." When you notice the inner voice of criticism, practice 'The Joy of Letting Go' exercise.

Let's Practice:

You may begin with some aromatherapy for relaxation. Place a calming essential oil on your wrist. Breathe in the essential oils for opening up passageways and for deep relaxation. Play your favorite calming and relaxing music or nature sounds.

The Joy of Letting Go:

Step 1. Notice how you are feeling or what emotional state you are experiencing.

Step 2. Welcome and be kind to the emotion. Give it your full attention.

Step 3. Notice how it feels and where it's located in your body.

Step 4. Notice any tension in your body and mind and take deep breaths. Relax and let go.

Step 5. From this place allow yourself to see the goodness in you in the moment.

Step 6. Stay with this feeling, even if uncomfortable, until it feels like a more natural state.

Another wonderful mantra you can say anytime is The Serenity Prayer:

God, grant me the serenity to accept the things I cannot change,
the courage to change the things I can,
and the wisdom to know the difference.

This simple yet profound prayer invites you to reflect and discern in any given moment what is your responsibility and what is not, guiding you to choose a thoughtful response.

4. Yoga Asanas: Yin Yoga

Homeostasis means that all of the systems of our body are in harmony and Yin and Yang are balanced. Yin is our female, cool energy. Yang is our male, fiery energy. In our society we tend to operate more in the fast-paced fiery energy of Yang. A Yang yoga practice would be ashtanga, vinyasa or power flow. To balance this energy, we need the slower paced, held postures of Yin. Yin yoga practice helps to reduce stress and provide restoration to the body. The postures are held longer to facilitate increased mobility and circulation and to calm the nervous system.

For the following Yin yoga sequence of seven postures gather some props like blocks, blankets, bolsters, and pillows. Hold each pose for three to five minutes or even longer. When transitioning between poses, choose a relaxing pose and hold it for 1 minute to allow the connective tissue to rehydrate. {Some postures are not pictured}

1. **Supported Child's Pose** - Place a rolled blanket or bolster on your calves and rest your hips back towards your heels. Reach your arms forward and rest your head on a block or blanket. {pictured below}

2. **Sleeping Swan Pose** - From all 4's bring your right knee forward directly below your chest. Extend your

left leg back behind you in line with the left hip. Keep the heel aligned with the toes. Rest your chest over your right leg. Choose a transition pose and then repeat with the left leg forward. {not pictured}

3. **Seated Forward Fold** - Sit up in staff pose, extend your legs forward and open them a little wider than hip distance. Place blankets on the floor between your legs and rest your chest on them. {pictured below}

4. **Thread the Needle Pose** - From all 4's Position thread the right arm under the left and rest the upper right corner of your skull on the floor. Slide the left arm forward. Choose a transition pose and then repeat with the left arm under resting on the upper left corner of the skull. {not pictured}

5. **Deer Pose** - Sit up with both knees pointing to the right. Place a bolster or stacked blankets or pillows near the right hip. Rotate your upper body and rest on the bolsters. Choose a transition pose and then repeat with the knees to the left. {not pictured}

6. **Legs in the Air Pose** - Extend the right leg in the air. Extend the left leg straight on the floor or bend the knee and place the foot on the floor. Choose a transition pose and then repeat with the left leg in the air and the right leg extended or foot on the floor. {pictured below}

7. **Savasana** - Rest in corpse pose for as long as you like. Feel the benefits of Yin. {pictured below}

Add: rest a blanket on your
calves and one on your forehead

Add: blankets on the floor
between the legs to rest on

Add: away from the wall, extend 1 leg up and the other down

5. Technique #2: Guided Nature Visualization

The following two nature visualizations are designed to ease your body, mind and spirit. By vividly imagining the sights, sounds and scents of nature as if you are experiencing them in the present moment you can let go and relax. {You may find these recordings on www.Y4ES.com}

Guided Forest Visualization:

Come into a restorative posture either lying down or reclined back in a chair. Close your eyes and begin to feel a sense of calm and relaxation wash over you. Take a full deep breath in and with a longer breath out relax even further releasing any remaining tension. Imagine you are walking down a path deep in the forest. All around you there are tall trees: pine, fir, redwood, oak. See them standing tall and majestic. The sound of wind blowing through the treetops is so soothing. You take a deep breath and smell the rich dampness of the forest floor, earth and seedlings. Now you look up through the treetops until you see a light blue sky. As the sun enters the canopy of the treetops it splinters into rays that penetrate through the trees to the forest floor. You marvel at the patterns of light and dark created as the sun filters down through the trees. The forest feels like a great cathedral filling you with a sense of peace and reverence for all living things. Off in the distance you hear the sound of rushing water echoing through the forest. It gets louder as you approach, and soon you are at the edge of a mountain stream. Now you sit down and make yourself comfortable. You can see the mountain stream creating rapids as it moves, rushing around an array of large and small rocks that are many shades of grey, brown and white. Some are covered with moss. The sound of rushing water is so peaceful that you can just let yourself drift off...relaxing more and more. You take in a deep breath of fresh air and breath out. The subtle smells of the forest are so refreshing. As you relax more and more you let go of any concerns or worries and you are filled with a deep sense of peace.

Guided Stream Visualization:

Come into a restorative posture either lying down or reclined back in a chair. Close your eyes and relax. Bring your attention to your breathing. Notice the natural flow of the breath without trying to control it. Now imagine that you are going for a morning walk in the woods near a stream. It's a cool, crisp day and the sun is just beginning to rise. You see the sun beams peeking through the trees. As you walk through the woods you breathe in the fresh air and the scent of forest and pine all around you. You hear the leaves crunching beneath your feet. Now you begin to walk towards the stream and hear the gentle trickling sounds of water passing over rocks. A leaf releases from a tree above and you watch as it floats on the air down to the water and lands in the trickling stream. It navigates its way along and as you walk near the water, and you are mesmerized by the way it floats, gliding over the rocks and branches. A gentle breeze comes and you take a deep breath in, enjoying the fresh morning air. Now the leaf meets with the larger creek and gracefully floats away. You lift your gaze to take in all of nature's beauty; trees, sky, water and the sandy banks of the creek. A deep wave of relaxation washes over you as you take in all of nature's wonders. As the birds wake up to the morning you pause to listen and appreciate their sweet songs carried on the breeze. The trees sway and gratitude fills your whole being. You are grateful to be alive, experiencing such beauty. You feel a deep connection with all of nature and the positive flow of energy that engulfs you. As you turn to walk back home you marvel at how just seeing the beauty of nature all around you brings a sense of peace and calm.

Guided Beach Visualization:

Come into a restorative posture either lying down or reclined back in a chair. Close your eyes and relax. Bring your attention to your breathing. Notice the natural flow of the breath without trying to control it. Picture yourself descending down a long, narrow, wooden stairway towards a beautiful white sand beach stretching as far as you can see. The ocean is a wonderful blend of deep to light blues closer to the shore. You come to the end of the stairway and step down into the warm soft sand. You pause to take in the sensation of sand on your feet and a cool breeze in the air. The sound of the waves crashing to the shore calms and soothes you and a smile comes to your heart as you sigh with relaxation. You begin to walk towards the water's edge as you feel the warm sun on your face. The smell of the sea air invigorates you, and you take in a deep breath feeling refreshed and renewed. You reach the water's edge and allow the water to wash over your feet as you wiggle your toes in the sand. You hear the sound of seagulls and look up to watch them glide overhead. All of these sights, sounds, and sensations allow you to experience a sense of calm and well-being. You feel a cool gentle breeze pressing lightly against your back. As you continue your walk down the beach, you notice a colorful beach chair resting in a peaceful spot on the sand. You approach this comfortable looking chair and sit down, lie back, and relax. The warm sun beams down on your whole body and you experience deep peace and serenity. Nothing else matters except for this quiet and comfortable moment.

6. Restorative Yoga Asana #2: Side Lying with Bolsters

Essential Oil Suggestion: Lavender

Set-up: Prepare a blanket or pillow to place under your head. Place a bolster or blanket between the thighs or just rest the top leg over the bolster or blanket with the bottom leg straight, and roll to your side. You may also choose to hug a bolster or pillow. Rest your head down and make sure your shoulder and head feel comfortable and fully supported. You may also place a bolster or a rolled blanket against your back. Relax and release any tension. Focus on the breath, silence, and stillness. After 5 minutes or so you may roll to the other side and relax there for 5 minutes or more.

EO's: You may place *Lavender* essential oil on your wrists or diffuse it in the air. Breathe in the essential oils to open up the passageways in the nostrils and the whole body. Take long, deep relaxing breaths. Play relaxing spa music, theta music or Tibetan singing bowl sounds with or without nature sounds. Rest and Relax.

7. Technique #3:
Brainwave Frequencies and Binaural Beats

Our brains produce five types of brainwave frequencies. They are Gamma, Beta, Alpha, Theta and Delta. Each of these frequencies represent the specific mind states we move through each day from fully awake to deep sleep.

Brain Wave	Mind State	Frequency in hertz
Gamma	Learning and Processing	40-100
Beta	Fully Awake	14-30
Alpha	Light meditative state	8-13
Theta	Light sleep/Deeper meditative state	4-7
Delta	Deep Sleep	3.5 and below

Sound therapy is designed to assist a person in experiencing a relaxed state of mind, residing between Alpha and Theta brainwave frequencies. Various instruments such as crystal or metal singing bowls, Native American flutes, drums, gongs, harmoniums, chimes and more are utilized in sound baths, offering a soothing experience that is like 'floating on sound'. Additionally, binaural beats or brain entrainment, which involves presenting two different tones (one for each ear) is another type of sound therapy used to induce a meditative and relaxed state as the brain perceives them as a single tone.

Let's Practice:

Select relaxing music of instruments, nature sounds with music or binaural beats. Come into a restorative lounge chair Savasana (See Restorative Yoga Asana #3) and envelope yourself in sound.

8. Restorative Yoga Asana #3: Lounge Chair Savasana with Binaural Beats or Relaxing Music

Essential Oil Suggestion: Tangerine

Set-up: Place two blocks next to each other; one on the highest level and the other on the medium level or one on the medium level and one on the lowest level. Lean a bolster or a tightly rolled blanket against it. Lie down with your bottom close to the bottom edge of the bolster and recline back. Use rolled blankets or pillows under your arms for arm rest support. Place a rolled blanket or bolster under your knees if you wish. Place an eye pillow on your eyes.

EO: You may place *Tangerine* essential oil on your wrists or palms or diffuse it in the air. Breathe in the essential oils to open up the passageways in the nostrils and the whole body. Take long, deep relaxing breaths. Play relaxing spa music, theta music or Tibetan singing bowl sounds with or without nature sounds. Rest and Relax.

9. Closing. Burning or Dissolving Ritual

◇ **Letting Go:**

Get a lighter and a heat resistant bowl (for the burning ritual) or a bowl filled with room temperature or warm water (for the dissolving ritual). Take the paper with the answer to the letting go question and say the following out loud:

"Dear Universe–I no longer need these thoughts, feelings, or circumstances that do not serve my highest and best good. I vow to be open to the lessons presented to me in order to create positive habits and improve my outlook on life."

Now light the paper on fire and place it in the bowl and watch it burn or take the special dissolving paper and place it in the water and watch it dissolve. Let it go.

◇ **Inviting in:**

Read one of the following quotes of inspiration below or choose your own. You may choose to print it on a paper or sticky note to post where you will see it. Say the following out loud: *"Dear Universe–I invite this message of inspiration into my life at this time to serve my highest and best good. I promise to be more present and kinder to myself every day."*

What will you invite into your life today?

1. Statement of gratitude to the universe about what you wish for today:

   "Thank you Universe for helping me to practice non-harming in thoughts, words, and deeds."

2. Two quotes of inspiration

   "The moment judgement stops through acceptance of what is, you are free of the mind. You have made room for love, for joy, for peace." ~Eckhart Tolle

   "Feed the body food and drink, it will survive today. Feed the soul art and music, it will live forever." ~Julie Andrews

Story #14. Think Twice. Be Nice.
(Think before you act)

All of these trucks kept crashing into or getting stuck under the overpass in my hometown, Newark, Delaware. To address this, the city decided to install signs that bluntly declared, "Think Twice!" as a warning for drivers to consider the height of their vehicles in comparison to the height of the overhead railroad. This scenario brought a metaphor to mind that we often need reminders to focus on our own thoughts, words, and actions before they turn into regrettable decisions.

Consider a time when you wished you hadn't said or done something that ended up causing harm. Maybe you sent a hasty text or email in anger or perhaps you misunderstood something someone said and reacted harshly. Or maybe you turned the focus inward and you beat yourself up with negative self-talk, alcohol, over eating, impulse buying, or other unhealthy activities.

Whenever you feel your emotions rising and you have an initial knee jerk reaction (thinking once), pause to reset and "think twice." Ask yourself crucial questions to process the situation for a more positive outcome. Ask yourself: Is this true? How important is this? Do I really need to say or do this now? Can it wait? Will this harm me or others? Most importantly, an interesting question, consider: What would love do?

By taking this momentary pause after thinking once and then thinking twice before responding, your relationship with others and especially with yourself will likely see improvement. Avoid regrets by choosing to "stop now", as the final warning sign before the overpass advises. Just as the driver might reconsider attempting to fit under the bridge after initially thinking they could, you too can steer clear of potential impacts on your well-being and the well-being of those around you. So, think twice and be nice. Be kind to yourself and others by pausing to consider the effects of your thoughts, words, and actions. Respond out of love and kindness and not on impulse.

In practicing this thoughtful approach, you align with Byron Katie's method, "The Work"; four questions to help you to reconsider your thoughts and emotions, leading to better relationships and fostering contentment. Give 'The Work' a try and see how it helps you to think twice. (See description and practice of "The Work" in Heart Opening #2 or on www.thework.com).

What we resist persists

YES for Relaxation #3

1. Opening

◇ Letting Go

Questions of the day. On a piece of paper, that you will burn or dissolve at the end, write your answer to the question(s) below about what you wish to let go:

1. *What limiting beliefs or critical thoughts keep me from feeling joy and happiness?*

2. *What blame, guilt or shame am I holding on to?*

◇ Hand on Heart Affirmations

"I feel more at peace every day."

"It is easy for me to rest and relax."

"I can relax my body and mind through visualization, focus and deep breathing."

◇ Personal Mantras

Choose a mantra of your own that speaks to you today. Begin with "I am," and say it in the present moment as if it already exists! Your personal mantra should be something you truly believe. Say it out loud with energy, emotion, vigor, enthusiasm, and intention to grow these positive seeds within you!

Example Mantra: *"Relaxing into the present moment releases any regrets from the past or worry about the future. In the present moment I am free!"*

◇ **Gratitude and Energy**

Say to yourself or out loud what you are grateful for and what positive energy you wish to invite into your life today! You may also choose an angel card with a word or message of inspiration for the day.

2. Restorative Yoga Asana #1 and Breath Assessment: Child's Pose

Set-up:
Come to all 4's. Touch your big toes together and take your knees wide. Rest your hips back to your heels. Rest your chest between your legs or on a bolster in front of you. Allow your forehead to rest on the floor or turn your head to the side to rest on the bolster. Come into a restful, supportive position.

◇ **Breath Assessment:**

Come into the posture and begin to release any past or future thoughts. Relax and surrender more with every breath. Notice your breathing pattern without trying to change anything. Notice the rise and fall of the belly and chest. Observe the length of the breath. Is it flowing naturally helping you to become calmer or does it feel rapid or shallow creating tension? Just observe. Next, count your inhales and exhales. Cultivate longer exhales. Allow your body to surrender to the present moment and just be.

3. Technique #1: Samskaras and The Untethered Soul

During a 200-hour Yoga Teacher Training that I was leading, a student and friend, Kelly, introduced me to Michale A. Singer, author and founder of a meditation center in Florida. His books, "The Untethered Soul" and "The Surrender Experiment"[35]. captivated me, leading me to delve deeper into the yogic concept of samsara, a sanskrit term referring to the impressions that the mind clings to from the past. These impressions, whether positive or negative, manifest as ingrained, unfinished energy patterns. The ones that keep us stuck and blocked are the negative ones tend to resurface in our lives in the form of re-experiences, energy stimulations or a triggers-reminders of past impressions that we haven't fully processed. As Michael puts it, '...unfinished mental and emotional energy patterns are getting stored and reactivated' ("The Untethered Soul"). The key, according to him, is as simple as allowing the experiences to come in and pass through. Open and relax your heart and let them pass without suppressing them.

Some of my favorite takeaways from "The Untethered Soul" are:

- Become an observer of your inner roommate- the voice in your head
- Allow the old stories to pass through
- Keep your heart open
- Release preconceived notions of how things *should* be

---

35 https://untetheredsoul.com/

Let's Practice:

Practice the following whenever a samskara or past impression arises that triggers a response from te past. When the old story resurfaces, choose to let it pass through.

Imagine a tightly woven sieve with tiny holes. Initially, the impression may be difficult to pass through, like navigating a sieve. The next time the samskara emerges, allow more of these past impressions to pass through. Picture the sieve transforming into a tennis racquet with a slightly larger holes so more passes through without evoking a strong reaction. Each time the impression arises, allow it to pass through with more ease as the holes expand- progressing from a net to a chain-link fence, until eventually it just passes through you with ease. Over time you will begin to replace the old stories with a newfound sense of hope until nothing remains, and the story ceases to arise altogether.

4. Yoga Asanas: Relaxation flow

In the following flow, move slowly and with ease of body and breath. You may hold the poses as long as you like easing your way in, breathing to release and relax and then moving to the next posture.

1. **Supine Pose.** Lie on your back with your knees bent and feet wide. Touch your knees together and rest. Notice your breathing. Extend your exhales longer than your inhales. Release any tension and relax.

2. **Supine Twist.** Hug your knees to your chest and then bring them to a 90° angle with your knees stacked over the hips. Extend your arms to the side and allow your knees to drop to the right for a few breaths as you relax into the stretch and then drop the knees to the left.

3. **Easy Seat (Sukasana).** Sit in an upright relaxed and stable position with your legs crossed. Remain here for a few relaxing breaths.

4. **Neck Stretches and Rolls.** Allow your head to drop to the right and left, ear to shoulder. Look to the right and left with your chin over your shoulder. Tilt your chin up and down. Circle your head clockwise and counterclockwise in small circles like you're drawing a circle with your nose in front of you.

5. **Shoulder Rolls.** Circle your shoulders in forward and backward circles.

6. **Cow/Cat:** Come to all 4's and arch and round the back moving in and out of cow and cat pose with each breath.

7. **Bird Dog.** From all 4's, reach out with the right arm and the left leg and back to the starting position. Reach out with the left arm and right leg.

8. **Child's Pose.** Rest your hips back towards your heels into child's pose.

9. **Downward Facing Dog.** Straighten your legs into Downward Facing Dog. Stay here with a focus on your breath and body. Walk your feet to your hands one step at a time until you are hanging and releasing in a forward fold.

10. **Forward Fold.** Hang and just let go in a forward fold. Slowly roll up to standing.

11. **Mountain Pose.** Stand with good mountain alignment posture and breathe.

12. **Lunge.** Step your right foot back to a lunge and place your knee down. Extend your arms up. Lift the knee and step forward. Step your left foot back to a lunge and place your knee down. Extend your arms up.

13. **Plank.** Transition into plank pose. Hold and breathe. Lower to your stomach.

14. **Sphinx Pose.** Place your elbows under your shoulders and your forearms on the floor. Lift your chest into sphinx pose.

15. **Child's Pose.** Stretch back into a child's pose.

16. **Seated Dandasana.** Sit up tall with your legs extended forward and your hands next to your hips.

17. **Forward Fold.** Lengthen your spine and fold forward hinging from the hips.

18. **Bridge Pose with a block.** Roll down to the floor and bend your knees. Place your feet on the floor and begin to lift your hips into bridge pose. Slide a block under your body and across the hips. Rest on the block.

19. **Legs in the Air.** Lift your legs into the air. Point and flex your feet and circle your ankles in both directions.

20. **Savasana.** Rest in corpse pose for as long as you like feeling the benefits of this relaxing flow.

5. Technique #2: Walking Meditation

Walking meditation is something you can do anytime. I used to take my dog for a walk around the neighborhood and my mind would be preoccupied with checking my phone, texting, or running through my to-do list for the day. My thoughts would wander, commenting on the weather, the people passing by, or various other things. However, on some days, I would make a conscious decision to embrace presence and go on a walking meditation.

This walk looked distinctly different. I would simply walk, placing one foot in front of the other, fully aware of my surroundings without any mental commentary. I observed each footfall and synchronized it with my breath. A sense of peace and calm came over me just experiencing the here and now. There was no excessive thinking, dwelling on the past or anticipating the future- just walking and being.

In walking meditation there is no arriving, other than continually arriving in the present moment. Walking provides an opportunity to inhabit our bodies differently than when sitting or lying down.

Let's Practice:

Step 1: Decide to begin your walking meditation. It can be integrated into your routine while walking somewhere or you may choose to dedicate specific time to walk inside or outside.

Step 2: Focus your attention on your feet. Feel the contact of each foot with the ground. Acknowledge when your mind starts to wander, noting where it went, and then gently guide it back to this moment, your breath, and the step you're taking.

Step 3: Maintain a steady even pace to assist in the rhythmic movement and pattern of each step and breath.

Tips:

- If you are staying in one place, minimize distractions by walking slowly back and forth or in a large circle.
- Keep your eyes soft, gazing ahead.
- Practice at a speed that suits you from very slow to even running.
- Try to eliminate inner commentary or dialogue about your environment or wandering thoughts.

Try Forest Bathing: Another popular practice is Forest Bathing[36.] This is simply a practice of walking in a forest. Surrounded by trees and nature, this allows you to disconnect from the fast pace of life and immerse yourself in the healing and relaxing powers of the natural world.

6. Restorative Yoga Asana #2: Twist with Chest on Bolster

Essential Oil Suggestion: Ylang Ylang

Set-up: Place a blanket on the floor or mat and another one for the head. Lie on your Right side with a bolster in front of your body from the hips down. Keep the right leg straight and place your left leg on the bolster. Rest your head on the blanket or on your arm for support. You may stay in this position for 5-10 minutes and then roll to the other side if you wish.

---

36 https://time.com/5259602/japanese-forest-bathing/

EO: You may place *Ylang Ylang* essential oil on your wrists or diffuse it in the air. Breathe in the essential oils to open up the passageways in the nostrils and the whole body. Take long, deep relaxing breaths. Play relaxing spa music, theta music or Tibetan singing bowl sounds with or without nature sounds. Rest and Relax.

7. Technique #3:
Point to Point Guided Breathing for Relaxation

Practice this guided breath during savasana. The focus is on breathing from one body part to another. The inhalations move up the body and the exhalations move down the body. The first part of the practice is a focus on the exhales moving down the body to release tension and let go. The second part focuses on the inhales moving up the body to help sense the energy that you are.

Begin by letting your body rest on the floor. Breath smooth and evenly. Breathe deeply into the abdominal area without much effort. Scan the body from the crown of the head to the feet. Now scan from the feet up the legs and the spine to the crown letting go of any tension you notice along the way. Let your entire body rest in the breath. Now let the focus go to the nostrils. Notice a cooling sensation as the air moves in and a warming sensation as the air moves out.

Inhale to the crown of the head and exhale to the toes, letting the exhale release tension. Inhale to the crown and exhale to the ankles. Inhale to the crown, exhale to the knees allowing the lower legs rest. Each breath carries away any stress, strain, or worry that you may hold in your tissues. Inhale to the crown and exhale to the hip joints, relaxing deeper around the pelvis and torso. Let go of worry, stress, doubt and fear. Inhale to the crown and exhale to the pelvis area, releasing stress around relationships, longing or desires. Inhale to the crown of the head and exhale to the abdomen. Release stress around fatigue or indigestion and loosening any holding on to self-doubt, self-criticism, or judgement. Inhale to the crown and exhale to the heart center. Soften around heartache, loss, grief, or sorrow. Inhale to the crown of the head, exhale to the throat. Release any tightness around the throat and the voice. Inhale to the crown and exhale to the arms. Inhale to the crown of the head and exhale to the fingertips. Inhale to the crown, exhale to the forehead. Release all worries, mental anxiety and stress.

Now shift the focus to the inhales. Let each inhale nourish and protect you. Each inhale moves deeper and deeper into the region of the mind comforting and soothing and inviting in harmony. Inhale from the throat to the crown of the head. Exhale to the heart. Inhale from the heart to the crown. Allow each inhale to comfort and soothe the tissues deep within the heart. Exhale to the abdomen. Inhale from the abdomen to the crown. Soothe the abdomen. Exhale to the pelvis. Inhale from the pelvis to the crown. Allow each inhale to soothe all the tissue in the pelvis that has held on to doubt or worry or fear or shame. Let each one of the cells be nourished with the inhale. Exhale to the knees. Inhale from the knees to the crown. Each inhalation brings comfort and compassion and kindness deep into the bones, reestablishing courage and faith in the body and faith in yourself. Exhale to the ankles. Inhale from the ankles to the crown. Move deeper and deeper into the marrow of the bones restoring faith, courage, strength and will. Exhale to the toes. Inhale from the toes to the crown to strengthen and establish courage and faith. Exhale to the soles of the feet and beyond to infinity and inhale from the soles of the feet all the way up the body to the crown and beyond to infinity. Rest in this breath and surrender to it. Let the breath move completely through you nourishing, replenishing, restoring, cleansing, releasing. Rest in the space of the breath. When you are ready simply roll over to the side and pause. Notice how you feel.

8. Restorative Yoga Asana #3: Lounge Chair Savasana with Point to Point Guided Breathing for Relaxation

Essential Oil Suggestion: Pine or Thyme

Set-up: Place two blocks next to each other; one on the highest level and the other on the medium level or one on the medium level and one on the lowest level. Lean a bolster or a tightly rolled blanket against it. Lie down with your bottom close to the bottom edge of the bolster and recline back. Use rolled blankets or pillows under your arms for arm rest support. Place a rolled blanket or bolster under your knees or come into a bound angle pose by placing the bottom of your feet together and place blocks under your legs for support if you wish. Place an eye pillow on your eyes.

EO: You may place *Pine or Thyme* essential oil on your wrists or palms or diffuse it in the air. Breathe in the essential oils to open up the passageways in the nostrils and the whole body. Take long, deep relaxing breaths. Play relaxing spa music, theta music or Tibetan singing bowl sounds with or without nature sounds. Rest and Relax.

9. Closing. Burning or Dissolving Ritual

◇ **Letting Go.**

Get a lighter and a heat resistant bowl or a bowl filled with room temperature or warm water. Take the paper with the answer to the letting go question and say the following out loud:

"Dear Universe–I no longer need these thoughts, feelings, or circumstances that do not serve my highest and best good. I vow to be open to the lessons presented to me in order to create positive habits and improve my outlook on life."

Now light the paper on fire and place it in the bowl and watch it burn or take the special dissolving paper and place it in the water and watch it dissolve. Let it go.

◇ **Inviting in.**

Read one of the following quotes of inspiration below or choose your own. You may choose to print it on a paper or sticky note to post where you will see it. Say the following out loud: *"Dear Universe–I invite this message of inspiration into my life at this time to serve my highest and best good. I promise to be more present and kinder to myself every day."*

What will you invite into your life today?

1. Statement of gratitude to the universe
   about what you wish for today:

   "Thank you, Universe, for all the joy in my life that comes in the form of deep breathing, seeing clearly, high vibrational energy, opening my heart and relaxing. I will invite these into my life every day."

2. Two quotes of inspiration

   "The moment judgement stops through acceptance of what is, you are free of the mind. You have made room for love, for joy, for peace." ~Eckhart Tolle

   "Feed the body food and drink, it will survive today. Feed the soul art and music, it will live forever." ~Julie Andrews

Story #15. I Could Easily Freak Out Right Now!
But I Won't.

(Freak out or be calm. Which do I choose?)

Try this exercise: sit still, take long, deep breaths, and close your eyes. Find the stillness within, feeling calm and at ease. Now bring your mind to a challenging situation or a person with whom you've had conflicts. Remember the cause, your emotions, and the physical sensations. Notice how you feel in your physical body. What thoughts are racing in your head? What emotions are arising? Picture it. Acknowledge it and...let it go.

Return to the stillness and calm within. Now focus on a joyful experience, recent or from the past. Envision it vividly, recalling sights, sounds, and feelings. Feel the happiness and now...let it go.

Return to the stillness and ease within. Now think of a memory, good, bad, clear or foggy. Who was there? What were you doing? How did you feel in your body, mind and spirit? Relive the details and now... let it go.

Take another deep breath, open your eyes, and reflect on this journey through experiences, emotions, thoughts, and sensations. This exercise reveals the power of our thoughts and how they can lead to joy or despair. Recognize thoughts like 'I don't have enough time or money', 'I can't handle this situation', 'I am not enough', or 'nobody cares about me,' but avoid letting them lead to despair.

Believe me, I have had my share of freak outs. They have been loud with a full out tantrums inside my head as I criticize myself mercilessly. I experienced my father dying while my husband was asking for a divorce and my daughter was going into another rehab all at the same time. I could have easily freaked out and gone into a deep depression or run away or turned to some addiction to manage it but in those moments I said to myself, 'I could easily freak out right now.'

I acknowledged it. Then I said to myself, *but I won't.* I chose to find my strength and take one thing at a time.

Despite challenging moments, choose not to freak out. Acknowledge the difficulty, find strength, and take one step at a time using the *YES* techniques. Over time, stability in emotions grows, allowing observation, reflection, gratitude , and a smoother flow in the stream of life.

These lessons can also be found in the ancient text The Bhagavad Gita (2.14 and 2.15) which teaches that we will experience pairs of opposites: pleasure and pain, joy and sorrow, cold and heat. These sense perceptions are temporary and fleeting. To navigate them successfully, it is essential to cultivate self-discipline, allowing us to remain unaffected by the impermanence of both material happiness and material distress.

Here are few things to do when you decide **NOT** to freak out:

*sleep	*meditate
*take a walk in nature	*sing
*pat your dog	*use essential oils
*take a bath	*journal
*do some yoga postures	*chant
*listen to calming music	*say affirmations
*read	*light a candle and enjoy the scent
*talk to a friend	*dance
*exercise	*watch a movie

Story #16. Is This 1 Breath or 1,000 Breaths-Worthy?

(Remember to breathe)

I live in a house in nature. I love it! I wake up every morning to the beautiful sky, trees, horses and spiders! Nature often finds its way indoors, especially in the form of spiders. Rather than resorting to harm, I've developed a system- the "tissue worthy" or "cup worthy" classification. When I see a spider and it's tiny and cute, I reach for a tissue to release it outside. For the larger, leggier friends, I grab a cup and gently ease it over the spider, then I slide a paper under the cup and with a squeamish "eeeee" sound release it back outside.

So, why am I talking about spiders? Because the other day when I was reflecting on some recent interactions and circumstances in my life, I noticed emotional responses starting to surface. Unkind emails, rude remarks, gossip, or even the way someone cut me off in traffic all required an appropriate response. I know that deep breathing is the answer and an anchor in these situations. The question arises: How many breaths do I need to help me respond appropriately in each situation? Is this situation 1 breath-worthy or 1,000 breaths-worthy?"

Focusing my attention on deep breathing helps to calm not only my body but also the monkey mind and ego mind that tend to react impulsively. It helps me to activate the parasympathetic nervous system and avoid knee jerk reactions. Taking responsibility for my emotions and actions, I recognize that my ultimate goal is inner calm and happiness. Regardless of external circumstances I aim to maintain that state!

Now, when faced with challenging situations, I can pause and assess how many breaths it will take for me to regain composure and return to balance.

Here are some examples, each requiring a different number of breaths to navigate:

Situation	Breath-Worthy (# of Breaths)
A squirrel runs across the road in front of the car	1 breath
Someone says "No" to a favor	4 breaths
Overheard gossip	8 breaths
Receiving a mean email	15 breaths
A trigger of a bad car accident comes to mind	30 breaths
Something huge that activates a panic attack or state of anxiety	100+ breaths

I calculated that 1,000 breaths = approximately 167 minutes or 2.78 hours

That would be a serious breath-worthy incident!

In meditation we are taught that when our mind starts to wander to bring the attention back to the breath. A regular meditation practice offers us a way to focus on the breath and allow our body and mind to assist us in coming back to balance. When we do, a surprising thing will happen! People around you will see your responses and that you remained calm, content, loving and compassionate because you took the time to take care of you by simply pausing and breathing!

Let's Practice:
Step 1: Notice
When you begin to feel frustrated, blamed, unsupported, criticized, depressed, worried, upset with yourself or others, or in a scary or uncomfortable situation, pause and prepare to take some long deep breaths, knowing your intention is to calm your body and mind.

Step 2: Breathe

Inhale fully and exhale fully and say "that's 1," then again breath in and out and say "that's 2." Inhale, exhale 3." Assess and decide if you need to take more breaths. If so, inhale and exhale "4." Inhale, exhale "5." Notice if you are feeling calmer and decide if you have come through the difficult situation and accompanying emotions and are ready to move on.

Step 3: Let Go

Now you can begin to let go. First, Congratulate yourself for using your breathing technique. Let go of the situation and of the pattern to blame others or yourself. Return to the breath if needed. With every exhale, feel the emotion ease a little more. Once the emotion has come down to a zero where there is no tension, worry or anxiety, you can decide what you will do next.

Step 4: Move on

Now you can move on with your day. Go for a walk, eat a nice meal, read a book, rest, think of positive aspects or whatever you were in the midst of doing when the situation arose. There's no need to bring that situation up in your mind or with that person again. You already worked through it, took your deep breaths and let it go! Focus on what you wish for now. Time to move forward with joy!

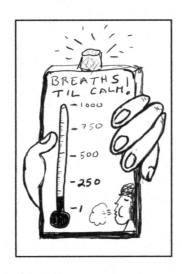

Story #17. Poop on the Path

I am so very grateful for the home where I currently live. It is a peaceful and healing place surrounded by nature on all sides, near Fairhill park in Maryland. I can walk down the lane and visit the horses who are right there. I love to pat them or just watch them eating grass and enjoying life out in the great wide open spaces. When I walk down even further there's a magical path with a canopy of bamboo creating a passageway to the other end, opening up to more trails for bikes, people and horses.

One day I was walking with Sosa down the path. Actually, he was running and sniffing and enjoying the freedom and fresh air of the day. I was looking up to the sky and also appreciating all of nature when I happened to look down and "oops!" a huge pile of horse poop was in the center of the path! I almost stepped right in it! Ack!!! I guess that's to be expected on a horse trail. I did a quick side step around it and kept going. Then I paused and thought "If I almost stepped in that then chances are others may too." I looked around for something to push it over. I found a big stick and slid the poop to the side.

Of course, my mind went right away to a poop analogy! I liken poop to the crappy life challenges that are presented to us in the form of difficult work situations and goals to be met to battling an illness or injury to even more serious situations like the results of past trauma that affect our present life. In any case when life presents us with poop we have options. Here are the four options I came up with.

Poop on the path choices:

1. **We can ignore or avoid it** by walking around it or looking the other way. When we do this we are never really addressing the problem or emotion or any associated results which may result in us pushing our feelings down and creating more distress and disease.

2. **We can walk through it** and get poop all over us. We might act as if it doesn't bother us or we can handle it but it is still sticking with us and hanging around in our thoughts because we haven't processed it.

3. **We can scoop it up** and move it off of the path. This choice is addressing the situation in order to move through it. We may seek support from friends, or family, a therapist, or tools we have learned. With this choice we can gain insight to process and move through to the solution and find resolution and release.

4. **We can use it for something good**, like fertilizer. After resolving the challenge we can use the lessons we learned and move through and forward with a positive focus in life. What we learned can help us to grow, change, and improve. Then we may use what we discovered to help others on their path with similar challenges.

I'm actually appreciative of the poop that shows up in my path. I may not like what shows up but I enjoy the process of being faced with poop and then deciding what choice I will make to have the outcome I desire.

Sometimes when Sosa is trotting or sprinting along on the path he steps in the occasional poop and just keeps going! We could all learn a lesson from dogs. A little poop never hurt anyone.

YES Sessions for Specific Emotional States

This table shows the emotional states you may be experiencing and the suggested themed class as well as suggested techniques and practices to calm the body and mind

Emotion	Themed Session	Suggested Technique/ Lesson /Reading
Anxiety	Relaxation & Clarity	Mantras/4-7-8 breath/ Emotional Guidance Scale
Worry	Heart Opening/ Relaxation	Meditation / Happiness Bubble
Sadness	Breathing /Energy	Affirmations/Yoga Asana/Breath of Joy
Grief/Loss	Breathing	Alternate nostril/ The hook up & Heaven and Earth
Anger	Breathing	Emotional Guidance Scale / The 4 Agreements
Disappointment	Clarity /Heart Opening / Relaxation	Point to point breathing / acupressure
Uncertainty/Doubt	Clarity	Letting go / Heart Brain Coherence
Loneliness	Energy/Clarity	Raise your Frequencies /Yoga Asana / Chakras, Vayus, Nadis
Shame	Heart Opening	Chanting / Pratyahara / Metta meditation / positive affirmations
Blame	Heart Opening	'The Work' / Tendency to Judge
Jealousy /insecurity	Heart Opening/ Relaxation	Octopus technique / Detachment
Fear	Relaxation/Clarity	Cure for Fear Albert Brooks/Breath of Joy
Depression	Relaxation/ Heart Opening / Breathing/Energy	Essential oils / Mantra Parusha/ 5 Kleshas

YES Sessions for Specific Situations

This table shows a situation you may be experiencing and the suggested themed class as well as techniques and practices to calm the body and mind

Situation	Themed Session	Suggested Technique /Lesson/Reading
Triggers Arising	Relaxation/ Heart Opening	Yoga Nidra, Emotional Guidance Scale, Raise your Frequency, Samskaras
Conflict	Clarity/ Energy	Octopus Technique, 'The Work', Fear
Addiction	Energy/ Relaxation	Manifesting your reality, Energy Exercises
Headache	Breathing	Buzzing Bee
Body Aches and Pain /Sickness	All	Yoga Asanas, Yin Yoga, Grounding taps
Panic Attack	Breathing / Clarity	Breathing practices, EFT- Tapping
Tension	Breathing/Relaxation	Fierce Lion, Acupressure, PMR
Rejection	Clarity / Breathing	12 Pathways, Breath of Joy
Death of loved one	Relaxation/ Breathing	R.A.I.N., Kapalbhati & Sitali Breath,
Break up	Heart Opening / Clarity	Metta meditation, Detachment
Loss: relationships/ home /job	Relaxation	Walking Meditation, Nature Visualization
Aging	Heart Opening	5 Invitations

PART III

7

Aromatherapy - Essential Oils

Essential Oils are highly concentrated phytochemicals that are distilled from plants. They are best used diffused in the air. They can be placed directly on the skin or ingested. Be sure to research essential oils to fully understand the proper use and care. The quality of essential oils varies greatly. I recommend reputable companies such as DoTerra and Young Living. It is advisable to dilute the oils in a carrier oil like sunflower, jojoba, almond or avocado. Although essential oils do possess many of the healing properties listed below, be sure to consult a certified holistic doctor or other professional to understand and follow the correct use of essential oils.

The following are the essential oils used in this book:

Breathing

Peppermint: Invigorating scent that helps clear the mind from overactive thinking. Eases digestion, relieves headaches, freshens breath and opens sinuses. Helps give the feeling of being energized and awake. (B#1)

Lavender: Offers comfort and relaxation. Soothing to the skin and supports our overall well-being. May improve sleep and lower blood pressure. (B #1)

Eucalyptus: Helps inspire clarity, focus and easy breathing. Inspires movement when the body feels tense. Has anti-inflammatory properties. (B #2)

Cardamom: An antioxidant and anti-inflammatory. Helps with digestion, treats infections and gives a feeling of clear breathing. (B#2)

Cedarwood: A woodsy scent that brings a sense of grounding and well-being. It helps with anxiety and improves sleep. (B #3)

Clary Sage: Reduces stress and anxiety. Is a natural antidepressant and helps to reduce menstrual cramps. (B#3)

Clarity

Patchouli: Calms nervous energy and soothes tension. Helps diminish intense emotions. (C #1)

Coriander: Has antiseptic, antibacterial and detoxifying properties. (C#1)

Sandalwood: Helps promote mental clarity and cognitive function to stay calm under stress and see things more rationally. (C #2)

Grapefruit: May promote weight loss, balance mood and reduce stress and lower blood pressure. (C#2)

Tea Tree: Supports clear skin, sharp thinking, reduces germs, antiseptic and anti-inflammatory (C #3)

Jasmine: Helps ease stress, anxiety, depression and fatigue (C#3)

Energy

Lemon: Powerful in cleansing, clearing and detoxifying. The zesty aroma radiates high vibration energy, is calming and inspires motivation and ambition. (E #1)

Juniper Berry: A natural antiseptic that boosts digestion, and aids in sleep and relaxation. Assist in protecting the skin and reducing heartburn. (E#1)

Rosemary: A cooling and earthy scent that activates sharp thinking and motivation. Antioxidants, anti-inflammatory, boosts the immune system and improves blood circulation. (E #2)

Lime: Clears the mind, encourages mental energy and supports the immune system. (E#2)

Lemongrass: Relieves pain and anxiety and soothes an overactive mind. When diffusing it uplifts the energy in the room. (E #3)

Melissa: Boosts mood, prevents and treats infection with anti-inflammatory properties. Lowers blood pressure and relieves menstrual symptoms. (E #3)

Heart Opening

Rose: Raises vibration and enhances mood. Decreases anxiety and stress. Eases depression (HO #1)

Orange: Helps to reduce the symptoms of anxiety and depression and assists with pain relief and weight loss. (HO#1)

Bergamot: Creates a feeling of joy. Is considered one of the best emotional balancers. It is uplifting, soothing and nurturing (HO #2)

Sage: Helps to ease muscle and joint pain, addresses bacterial infections, and assists with digestion.(HO#2)

Sweet Orange: Offers a feeling of contentment and joy. The aroma lifts your mood and dispels negative feelings. Helps treat insomnia. (HO #3)

Sweet Marjoram: Promotes blood circulation and helps with digestions, depression, migraines, coughs, and pain. (HO#3)

Relaxation

Frankincense: The woodsy herbal aroma gives a grounding, relaxed feeling. It helps to balance the emotions and supports the immune system. The body feels peaceful and at ease. (R #1)

Spearmint: Improves memory, reduces stress, and fights bacterial infections. (R#1)

Lavender: Offers comfort and relaxation. Soothing to the skin and supports our overall well-being. May improve sleep and lower blood pressure. (R #2)

Tangerine: Has a calming effect, reduces tension and emotional imbalances. Helps to alleviate mood swings. (R#2)

Ylang Ylang: Decreases stress and anxiety, calms the nervous system. It enhances digestion, improves circulation, and acts as an aphrodisiac. (R #3)

Pine or Thyme: Eases symptoms of inflammatory skin conditions or arthritis and muscle pains. (R#3)